Why

[SMART COMPANIES]

Do Dumb Things

Why

[SMART COMPANIES]

Do Dumb Things

Lessons Learned from *INNOVATION* Blunders

Avoiding Eight Common Mistakes
in New Product Development

Calvin L. Hodock

Prometheus Books

59 John Glenn Drive
Amherst, New York 14228–2119

Published 2007 by Prometheus Books

Inquiries should be addressed to
Prometheus Books
59 John Glenn Drive
Amherst, New York 14228–2119
VOICE: 716–691–0133, ext. 210
FAX: 716–691–0137
WWW.PROMETHEUSBOOKS.COM

11 10 09 08 07   5 4 3 2 1

Library of Congress Cataloging-in-Publication Data

Hodock, Calvin L.
    Why smart companies do dumb things : avoiding eight common mistakes in new product development / by Calvin L. Hodock.
        p.   cm.
    Includes bibliographical references and index.
    ISBN 978–1–59102–568–9 (alk. paper)
    1. New products. I. Title.

HF5415.153.H62 2007
658.5'75—dc22

2007027083

Printed in the United States of America on acid-free paper

[CONTENTS]

(1)

[THE INNOVATION CHALLENGE]
Damned If You Do and
Damned If You Don't

" **I**n 1882 in lower Manhattan, Thomas Alva Edison flicked the switch to electrify Pearl Street."[1] However, it would be almost four more decades before electric appliances were widely available to American homes. Following the dawn of the twentieth century, the urge to innovate turbocharged America. The everyday landscape of the country was permanently altered, fueled by a passion for innovation. The next hundred years are likely to be equally rich in innovation and scientific progress. It's the American style.

A NEW DAWN IN MARKETING

With the return to normalcy after the Second World War, America experienced an evolution of factors in the '50s and '60s that changed the way we lived and fueled a seeming hunger to invent a new order of living structured around goods and possessions.

Lifestyle Changes

Immediately after the War, the country experienced a tidal wave of innovation in consumer goods and services. The flight to the suburbs mushroomed. Many of the expatriates from the cities were discharged servicemen. They were not passive consumers. They were receptive to the challenge of finding the American dream. They flocked to the suburbs with pent-up aspirations and a strong desire to implement their dreams. Buying behavior was no longer suppressed by the war effort. Newly minted shopping centers spanned the suburban terrain, offering a bazaar of possibilities to satisfy the pent-up demand.

Marketing Sophistication

The merchants of marketing became increasingly more sophisticated. They learned to sell not just products, but to sell benefits. Don't just sell a car; sell a lifestyle. Don't just sell tonic water; sell elegance and romance. In selling dreams, television became a wonder drug, with its massive reach for the advertising hucksters dedicated to aggressively peddling their wares.

Credit Card Craze

Plastic made it easier to acquire goods and services. Credit card debt soared as consumers played credit card roulette by carrying several different cards in their wallets. To this day, the beat goes on in the game of credit card roulette. In a recent focus group on the west coast, we found the ultimate player: a woman with thirty-six active credit cards in her purse.

New Product Mania

In the early '50s, product innovation was not a compelling issue. Companies were content to focus on shop-worn brands like Halo Shampoo, Carter's Little Liver Pills, Jergens® Lotion, Chesterfield cigarettes, and other familiar names. Relics from an earlier era were made popular through the broadcast medium of radio. However, the marketing game was about to change dramatically.

Marketing research techniques became more sophisticated. Ernest Dichter, a Viennese psychoanalyst, started to use Freudian psychoanalytical techniques to probe the consumer psyche. This approach, labeled motivational research, was widely used to discover hidden meanings and hidden resistances to buying products. Women wanted a shampoo to do more than clean their hair. They wanted one that reflected their self-concept. The insights from the depth manipulators spawned a galaxy of new products. Innovate or perish became the mantra, replacing the status quo of the early '50s.

A new product mentality surfaced in America. We were on our way to swimming in a pool of materialism. Our culture evolved into one where marketing induced Americans to try new things, and consumers found that their quest for new was addictive. The consumer love affair with "new" knows few limits or boundaries, whether it's new colors, new flavors, new fragrances, or just about everything else labeled new. Americans became conditioned to eagerly anticipate the annual arrival of new styles in apparel and automobiles. We learned to value stuff, worshiping at the "altar of new."

The Magic of Segments

During the two decades after World War II, America became a mosaic of consumer segments that has continued to this very day. Each segment cried out for its individuality to be recognized and served. One size no longer fit all. Mass marketing became a cadaver. In the '80s market segmentation—the practice of carving up large monolithic markets into smaller segments that could be reached more effectively and efficiently—spread like a California brush fire in the marketing community. At one point, Procter & Gamble was selling eleven laundry brands in the United States, each directed to a different market segment.

The high priests of marketing scrambled to find niches and subsegments before their competitors and, once unearthed, to build share quickly in the discovered segments. Consumers suddenly had a cornucopia of choices that continues to this day. We now have forty-eight versions of Tylenol®, and Quaker® Oats Instant Oatmeal has thirty-eight SKUs (Stock Keeping Units) on supermarket shelves. There is choice for everyone.

In their aggressive pursuit of segments, the merchants of marketing fell into an innovation trap. They became enamored with line extensions. Line extensions were easy to do; they were relatively inexpensive to introduce, because they carried the equity mantle of the parent brand.

But many of these line extensions were parasites. They did not bring growth to the overall business. In many instances, they simply stole sales from the parent brand and diluted its core value. Many were miserable failures. Coke and Pepsi typified the problem. Both had done many line extensions over the years. Most of them are no longer around. Coke has not unveiled a major successful new brand since Sprite® in 1960, excluding Diet Coke® and Coke® Zero, which are really line extensions. The surfacing of line extension addiction chasing down miniscule segments contributed to the increasing mortality rate for new products.

Disposable Society

The merchants of marketing moved consumers toward an obsession with obsolescence. Throw good products out on the trash heap. Everything was disposable. New was better than old. Buy the same thing again with the latest bells and whistles. The throwaway strategy became part of our everyday culture, ranging from products to marriages.

More Choices

Women roam the malls of America with T-shirts declaring, "Shop till you drop." Shoppers enjoy browsing through stores simply seeking out newness. For a very modest investment, they can experiment with relatively little risk. It's a cheap thrill. Long ago, ad agency copywriters discovered that among the most powerful words in the advertising language were "new and improved."

On the surface, our choices in the pursuit of "new" can be a paradox. Who would have prophesied ten years ago that Americans would abandon Coke® and Pepsi® to buy bottled water at supermarkets, convenience stores, and vending machines? Isn't water supposed to be free?

Is Martha Stewart or Ralph Lauren™ paint really better than reliable Glidden or Sherwin Williams? "With the increased amount of time Americans are working, housework ranks lower on the priority scale. But, despite more dust balls on the floors, our homes smell squeaky clean."[2] Sales of new aromatic products like air fresheners and scented candles proliferate.

With our consumer thirst for new, isn't product innovation a cinch? Wrong. Consumer judgments are harsh, even brutal, in casting votes for the myriad of choices in today's marketplace.

THE STATISTICS OF INNOVATION

Product innovation is a paradox: It represents two seemingly irreconcilable sides of the same coin:

- One side involves the statistics of innovation, which documents that the odds of failure are high in the pursuit of product innovation.

- The other side consists of substantive reasons to innovate, despite that failure rate.

The statistics of innovation are heartless. In the pharmaceutical industry, innovation focuses on an empirical screening of compounds. Richard Foster describes the process:[3]

"Companies try hundreds of variations of chemical compounds until one combination works—molecular roulette."

Only one in ten thousand compounds ever reaches an end user. A medicinal chemist can work for thirty years in the lab and never be associated with a compound that reaches the marketplace. If five drug products are granted NDAs (New Drug Applications), only one of these new drugs is likely to achieve even a modicum of marketplace success.

In writing about the math of innovation in Silicon Valley, Gary Hamel observed:

Out of a thousand nascent business plans, maybe 100 will have enough merit to justify a few thousand dollars of angel investment. Out of these 1,000, perhaps ten will demonstrate enough promise to warrant a few million dollars of venture capital money. And out of these, only one or two will ever make it to the public market and achieve the success of an eBay or a Juniper Network.[4]

Nine out of ten packaged goods products fail. About two-thirds of the high-tech products are destined to fail. In industrial products, the failure rate is 50 percent. The beat goes on.

These brutal statistics apply even to the entertainment field. Many Broadway shows flop rather than succeed. Nine out of ten television shows are doomed to fail. Just ask Michael Richards, Julia Louis-Dreyfus, and Jason Alexander of *Seinfeld* fame.

In discussing the math of innovation as applied to life itself, Gary Hamel noted,

For every 1,000 eggs laid, only one sea turtle will survive to adulthood.[5]

In every act of human procreation, Hamel further noted, "60 million sperm swim upstream but only one penetrates an egg."[6] Ah yes! The math of innovation. It's everywhere we want to be, just like our Visa cards.

Conclusion

The math of innovation is formidable. The odds of success are better at any casino in Las Vegas or Atlantic City. There has been no appreciable change in the success rates for new products in almost six decades, despite increasing marketing sophistication. The issue this book is devoted to is: What is the difference between innovation that works and innovation that doesn't?

FIVE REASONS TO INNOVATE

There are five compelling reasons to tackle the risky turf of product innovation.

Reason #1 Adapt to Today's Shorter Product Life Cycles

Companies can no longer expect their brands to be living annuities. Establish a viable beachhead with the new product or service as the following examples portray, but don't plan on occupying the turf forever.

Febreze®

Febreze® spray is a breakthrough innovation from Procter & Gamble designed to eliminate smells in fabrics. The product immediately encountered competitive response from Clorox and SC Johnson, who launched their own improved version of Febreze® in less than a year.

Mach 3®

To develop Mach 3®, Gillette spent a bloody fortune—a billion dollars—over a period of ten years. A few months after the Mach 3® launch, *Economist* noted, "Gillette saw Asda, a British supermarket, rush in with its own product, Tri-Flex, claiming that it was just as good and 40% cheaper."[7]

Johnson & Johnson Coronary Stents

Johnson & Johnson was feeling good vibrations, because they were the only game in town. Through the acquisition of Cordis, Johnson & Johnson had ventured into the coronary stent business, the tiny metal-mesh cylinders that keep arteries from closing after angioplasty.

But Johnson & Johnson got a bit cocky. Their stent monopoly alienated the cardiology profession with high prices and arrogance. When competitors Guidant and Boston Scientific came out with superior stents at better prices, cardiologists eagerly bid au revoir to the Johnson & Johnson stents.

In retrospect, Johnson & Johnson realized they miscalculated the longevity of their product line. The company bounced back with the first drug-coated stent, which dramatically improved the incidences of arteries that stayed unclogged after surgery. They also discovered new-found humility in dealing with cardiologists.

Conclusion

Innovate or perish. Product life cycles are fragile. Consumer and technology trends wash over existing brands and businesses like crashing waves. Competitors are too nimble to allow a product innovation the luxury of a long, comfortable residency in the category sandbox.

Reason #2 Innovate to Attack Yourself

Innovation requires marketing courage. It mandates that companies attack themselves. But resistance to attacking oneself is a powerful force—sometimes called "incumbent inertia"—and many companies discover that the hard way.

The prolific explosion of bottled water as an everyday beverage is a good example of how two rivals responded to the innovation challenge. Both Coke and Pepsi watched their customers drift toward bottled water usage. Was this a trend or a fad? Was it a mere flirtation or a deep commitment?

The Coke and Pepsi Challenge

Trends tend to be anchored in multiple benefits. When women started drinking bottled water for weight control, it was not a good sign for diet sodas like Diet Coke®. Worker bees and exercise enthusiasts took to bottled water for replenishment. The only beverage allowed in many high school and college classrooms was bottled water. Bottled water benefited from a built-in health advantage. "Drink eight glasses of water a day" resonated favorably as a health mantra. There is no health benefit associated with the typical carbonated soft drink. However, there are multiple benefits associated with bottled water consumption.

Trends also tend to be anchored in acceptance by two important market segments—working women and Baby Boomers. Both were early adopters of bottled water's virtues.

After carefully reading the tea leaves, Pepsi jumped into the water, garnering a 12.6 percent share of the then $6 billion category. Coke remained on the beach, sunning itself under an umbrella of self-contentment. Coca-Cola® was holy water. Why drink anything else? Coke was in denial. Their holy water was on "the wrong side of the wellness and health trends that are restructuring their 'colafied world.'"[8]

The reality of the defection to bottled water was that it was better for Coke to lose these usage occasions to its own bottled water than a competitor's. This at least kept the business in the Coke family. Otherwise, this usage volume was gone forever. So, finally, Coke surfaced with Dasani®, but Pepsi had a two-year jump-start in the bottled water segment. New brands work best when they are first, other factors being equal.

What took Coke so long to attack? The dysfunctional Coke culture, awash in hubris, was in deep denial that consumers, especially the youth market, were seeking cola alternatives. It was a pivotal point in Coke's product innovation strategy. They abdicated the non-carbonated business to Pepsi, clinging to their shop-worn strategy: Here's your carbonated soda. Drink up, and shut up!

In contrast, archrival Pepsi was less sentimental about their flagship brands. While they supported them with lush budgets, they were not afraid to attack their core. The acquisitions of Gatorade® and new age SoBe®, along with their bottled water brands Aquafina® and Propel®, gave Pepsi a strong arsenal of noncarbonated brands. Pepsi had adapted successfully to changing consumer tastes; Coke had not.

Investors displayed confidence in Pepsi's innovation strategies; its market capitalization surpassed Coke for the first time in the history of the two companies. At one point, Coke had three times the "market cap" of Pepsi. But the days of wine and roses were over for the once formidable Coca-Cola; the company struggled to unshackle the chains of innovation malaise, attempting to regain consumer and investor confidence. In the US market, Pepsi had trumped Coke with superior innovation initiatives.

Gillette: The Grand Master of Attack Yourself

Gillette dominated the blade business around the world for decades. Therefore, the company refused to believe an obscure sword company from the United Kingdom could represent serious competition, and their sales plummeted with the US introduction of Wilkinson Sword® stainless steel blades.

Perhaps surprisingly, Gillette was already marketing stainless steel

blades in the Swiss and Swedish markets before Wilkinson Sword®
arrived on the scene. The company even owned the patent on the sili-
cone for the Wilkinson Sword® blades. Why was Gillette slow to adopt
stainless steel?

The company drooled at the rapid use-up rate associated with their
"nick and cut" blue blades. This meant juicier profits. Why market
longer lasting stainless steel blades? This might adversely impact the
bottom line. Men never complained about the inferior blue blades until
they tried the alternative—stainless steel.

Wilkinson Sword® came dangerously close to striking a mortal
blow to Gillette's supremacy in wet shaving. Stunned by this experience, Gillette embarked on a succession of product innovations, which
allowed them to regain category dominance.

Gillette learned to attack itself—going from blue blades to stainless
steel, Trac II, Atra, disposable blades, Sensor, Sensor Excel, Mach 3®,
and more recently the Fusion™ with six blades, premium priced over the
already very pricey Mach 3® blades. Gillette was even willing to accept
the lower margins of disposable blades when confronted with the reality
that Bic was bringing disposable blades from Europe to America.

Gillette's attack dog mentality remains intact. In a top-secret research
and development laboratory, Gillette's next wet shaving innovation can
be found. It is almost ready to go—waiting in the wings for Fusion™ to
run its course. Gillette always controls its future with aggressive innovation rather than letting competition shape its destiny.

Reason #3 To Provide Fuel for Profits and Survival

Marketing Management, a publication of the American Marketing
Association, featured an article focusing on the power of innovation.
Author Barton Tretheway made the following observation:[9]

> A new products and services best practices study we recently com-
> pleted looked at the results of more than 11,000 new products and
> services introduced over a five year time period. Companies were

divided into two categories: the "best" and the "rest." Best companies generated nearly twice the proportion of profits from products
and services introduced in the past five years. Additionally, best
companies had more than twice as many of these new products still
on the market compared to the rest. The study found that companies
that continually find new ways to serve markets enjoy better results.
The best companies derived 39% of their revenues from new products and services vs. only 23% for the rest.

Companies like Gillette and Toyota never lose their appetite for the innovation game. These are "best practices players." They are on their toes—
ready to reform, regroup, rethink, and restaff as necessary. They have put
into place the tools, the talents, and the discipline to tilt the innovation
game in their favor. Companies that are innovation prone consistently
derive anywhere from 30 to 40 percent of their profits from new products
that did not exist in the organization four or five years earlier.

Reason #4 To Restructure Category Dominance

Successful product innovation restructures market parameters. Followers become leaders. Leaders become followers.

A Success Secret

The secret to Colgate's success in introducing Total® toothpaste: innovative marketing of a magic ingredient. Colgate's research and development personnel labored for years in an effort to develop a new den-
tifrice formulation. Their painstaking efforts paid off with a patented
formula using triclosan, an antibacterial ingredient that keeps working
for twelve hours after brushing.

Colgate's Chairman Reuben Mark told the troops in the trenches to
"make it happen." The assigned mission: Deliver 46 million tubes of
toothpaste to the shelves of 13,000 stores in a mere three days. This
incredible deployment was a first for Colgate-Palmolive. It normally
takes three to four weeks to get this volume of product on store shelves.

The rapid delivery was a component of the $120 million US launch of Total®; the first toothpaste sanctioned by the FDA to claim it could prevent gingivitis, the early signs of gum disease. While Total® was first introduced overseas in 1992, the US introduction was delayed for years as Colgate scientists marshaled volumes of clinical data and documentation required for FDA approval. When finally unleashed in America, Total® leapfrogged over Crest®, becoming the category leader and duplicating that result in every country where the brand was introduced.

Beware Overconfidence

Procter & Gamble knew about triclosan. In the company's judgment, the ingredient did not merit years of haggling with the FDA. It represented at best minimal incremental value over their flagship brand, Crest®. Within a year, Total® snared almost one-third of toothpaste sales in the US.

Overconfidence is a fatal judgment trap for category leaders. Crest®'s success triggered complacency. After thirty years of dominance, Crest® was dislodged as the category leader. Colgate® became "king of the hill."

Procter & Gamble did not give up market share easily. It was back to the drawing board. What could we do about those rascals from Colgate? Despite the risks, continuing innovation was the key to survival. Procter & Gamble bounced back with Crest® Pro-Health™ in an attempt to trump Total®. And, it is a safe bet to speculate that Colgate has a trick or two up its sleeve in response to Crest® Pro-Health™. The toothpaste war thrives on innovation.

Reason #5 To Continue Category Dominance

Innovation helps category leaders retain and even grow their leadership positions. Audacity, audacity, and more audacity, and not caution, must be the norm.

A Slumbering Listerine® Wakes Up

For years, Listerine® and Scope® were the dominant mouthwash brands. Each had about one third of the business. The makers of Listerine® were reluctant to tamper with their bad-tasting mouthwash. They believed that the brand's unpleasant taste was a barometer of its perceived efficacy. However, they also knew that younger consumers were not buying Listerine®. The brand's core users were older and dying off.

Listerine® woke up from its increasingly unpleasant dream of incumbent inertia. It finally attacked itself, with the introduction of several line extensions that were better tasting than the parent brand. The flavor strategy had been around for years, but Warner Lambert's (now Johnson & Johnson) nervousness about denigrating original Listerine® had prevented the essential audaciousness.

The strategy worked. While there was some cannibalization of the original Listerine®, these were smartly executed line extensions. Citrus Listerine® used proprietary technology from Pfizer's pharmaceutical side of the business. Each new product was aggressively detailed to dentists, and Listerine® replaced Lavoris® and Cepacol® as the "dentist recommended mouthwash brand."

After years of timidity, Listerine® solidified its marketplace position, passing Scope® in sales to become the top mouthwash brand. Younger consumers were drawn into the Listerine® franchise with new flavors and portable Listerine PocketPaks®. Listerine® was no longer the brand for the nursing home crowd.

Scope® sat in the grandstand watching the innovation game being played. Its ad budget was slashed to almost nothing at the same time Listerine® was shaking and baking. The lack of Scope® media support was an internal decision to free up money to fight the rascals from Colgate on the toothpaste front.

After letting Scope® languish for over five years, Procter & Gamble has attempted CPR "with flashier packaging, new flavors, and a revitalized ad budget."[10] It didn't work, and then Procter & Gamble dropped their atom bomb on Listerine®—alcohol-free Crest® Pro-

Health™ Rinse. Surely, the leveraged Crest® name, a unique product formulation, and a $100 million marketing budget could stop the Listerine® juggernaut.

Consumers liked the tingling sensation in Listerine®. It was a sensory cue that the mouthwash was working. Gillette learned the sensory cue lesson the hard way years earlier when they attempted to market an alcohol-free after-shave lotion. Men wanted bite when lathering their faces with after-shave lotions; consumers wanted a tingling sensation when swishing around their mouthwash.

Crest® Pro-Health™ was homeless—straddled between Listerine®'s dominance and an irrelevant consumer promise. The trade was unhappy because Procter & Gamble failed to deliver on its promise of a 15 percent market share for Pro-Health™, because it did not like giving up inelastic shelf space to a loser that was promised to be a winner. Listerine® rolled on as Procter & Gamble's mouthwash nightmare continued.

The pattern was clear. Have the audacity to attack. Line extensions work when smartly executed. When a marketer takes the position of "why fix it if it ain't broke," somebody else is out there looking for a way to fix it, and they'll find it. Better to be on the offensive side of the football field, like Listerine®, than playing defense, like Scope®.

WHEN INNOVATION FAILS: EIGHT FATAL MISTAKES

There are eight common mistakes associated with flawed innovation.

1. Marketing Misjudgment: An important marketplace element relative to category behavior is fatally missed or misunderstood. This leads to overestimating the magnitude of the marketplace opportunity.

2. Positioning Poison: David Ogilvy said the most important decision in marketing is how the product or service is positioned.

Positioning carves out a unique niche about a brand in the minds of consumers. For example, Volvo® stands for safety in the mind of car buyers. If the product suffers from positioning poison, it's launched with a high probability of having a short life cycle, because the positioning is fatally flawed.

3. Dead-on-Arrival Product: The product is inflicted with an incurable disease. It may not work, like the Iridium™ phone. It may be a food product that tastes like medicine. It may have ugly duckling styling that "turns off" the car buying public, like the Pontiac Aztek®. It may even be the ultimate in deadly— think Vioxx®—a pain reliever with the potential risk for strokes and heart attacks. These and other maladies make it cadaverous—a flawed product that never should have surfaced from the research and development lab or slipped through the security checkpoints in the development process.

4. Competitive Delusion: Not being concerned about the competitive response. Competitive delusion lurks in the shadows, ready to impinge upon the best-laid plans of mice and men.

5. Defective Marketing Research: Product innovation is marketing research intensive. Not doing the required marketing research homework undermines the prospect for success. This doomsday scenario can be either a sin of omission or commission. Sins of omission occur when needed research steps are skipped. In sins of commission, the homework assignment is handed out, but the research steps undertaken are wrong, as was the case with New Coke®.

6. Fatality in Frugality: Be a cheapskate and fatal frugality is ready to strike. New ventures must be marketed with impact. This means appropriate financial support.

7. Timetable Tyranny: This malady strikes when marketers are unrealistically compressing the development timeline in the rush to the marketplace.

8. Marketing Dishonesty: This involves consciously or unconsciously ignoring disquieting signals or evidence that strongly suggests the product will not cut the mustard.

WHY WE SHOULD CARE

The cornerstone of our book—flawed product innovation—impacts the very fabric of our lives. Nobody escapes its consequences—shareholders, corporations, employees, and even our free enterprise economy.

Consequences for America

We need to look no further than our domestic automobile industry to witness the broad social and economic disruptions from a flawed innovation virus at work. In the '50s, General Motors CEO Harlow Curtice joked in the GM boardroom that a 50 percent share was not enough—he wanted to shoot for 75 percent market share. Those were exuberating days, before Honda and Toyota showed up. It now takes more than three months to move many General Motors cars off their dealer lots. Generations of Americans have grown up with the perception that it's not cool to drive American-made cars.

The demise of the American automobile industry—our economy's second most important business sector—was the direct result of three decades of innovation malaise. While William Ford pontificated about the "new spirit of innovation" at his company, the reality is simply this: the Asian connection did not give up market share, and they now compete in all of the market segments that once belonged to Ford and General Motors. Detroit's Big Three will be lucky to retain what they have.

The ripples of Detroit's innovation virus are widespread in terms of social and economic disruptions. Cities and states lose tax revenues, hampering their ability to provide basic services for their citizens. Employees lose their jobs, pensions, and health care benefits. Yet, the automobile industry thrives in Ohio, Indiana, Tennessee, and Alabama—states where foreign brands have established manufacturing facilities. The newfound prosperity for employees at these plants is simple. Foreign brands have the Midas touch—seductive value-added features, options, and designs that synergize into "gotta have" cars. Meanwhile, Detroit continued to believe that not much had changed from the '50s when big, clunky cars rolled off their assembly lines.

Losing the North American automobile market has formidable implications for America. We assume that America's future lies in product innovations and design while global competitors such as Eastern Europe, China, and India perform routine tasks for us using their skilled, lower-paying labor. It is a page from David Ricardo's nineteenth-century theory of "comparative advantage," explaining why we export software to China, which in turn exports cheap textiles to the United States. The solution to the controversial issue of outsourcing appears to be that America must continue to innovate.

On the surface, this proposition seems plausible, because innovation has been historically America's stew. About half of the Nobel Prize winners are Americans. We gave the world the airplane, the first browser—making Internet surfing an easy, common everyday happening—and much of the software to navigate it. The Italians may have invented pizza, but it was American ingenuity that made it an everyday food by serving slices with toppings on it. However, Ricardian reasoning, based on our preordained natural endowments, might explode on us.

The global competitors performing routine tasks are going to want to develop the software that makes performing the task possible. Global competitors aren't going to leave product innovation and design to the sole province of American corporations. Comparative advantages are not permanent in the new world economy—just ask the besieged executives at Ford and General Motors.

Is the Detroit demise a harbinger for other American industries struggling with product creativity? It will be unless America undergoes an innovation tune-up. Many of the dreary products cranked out by American companies lack electrifying design. The Asian connection will notice this. So will the design-conscious German and Scandinavian companies.

Depleted Shareholder Value

Innovation mistakes destroy shareholder value. The price tags associated with failures are steep. Iridium™, the global satellite-based wireless telephone system, cost $6 billion. Procter & Gamble spent about $1 billion on olestra, the anti-fat ingredient, with very little to show for the investment. RCA lost almost $600 million on its Selecta Vision videodisk player. R.J. Reynolds' accounting ledger shows about $600 million in red ink for its smokeless cigarette debacle. This is not chump change. It's investor money that should go to shareholders in the form of higher dividends or a handsome profit when the broker gets the sell order.

Shareholder value is diminished with each act of submarginal innovation. Companies are banking on the fact that their shareholders probably won't notice their mistakes. They are too busy raising families, working sixty hours a week to make their mortgage payments, and saving for college tuitions. Innovation mistakes disappear into the bowels of the balance sheet. Nobody notices.

The Widespread Repercussions of the Merck Meltdown

Merck is a good example of how bad innovation decisions have widespread consequences. The drug business changed with the emergence of biotech companies discovering drugs via genes rather than chemical compounds. Every pharmaceutical company faced a decision. Should strategic alliances be developed with biotech companies? The biotech company provides the new drug. The pharmaceutical company provides the selling and marketing muscle. This is the arrangement that Johnson & Johnson and Amgen made for Procrit®, a drug prescribed to help cancer patients cope with chemotherapy.

Merck's CEO, Raymond Gilmartin, believed the company's pharmaceutical research and development resources were sufficient to develop new drugs. Merck stayed on that course, leveraging the capabilities of its internal scientists in the pursuit of blockbuster drugs like its own Zocor®, a drug that lowers bad cholesterol. There was no perceived need for alliances between emerging biotech companies with promising research. Gilmartin made the wrong innovation decision, and innocent bystanders paid dearly for it.

Merck scientists moved forward in a futile journey of clinical testing on five developmental drugs. All were discontinued due to disappointing clinical testing. Two of the drugs were in the final stages of clinical testing, ready to be submitted to the FDA for approval. Merck's product cupboard was suddenly bare. Wall Street was not happy.

When Merck was the poster child on Wall Street, the stock sold in the '90s. Merck investors took a bath as the stock sunk below thirty because of Gilmartin's stubborn dependence on in-house product development for breakthrough innovative drugs. The Vioxx® bombshell, the withdrawal of its COX 2 pain reliever due to heart and stroke risks, simply reinforced the misfortunes of an already brittle company.

Business Week named Gilmartin the worst CEO in 2004. In the insane world of CEO compensation, what did he get for innovation myopia and the Vioxx® flameout? A $1.4 million bonus! But there was heat in the executive suit—Vioxx® lawsuits were up, and Merck profits were down. Gilmartin was forced to take early retirement, riding into the sunset with $1.68 million a year in pension benefits and lots of Merck stock. What did Merck shareholders get? The shaft—they lost over $120 billion in shareholder value.[11]

The shaft for Merck employees was further down the road. The new CEO Richard Clark inherited the Merck meltdown; he had no choice but to finally pull the trigger—closing eight plants and research facilities and terminating 7,000 Merck employees—while Gilmartin, the architect of the Merck mess, enjoyed a very comfortable retirement. Gilmartin's pay and performance were out of alignment—a common problem for underperforming companies like Merck—but the ultimate victims were Merck employees and shareholders. And this doesn't even take into consideration the thousands of plaintiffs and their grieving families waiting in the wings to confront Merck in the courts for allegedly marketing a high-risk drug for pain management.

Conclusion

Innovation is everybody's business. Its shape and form touches all of us in numerous ways.

Lessons Learned From Innovation Blunders

There exists a consistent failure pattern among corporations with regard to the innovation process. Since the reasons behind failure represent a rich instructional tool, the prescription for successfully harnessing the power of this process becomes straightforward:

- Focus attention on the elements of innovation failure.

- Integrate the learning into the company culture.

Let the journey begin.

NOTES

1. Karren Pennar, "One Hundred Years of Innovation," *Business Week* (Summer 1995): 8.
2. Helen Stapinski, "Dusty Trails To You," *American Demographics* (November 1999): 38–40.

3. Richard N. Foster, *Innovation: The Attackers Advantage* (New York: Summit Books, 1986), p. 260.

4. Gary Hamel, "Innovations New Math," *Fortune* (July 9, 2001): 131.

5. Ibid.

6. Ibid.

7. Jagers Gamble, "Gillette's Pricey Razor," *Economist* (October, 1999): 75.

8. Kate MacArthur, "Coke Commits $400M to Fix It," *Advertising Age* (November 15, 2004): 50.

9. Barton G. Tretheway, "Everything New Is Old Again," *Marketing Management* (Spring 1998): 5–7.

10. Christine Bittar, "Scope Mouthwash to Get Second Wind," *Brandweek* (November 29, 2004): 6.

11. Gary Strauss and Barbara Hansen, "Special Report: CEO Pay Business as Usual," *USA Today* (March 30, 2005): B1.

②

[AVOIDING MARKETING
MISJUDGMENT]

In flawed innovation, marketing misjudgment has two dimensions.

- Not Understanding Category Dynamics. Understanding the fundamental dynamics in the category is critical. Without this basic knowledge, there is a propensity to overestimate the magnitude of the marketplace opportunity.

- Straying from Core Competency. This misjudgment involves drifting away from the company's strengths. Robert Waterman and Tom Peters emphasized the phrase "stick to the knitting" in the '80s.[1] It means focusing on the corporation's core competency, avoiding the drift into unfriendly waters. McDonald's core competency is delivering 50 million meals worldwide everyday with uniform consistency. It would make no sense for McDonald's to rent DVDs like Netflix or Blockbuster.

What follow are practical examples of these two dimensions of marketing misjudgment.

CATEGORY DYNAMICS MYOPIA

First, we shall review how Campbell's Soup failed when it tried to "soup up" a sales problem by innovating an entire new product category called Intelligent Quisine®. Even worse, the soup master tried to solve a problem that Americans did not know they had, at a price point as high as a visit to the doctor.

For the other example, we will look at how Procter & Gamble stumbled going up the Citrus Hill™. Here we'll see how some smart marketing managers mistakenly thought taste was a key differentiating dynamic and got beaten on the battlefield of trade promotions.

Case #1 Not Understanding Category Dynamics: Intelligent Quisine®

The Market

If you flip through the pages of Campbell's Soup's history, John T. Dorance is the man. As a new employee hired by his uncle, the nephew quickly made his mark with the invention of condensed soup. By eliminating the water in soup, the costs for packaging, shipping, and storage were dramatically reduced, providing the company with a huge marketplace advantage.

The success of condensed soup triggered a company name change from Joseph A. Campbell's Preserve Company to simply Campbell's Soup. As condensed soup thrived, millions of Americans enjoyed the "M'm! M'm! Good" experience.

Nothing is forever. In America, thirty-five new food products are introduced every day. Condensed soup immediately encountered alternative products competing for occasions where soup could be served—including pizza, Pop Tarts®, or a grilled cheese sandwich. Per capita consumption of condensed soup drifted into decline, and so did Campbell's earnings.

Aggressive competition also invaded the soup category. ConAgra Foods leveraged its potent brand name, Healthy Choice®, across a line of soups. The name implied a healthy alternative to Campbell's condensed soups. Another company that ramped up its ads was Progresso®, positioning condensed soup as the "soup for kids." These ads showed the thin, watery soups from Campbell's versus the hefty, bountiful ingredients in Progresso® and made Progresso® the adult choice for soup lovers. Campbell's condensed red and white soups wilted under the aggressive Progresso® attack, inexplicably allowing Progresso® to knock its brains out without any retaliatory response. What was the company's formula for sluggish soup sales? It was time to innovate.

The Company "Savior" Arrives

Enter Intelligent Quisine®, a complete line of meals and snacks conforming to the American Heart Association Step 2 dietary guidelines. The eighty items in the line were not sold in supermarkets, but delivered to homes via parcel post. Demand would be driven by two activities. The Campbell's sales force would detail doctors' offices with Intelligent Quisine® product literature, and an infomercial would create consumer awareness.

Much was expected of the savior. Campbell's chairman, David Johnson, speculated that Intelligent Quisine® could be a $250 million business. That was a lot of money to offset the company's soup woes. After five years in development, the savior had the perceived smell of triumph. The relationship between diet and disease prevention seemed plausible for this line of healthy foods.

The Flawed Dynamics

But here's the trap: Intelligent Quisine® targeted people with high blood pressure, high cholesterol, and high blood sugar. Sixty million Americans have these medical problems. This represents a lot of bodies. However, many people with hypertension and high cholesterol are unaware they have these medical problems. Only about 15 percent of Americans with elevated cholesterol levels are aware of their condition. About 16 million of us have pre-diabetes, a condition where elevated blood glucose levels could lead to diabetes, but don't know it. Both segments would have benefited from Intelligent Quisine® if awareness of these medical conditions existed.

Another flaw: the price was $80 for twenty-one complete Intelligent Quisine® meals—a week's worth of breakfasts, lunches, and dinners. Many of the 60 million Americans suffering the most from heart disease and diabetes couldn't afford the meals. Ten weeks of recommended meals cost $700. These steep prices were incompatible with lower-income consumers. Wealthier Americans with the financial means to manage their health problems would have been the best target, but those who could afford a regimen of physician visits and medication didn't need Intelligent Quisine®. The target market was miscalculated.

The disparity between healthcare and income was widely acknowledged in public policy papers and other sources. Indeed, "higher income and more highly educated people are less likely to die of heart disease, strokes, diabetes, and many types of cancers, and affluent Americans live longer and in better health than the middle-class who live longer and in better health than individuals at the bottom."[2] Campbell's management should have understood the relationship between "healthy and economic status."[3] Such understanding would have tempered senior management's enthusiasm for Intelligent Quisine®—a wellness formula the affluent didn't need and the economically challenged couldn't afford.

One of the final nails in the coffin of this product line was variety, the proverbial "spice of life," especially when it comes to planning meals. Committed users of Intelligent Quisine® soon got tired of eating the same meals over and over again. In addition, some of the items in the line did not taste good despite five years of testing. Everybody's favorite, pizza, was inexplicably absent from the line. Intelligent Quisine® had some noticeable flaws.

This Savior Does Not Walk on Water

Intelligent Quisine® moved into test markets in Ohio. Sales were miserable. The plug was pulled. The product's champion, David Johnson, gave up his CEO status and became Campbell's chairman. A new CEO came in to clean up the mess. Intelligent Quisine® was not the "Hail Mary" touchdown pass the company needed. Where was John T. Dorance when you needed him?

Lessons Learned

Innovation should not be used as a substitute for resolving basic business problems. Pick up the marbles and attack the problem. Use innovation for the right reasons. It is not a silver bullet for all the marketing woes in the company. Campbell's needed to do two things—smack Progresso® in the mouth and make soup portable to fit the trend toward eating on the go, sometimes referred to as "dashboard dining."

Marketers must understand the dynamics that drive category behavior. Most innovation begins in the marketplace, not the research and development labs. Campbell's should have known that the head count they anticipated—60 million—was a mirage. Most people don't know their cholesterol levels are elevated until they are rolled into the operating room for a triple bypass.

Perhaps the reason Campbell's could not see the forest for the trees was because both product development and marketing were under the auspices of the company's chief technical officer—a scientist, not a marketer. These are two very different disciplines. Scientists should practice science. Marketers should practice marketing. And never the twain shall meet.

In the development of Intelligent Quisine®, the role for price elasticity seems to have been forgotten. How responsive will target consumers be at various price levels? Not everyone has $80 a week to spend on meals. Test consumers should have been told what a week's worth of meals would cost. Without this important piece of information, the assessment equation was incomplete. This is what happens when technical people run things.

Case #2 Not Understanding Category Dynamics: Citrus Hill™

The Market

Americans love their orange juice, and Tropicana® and Minute Maid® are the dominant brands. Tropicana® is vertically integrated, owning everything from the orange groves to the trucks leaving the processing plants. Procter & Gamble wanted a piece of the orange juice action. The competitors are tough hombres, not necessarily scared off by the marketing goliath from the land of soap flakes and paper products.

A Blind Faith in Technology

Over the years, Procter & Gamble had pioneered many technologies. The company purchased the forests of America and created huge markets in disposable diapers, facial tissues, and paper towels. Tide® was a revolutionary washday miracle. This is the Procter & Gamble style—breakthrough products structured around pioneering technology.

It is not surprising that Procter & Gamble management was intrigued when their research and development scientists expressed confidence that they could make a better tasting orange juice. Blind product testing indicated that consumer taste buds preferred the company's orange juice to competitive brands. Since Procter & Gamble always looked for differentiated products, the better-tasting orange juice fit the company's development philosophy. Senior management crowed: "Now we can beat the competition. We have the best-tasting orange juice in the world."[4]

The adventure began in 1982, when the company purchased three processing plants from Ben Hill Griffin, a large processor of Florida oranges. Procter & Gamble's Citrus Hill™ refrigerated orange juice was introduced to America in the mid-'80s with much marketing fanfare. By the early '90s, the processing plants were sold to Cargill and Procter & Gamble bid bon voyage to the orange juice category. The adventure ended.

Procter & Gamble was confident its "whatever it takes" marketing formula would work in the orange juice business. They just had to outspend Tropicana® and Minute Maid® in media and marketing by anywhere from two to five times. They could leverage the principles of branding in a way that Citrus Hill™ occupied a pedestal alongside the company's power brands like Tide® and Pampers®. All it took was lots of money and Procter & Gamble's legendary marketing smarts.

The Highs and Lows of Citrus Hill™

During its tenure in the orange juice category, Citrus Hill™ was the first orange juice brand to introduce the pour spout package. Packaging innovations are always short lived. The pour spout quickly became the category standard. Another high was the development of the first calcium-fortified orange juice. This innovation really didn't make its mark until the late '90s when Tropicana® ran with it, licensing the technology from Procter & Gamble. Orange juice with calcium became a category killer under Tropicana®, but not Citrus Hill™.

There were several low points. Consumers never mentioned in survey research conducted by competitors that Citrus Hill™ was the better-tasting orange juice. Tropicana® and Minute Maid® dropped their prices, as a countermove, perfectly willing to take less profit. Tropicana® introduced a "not from concentrate" orange juice that test audiences claimed tasted better than Citrus Hill™.

Citrus Hill™ never garnered more than a 10 percent share of the orange juice market. Tropicana® and Minute Maid® rolled on, unfazed by Procter & Gamble's marketing reputation and the company's "whatever it takes" formula. Clearly they were saying, "This is our house, Procter & Gamble. Don't expect a pain-free entry into it."

The Missing Link in Citrus Hill™'s Woes

Procter & Gamble brought several innovations to the orange juice category, but here is what they did not understand about being in that particular business.

- Sales have relatively little to do with consumer's taste buds.

- The orange juice business is trade promotion-driven.

The supermarkets of America put a specific brand "on deal" every three weeks. A popular deal in the orange juice category was two cartons for $5, or occasionally two for $4. The promoted brand moves millions of cases during the deal period. A few weeks later another brand is on sale. It moves millions of cases, while the other brands in the category sit on the sidelines and watch the action.

Shoppers know the dealing patterns. They load up their household inventory and wait for the next deal. Taste has nothing to do with their behavior. Some consumers can taste the difference between orange juice brands. Others cannot. It doesn't matter. Only one thing really counts—two cartons for $4. Dealing patterns made orange juice a commodity product category; brands are differentiated based on their selling price.

Lessons Learned

Avoid category myopia. Understand the dynamics that drive category behavior. Procter & Gamble should have been sensitized to the promotionally driven dynamic in the orange juice category. Taste has nothing to do with orange juice sales.

A strong preference margin in blind product testing, like Citrus Hill™ achieved, means the company can proceed to the next spot on the Monopoly board, but it's not safe to count the money yet. In the real world of brands, Citrus Hill™ must contend with Tropicana® and Minute Maid®—brands with history, strengths, DNA, personality, emotional values, and, most importantly, deep pockets. The orange juice encounter is war, not some antiseptic product testing where brands are unidentified and their assets obscured.

STRAYING FROM CORE COMPETENCY

In the assessment of combat forces, author Richard Gabriel says, "It is a mistake to assume that an army successful in one type of war is likely to be successful in another type of war."[5] The assessment is analogous to business.

Banana Republic tried a magazine.
Anheuser-Busch attempted to get into the snack food business.
Sears tried to become a financial supermarket.
Miller tried to market 7Up®.
Gillette dabbled in calculators.

As we shall see, disaster lurks when companies move beyond their core strengths. It is important to give the customer what he or she needs and wants. But, the origin of your expertise has a lot to do with understanding how to fulfill that need.

Our first example of wandering off the yellow brick road looks at how McNeil, a Johnson & Johnson company, stumbled into the consumer products world of margarine spreads. The second example of diverting from core competency looks at Mueller's and Nabisco's flirtations with salty snacks, even though their expertise lies in pasta and cookies/crackers, respectively. Both learned the hard way that expertise in one category does not necessarily translate to expertise in another. Our final case histories show how easily core competency gets lost in translation at major companies like IBM, Bic, and KFC. These companies absolutely believed they understood their core competency, but that was a myth.

Case #1 Straying from Core Competency: Benecol®

The Market

Product innovation moves in cycles. New product gurus viewed the first decade of the millennium as an emerging era of functional foods. A functional food was defined as one that provided a health benefit. Orange juice fortified with calcium qualified because it promoted bone density. In its limited life, Intelligent Quisine® was a functional food, conforming to the American Heart Association's dietary guidelines. People could eat these healthy meals and snacks to control problems like heart disease and diabetes.

Three pharmaceutical companies—Novartis, Merck, and Johnson & Johnson—displayed varying degrees of interest in the promise of functional foods. If health problems can be handled with certain types of food products rather than popping pills, the interest of pharmaceutical companies was understandable.

McNeil Consumer Healthcare is a Johnson & Johnson Company. Its flagship business was Tylenol®, a monstrously successful brand encountering attacks from Advil® and Aleve®. The Tylenol® brand name had been extended across other categories beyond pain relievers. The brand sales and extendability had peaked. There was very little turf left for it to conquer. Today Tylenol® has forty-eight SKUs (Stock Keeping Units) reflecting its broad coverage.

Other ways had to be found to sustain McNeil's continued growth. Functional foods could be a path for expansion since McNeil already had a division marketing nutritional products such as Splenda®, a sugar substitute, and Lactaid® milk for those who are lactose intolerant. A Johnson & Johnson marketing executive found an intriguing functional food in Finland.

A "Gift" from Finland

Enter Benecol®, licensed from the Finnish food company Raisio. Benecol® was Raisio's trade name for the ester-plant sterol sold in Finland as margarine. Three servings a day could lower cholesterol levels within two weeks. Along with the margarine, McNeil launched a snack bar, salad dressings, and a single-serve form of Benecol®, reflecting its enthusiasm for the magic ingredient. This was a case of counting chickens before they've hatched.

Despite a $20 million ad budget, the marketplace response was weak. McNeil scaled back to a single spread, discontinuing the other items in the line. McNeil hoped to build the remaining Benecol® business with a marketing practice at which pharmaceutical companies excelled—detailing doctors. However, without advertising support, supermarkets were reluctant to give the brand shelf space. Benecol® never achieved critical mass despite a gallant effort on McNeil's part.

There were several issues associated with Benecol®'s rapid demise. The per capita consumption of margarine in Finland was extraordinarily high. The US market, however, was not Finland's. Margarine spreads had a checkered history in America. They flourished when butter was identified as high in saturated fat. Then margarine came under attack because it contained trans fat. Many confused consumers bounced back to butter. Want a healthy spread on your toast? Try jelly.

Margarine ended up with a mixed reputation. Many consumers viewed it as unhealthy. This made it difficult for some consumers to accept Benecol®'s proposition as the "healthy margarine spread."

Many shoppers were conditioned to buy margarine based on price. Margarine was margarine. There were no strong perceptual differences between brands. Margarine brands are rarely advertised on television because of their status as a commodity. Benecol® was higher priced than other spreads: twenty-one individual servings cost almost $6. This was truly the high-priced spread. Only the affluent could afford it.

There was one other paramount issue. It was easier to pop one cholesterol-controlling Lipitor® pill just before bedtime rather than scrambling around three or four times a day looking for something to spread your margarine on. Why not take the easy way out?

This doomed the euphoria about functional foods replacing medications to resolve health problems. In treating health problems, a critical issue was patient compliance—taking the medication regularly. This made once-a-day or once-a-week medications popular innovation initiatives in the pharmaceutical industry. It's too complicated for consumers, especially the older ones, to remember how many times a day they used Benecol® on their English muffins. Functional foods and pharmaceutical companies were not perfect together.

Benecol®'s Marketing Hemlock

Food marketing was a very different discipline from selling Tylenol®. What Benecol® needed was someone with food experience to shepherd the product through the marketing trenches, because McNeil was not "sticking to its knitting." The name, for example: "Bene" means good, and "col" stands for cholesterol. This was too esoteric for consumers to comprehend. The pharmaceutical-oriented name sounded like an antacid, an analgesic, or a cough syrup. While all these types of products were in McNeil's business portfolio, McNeil was now playing the innovation game in a different ballpark. Benecol® was not a name suggesting an appetizing food product. It sounded like a treatment, not a treat.

During Benecol®'s development, many names were evaluated and tested with consumers. The Benecol® name always finished last in the name tests among the alternatives under consideration. Consumers erupted with laughter when they heard it, but Raisio insisted that the name be used in the United States. A compelling marketing research finding was disregarded in an effort to please.

A food specialist probably would have fallen on the sword on the name issue. It was not a name that conveyed an image of a good-tasting spread. It suggested medicine. An astute food marketer would have used an in-your-face name like Healthy Harmony.

The package, with understated graphics and a lime green shade similar to the crud found inside a container of expired cottage cheese, was another problem. Robert McMath, a new product guru, pointed out that "Benecol®'s front illustration of a mountain valley vista was more reminiscent of country living than a product that promoted a healthy lifestyle."[6] The Benecol® package blended into the dairy case like muted wallpaper. A food company would have gone for dramatic, visual impact with appetite appeal. Benecol®'s therapeutic execution would have given Andy Warhol acid indigestion.

A marketing consultant who works for packaged goods clients tried both Benecol® and a competitive spread, Take Control, from Unilever. He believed that Take Control tasted better than Benecol®, a rather important criteria for a food product. Did McNeil do any taste testing in developing Benecol®? Judging by the taste, probably not. If it did, the results were likely ignored. A food company automatically conducts several rounds of taste testing for products moving through development. Its logic is simple: a food product must taste good, no matter what its health benefit might be.

McNeil had a strong reputation in OTC drug marketing. However, with Benecol®, the company sailed off into a sunset of uncharted waters, moving beyond its core competency. The name, packaging, and product taste reflected that very clearly.

Lessons Learned

There is good marketing research. There is bad marketing research. Know which is which. Never turn your back on good marketing research. The Benecol® name was problem-prone from the first day of the venture and repeatedly surfaced as a negative. A dear price was paid for not acting on this fact.

Smart companies should stick with what they do well. Companies that are tempted to go beyond core competency should do so with extreme caution. A strategic alliance or a partnership, like the one Pepsi had with Lipton in tea, can yield expertise. Both Campbell's and McNeil, with glaring weakness, rolled the dice in pursuing functional food products. Campbell's had no experience in detailing doctors. Intelligent Quisine® was a more lyrical name than Benecol®. Why not form an alliance between the two companies? Doing so would allow leveraging the core competency of each company, thereby enhancing the odds of success.

Case #2 Straying from Core Competency: Best Foods and Nabisco

The Market

Both companies had the savory snack itch. Best Foods wanted to expand its Mueller's franchise sold in the pasta sections of supermarkets. A project was undertaken to assess the viability of pasta snacks, which leveraged the Mueller's name.

Nabisco's Mr. Phipps™ snack line consisted of a pretzel chip and a tater crisp sold in the cracker section of grocery stores. Nabisco wanted to inject some snap, crackle, and pop into the line, especially the tater crisp. The crisp could best be described as a phony potato chip that cannot be called genuine because of the manufacturing process.

A company I worked for, Rainbow Consulting, was called in to work with both of these companies.

What is wrong with this picture?

Bridges Too Far from the Snack Aisle?

Both companies had mislaid their knitting needles. Shoppers do not go to the pasta section or the cracker aisle hunting for salty snacks. They go to the salty snack aisle, dominated by the eight-hundred-pound gorilla, Frito Lay, and several regional snack food manufacturers.

After a few group sessions with consumers, Best Foods wisely decided to permanently put pasta snacks into the closet, never again to see the light of day. However, Nabisco was out of the closet and actively selling the Mr. Phipps™ line.

How did Mr. Phipps™ get so far down the pike? Two group sessions immediately told us this snack line was destined for oblivion. Nabisco did not want to hear bad news. We were fired.

Snacks are sold in bags, not cracker-type boxes. The cracker-type box packaging format fit Nabisco's expertise, but it was the wrong expertise. Many shoppers passed Mr. Phipps™, thinking it was a cracker. With only two items in the line, Mr. Phipps™ lacked critical mass. Retail shelf space was too valuable for a slow moving two-item line.

Potato chip addicts wanted the real thing, not an artificial tasting tater crisp. An authentic potato chip has a unique salty, greasy taste and texture. Chip lovers have been known to lick the inside of their potato chip bags to satisfy their cravings for this unique taste. Tater crisps that taste like cardboard could not deliver this one-of-a-kind sensory benefit.

Nabisco could never match the marketing and distribution strength of Frito Lay. Just ask Anheuser-Busch: the company's Eagle® snack business was destroyed by Frito Lay's marketing muscle. Nabisco finally found its knitting needles. The Mr. Phipps™ snack line was quietly discontinued.

Lessons Learned

Pretzel chips are possibly a good line extension idea for a bonafide snack food marketer, like Frito Lay, with a pretzel presence in the snack aisle, but not for a cracker maker like Nabisco. Companies need to attack competition from positions of strength, not weakness: "Stick to the knitting."

Companies have to consider diversification strategies, but in doing so, they may not really understand their core strengths. Something gets lost in translation. Miller assumed naively that a beverage was a beverage. They were successful with Miller beer. So why couldn't they use the same marketing formula and be successful with a soft drink like 7Up®? They didn't realize the 7Up® brand they acquired lacked a critical core strength. Coke and Pepsi had the best bottlers tied up. Miller did not have the infrastructure to get 7Up® into the stores.

They eventually sold 7Up® to Cadbury Schweppes—a company that did have the infrastructure. Miller believed the soft drink game was basically one of good advertising and smart marketing—the same ingredients that made Miller beer a success. While these were core strengths of Miller, they weren't enough. Many companies make the Miller-type mistakes, because something gets lost in translation, as illustrated by the following cases: Bic, IBM, and KFC. A company's business portfolio must be true to itself no matter how seductive diversification might be. These three companies believed that they understood their core competency, but it was an illusion on their part.

Case #3 Straying from Core Competency: IBM

Big Blue Rediscovers Its Core Strength

At corporate headquarters, IBM had pressed the panic button. Senior executives were obsessed with the attention being paid to the Apple II desktop computer. IBM stood for computers. This turf had to be defended at all costs. The company needed a line of desktop personal computers in order to keep up with competition. IBM had a translation problem on its hands, but the company failed to realize the issue.

IBM sent twelve of its best employees to Boca Raton, Florida, to set up a skunk works free from everyday corporate interference. Their mission was to develop, as soon as possible, an IBM PC that the company could market and sell. Since speed to market was their mandate, the skunk works innovation team made a daring decision—use components from other companies, like an operating system from Microsoft, a smaller company just starting to show up on the radar screen. The decision helped make Bill Gates a wealthy man. It also was an early example of outsourcing the innovation process before it became fashionable to do this as a way to gain "speed to market" advantages.

IBM's PC was a historical innovation. It was instrumental in building the market for personal computers, but disruption lay ahead. As the market developed, the business drifted to competitors like Dell and Gateway, companies specifically set up to manufacture and market personal computers. They had better business models.

IBM's knitting needles had slipped between the floorboards. The lack of focus on its core competency was described as follows in *USA Today*:[7]

> IBM's core was never about computers even though that's what IBM has always sold. The company's core strength is a powerful ability to form relationships with customers to solve their information-based problems. The difference means everything.
>
> The key for IBM has always been people, not machines. Today, IBM's most successful unit is in consulting services, which lines up perfectly with the company's core strength.

When Lou Gerstner came aboard to clean up the mess at IBM, he realized that sticking to the knitting had gone astray. Something got lost in translation. He reengineered IBM, returning it to a primary core strength: sending an armada of bodies into a business environment to solve information-related problems.

Case #4 Straying from Core Competency: Bic

Bic's Brief Adventure

Bic offers another example of how "stick to the knitting" can get lost in translation. The company's core competency is cheap disposable plastic products—pens, shavers, and lighters "made from injection-molded plastic."[8] For some inexplicable reason, Bic ended up marketing disposable women's pantyhose. Bic failed to understand the limits of its core strength. Its "cheap stuff" product line shares common marketing, sales, and product technology. The women's pantyhose business shared none of these strengths in a new channel of distribution, and it required a different manufacturing process. "Consumers were unable to see any link between Bic's other products and underwear."[9] Bic's core strength—cheap plastic stuff—got lost in translation.

Case #5 Straying from Core Competency: KFC

Fried Chicken Still Rules the Hen House

In 1991, Kentucky Fried Chicken changed its name to the less ominous sounding KFC. It was an attempt to disassociate the franchise from that terribly unhealthy word, "fried." The change also sought to offer latitude in adding new items to the menu, but this turned out to be wishful thinking.

The company wanted to reconfigure its product line to better reflect the healthier eating patterns of Americans. Why not sell roasted chicken entrees as an alternative to the artery clogging, but delicious tasting fried chicken made from the colonel's original recipe?

The first attempt at roasted chicken was the Colonel's Rotisserie Gold Chicken, which capitalized on the founder's name. It also denigrated KFC's mainstream product line. "The roasters kept breaking down,"[10] and the customers were few and far between. So, the Colonel's Rotisserie Gold Chicken disappeared from the KFC menu.

The bad idea—roasted chicken entrees—resurfaced again several years later with the same result. The sales weren't there, and the venture was terminated for a second time. We are supposed to learn from our mistakes, but KFC didn't do that.

Olive Garden stands for Italian food. Pizza Hut is where we go for pizza. Want roasted chicken? Try Boston Market. KFC is where we go for a big bucket of fried, not roasted, chicken. And never the twain shall meet. Fried chicken ruled supreme at KFC. That's its core competency. Why fight it?

Lesson Learned

On the surface, "stick to the knitting" is an easy concept to grasp. The devil is in the details. There can be a wide gap between the concept's simplicity and its implementation. Be all that you can be, but beware of diversification's seductiveness. The grass always seems greener on the other side of the marketing fence.

SUMMARY

Marketing misjudgment can cause former winners to stray from their core competency when decision makers do not understand the fundamental dynamics of the category.

Joan of Arc's core competency was charismatic leadership. Napoleon was the master of maneuvers. Attila the Hun focused on terror. It's all part of doing what you do well. Companies must do the same.

Campbell's Soup, Best Foods, Nabisco, McNeil, IBM, Bic, and KFC: their sewing kits are secured. Knit one. Purl two. Stick to the knitting. That's the equation to prevent smart companies from doing dumb things.

The 3M company markets hundreds of products. On the surface, the company's portfolio looks like a smorgasbord of unrelated products, covering everything from Scotchguard™ to furnace filters. However, every 3M product revolves around a central core competency as Waterman and Peters note:[11]

> The company is dominated by chemical engineers that do most of their wizardry with coating and bonding technology. Sticking to that central discipline doesn't mean just mundane product line extensions.

As a result, 3M has a fabled reputation for major product innovations. Strengthen your strengths. Do well what you do well. Be true to yourself.

NOTES

1. Thomas J. Peters and Robert H. Waterman Jr., *In Search of Excellence* (New York: Harper & Row, 1982), pp. 292–93.

2. Schiffman, Leon G., and Leslie Lazar Kanuk, *Consumer Behavior Ninth Edition* (Upper Saddle River, NJ: Pearson Prentice Hall, 2006), p. 373.

3. Ibid.

4. Eric Schulz, *The Marketing Game: How the World's Best Companies Play to Win* (Holbrook, MN: Adams Media Corporation, 1999), p. 35.

5. Richard Gabriel, *Fighting Armies: Antagonist in the Middle East—Combat Assessment* (Westport, CT: Greenwood Publishing Group, 1983), p. 27.

6. Robert M. McMath, "Spread Alert Low Cholesterol, Low Fat and Low Sales," http://www.failuremamag.com/arch_McMath_Benecol.htm (accessed March 17, 2002).

7. Kevin Maney, "Pioneer IBM Finally Finds Its Way Out of the PC Wilderness," *USA Today*, December 8, 2004, p. 3B.

8. Matt Haig, *Brand Failures: The Truth about the 100 Biggest Branding Mistakes of All Time* (London: Kogan Page Ltd, 2003), p. 96.

9. Ibid., p. 97.

10. Bruce Horowitz, "Give Fried—Not Roasted Chicken, Customers Tell KFC," *USA Today*, July 15, 2004, p. 4B.

11. Peters and Waterman, *In Search of Excellence*, p. 225.

(3)

[ANTIDOTES TO POISONED POSITIONING]

In a moment of reflection, the masterful advertising genius David Ogilvy observed, "Positioning is the most important decision in marketing." In their first book on positioning, Trout and Reis offered this definition: Positioning is "not what you do to the product but what you do to the mind of the prospect for the product."[1] Because consumers are overloaded with information, positioning serves as an organized approach to find the right path into the mind of the customer. The positioning of a product or service is a kaleidoscope of perceptions, feelings, and impressions.

GET POSITIONING POWER

Good positioning involves isolating discernible niches that differentiate products or services from competitive offerings in certain reliable, identifiable ways. For example:

- Nordstrom's upscale retail stores stand for service.

- Volvo® owns safety.

- Pepsi is youthful.

These are positions that stick to the roof of the consumer's mind.

As a marketing weapon, positioning is so potent that even an inferior product can own the category sandbox. For years, competitive hand lotions would beat Vaseline Intensive Care® in blind product comparisons in which women would use two unidentified hand lotions. Test participants would always choose the competitive hand lotion over Vaseline Intensive Care®. But, the world is not a blind product test.

In the real world of brands, Vaseline Intensive Care® dominated the category sandbox for two decades because of its powerful therapeutic positioning reinforced by the Vaseline brand image. When Procter & Gamble introduced its hand lotion, Wondra®, it was perceived as a better hand lotion when it was pitted against Vaseline in product testing, forcing Vaseline Intensive Care® to reformulate. In the end, Wondra®, an excellent, efficacious hand lotion, disappeared while Vaseline Intensive Care® is still hanging around. That's the inherent power of positioning where inferiority can prevail over a competing product's superiority.

Bottled water is another example of positioning power. The source for major brands of bottled water is not a pristine, bubbling spring located deep in the Ozarks; the sources for Aquafina® and Dasani® are reprocessed municipal water near Pepsi and Coke bottling plants—the same stuff consumers drink from their kitchen faucets.

Aquafina® is positioned as the "young, edgy" brand. Dasani® is the healthy water. Evian® is the premium water that consumers pay more for based on its Swiss Alps heritage. And, if you do pay more for it, remember: Evian® spells naïve backwards. Consumers can't detect differences between any of these brands of bottled water in blind taste tests. Nevertheless, they'll swear up and down there are differences, because product positioning makes them believers.

Consumers pay 15 percent more for Purdue chickens, a commodity product, because they were swayed by the brand's strong initial positioning: "It takes a tough man to make a tender chicken." That tough man was Frank Purdue, the company's spokesperson. It didn't hurt the value proposition that he looked like a chicken in the commercials, but the positioning served the company well until they tried it in Spain, where the Spanish translation came across as "It takes an aroused man to make a chicken affectionate."

Campbell's Chunky™ Soup is another example of positioning power. It was originally part of Campbell's Bounty®, a line of canned entrées that turned out to be a major new product flop. One of the items in the line was canned stew, which had a negative image and a tinny, artificial taste. The canned stew became the base product for a marketing success.

The canned stew was repositioned as Campbell's Chunky™ Soup: "soup so chunky you'll be tempted to eat it with a fork." The positioning statement targeted men and urged them to chow down with a hearty can of Chunky™. The brand has used NFL football players like Mike Ditka and Donovan McNabb to pitch this hungry man's meal; advertising often featured an NFL player's mother, who teaches her son's team about the wholesome goodness of Chunky™ Soup. This marketing effort made soup man-food.

The brand moved from an abysmal failure to about a $500 million business. The product never changed from its days as a miserable failure—it was still the Bounty canned stew. What changed was the new thought planted in the minds of consumers.

Positioning is a critical issue in innovation initiatives. In working on hundreds of positioning problems, three mistakes with flawed positioning are common.

- Insignificant Positioning: The positioning benefit is irrelevant. It's a solution to a problem that America does not have. For example, think of dry beer from Anheuser-Busch. Shouldn't beer, as we know it, be wet and thirst quenching? Dry beer sounds like a dysfunctional beer that is not what we want it to be. When marketers make this positioning mistake, there is a lot of fuss about nothing, because the brand is underpositioned.

- Confused Positioning: Consumers do not understand what you are trying to sell them. The early light beer brands suffered from this problem until the right benefit promise came along. Gablinger's, one of the first light beers sold in America, failed because beer lovers were told they would lose weight drinking it. Beer drinkers were confused. Who drank beer to lose weight? Miller Lite®, a Gablinger's clone, came along and told beer drinkers that light beer meant they could drink more beer without feeling full. Beer drinkers heard what they wanted to hear even though both beers were essentially "identical products."[2] The magic of positioning won the day.

- Mismatched Positioning: The positioning and the product are not in synch. Fat-free or reduced-fat food products enjoyed temporary success but ultimately failed due to taste. They didn't taste like the real thing. Health was nice, but good taste was a paramount consideration in the consumer's mind. Consumers resist "good for you" foods that are lacking in taste. That's why sugar-coated cereals are more popular with kids than brussel sprouts.

INSIGNIFICANT POSITIONING: A LOT OF FUSS ABOUT NOTHING

Case #1 Insignificant Positioning: Bayer® Select

The Market

Tylenol® and Advil® were slaughtering Bayer® aspirin. With Bayer®'s share of the market in free fall, the decision was made to join the club rather than fight these prescription heritage pain relievers.

A Strategy for Self-Destruction

In 1993, the perceived solution to category survival was a $110 million advertising and marketing program for Bayer® Select, a line of aspirin-free analgesics that contained either acetaminophen (the core ingredient in Tylenol®) or ibuprofen (the active ingredient in Advil®).

There was nothing unique about Bayer® Select. Their pain relievers were already available, sold under the compelling brand names of Tylenol® and Advil®. Both were household words with a loyal customer base. Many users began taking Tylenol® and Advil® as a result of physician recommendations. Why would they abandon these professionally endorsed brands for Bayer® Select?

If aspirin-free Bayer® Select products were the manufacturer Sterling Drug's top of the line pain relievers, did the parent brand then become Bayer® "Ordinary"? The Select strategy denigrated the equity of Bayer® aspirin. The parent brand's credentials were emasculated, making it an egregious case of brand tampering at its worst.

Consumers aren't stupid. They are quick to spot a marketing scam. The company spent more in advertising Bayer® Select than it was getting back in sales. Moreover, the sales of Bayer® "Ordinary" continued its steep decline.

In retrospect, an advertising agency account executive working on the Bayer® Select business remarked, "We knew it was a flawed strategy, but we loved the forty-million-dollar ad budget." Unenlightened self-interest wins again.

The architects of Bayer® Select were a hang-tough group. Despite an inauspicious debut for the pain reliever line, they inexplicably raced off with a new Bayer® Select strategy, a line of cough and cold products. The same issues were in play. These were parity products basically identical to what was already available from powerful brands like Sudafed® and Actifed®. Not surprisingly, the marketplace response was anemic for these undifferentiated products. They weren't seen as any better than competing brands, so consumers stayed with what they knew. This meant two strikes against Bayer® Select, with a positioning strategy that offered a group of products already available to consumers. Both Bayer® Select ventures died a merciful death on the altar of blemished innovation.

An Alternative Solution

Rather than pursuing frivolous innovation, Sterling should have found a compelling position for Bayer® aspirin to compete effectively in its competitive milieu. Bayer® later regained market share with a value-added positioning strategy that stressed aspirin's value in cardiac therapy, illustrating once again that positioning can perform marketing miracles. David Ogilvy was right-on in his adoration for positioning power.

Lessons Learned

Do not use innovation as a substitute for solving a problem with the base business. Brand assets—the image and stored value of a brand—are precious; protect them. Bayer® Select is an example of severe brand malpractice. It takes decades for a brand to develop a core set of assets that uniquely define it in the marketplace. These hard-earned assets are diluted when a Bayer® Select type of innovation is cavalierly pursued.

Case #2 Insignificant Positioning: Arch Deluxe™

The Market

For some inexplicable reason, in early 1996 McDonald's decided it needed an adult hamburger. This presumably would make the Golden Arches more competitive with Wendy's and Burger King. Overlooked in this myopic strategy was the fact that McDonald's largest customer segment is kids.

Those Happy Meals® aren't for mom and dad. Indulgent parents tolerate a visit to the Golden Arches, but they would rather be someplace else. McDonald's reasoning became: "Let's feed these parents a hamburger while they watch their kids munch on a Happy Meal®."[3] The Arch Deluxe™ adult hamburger was conceived from this thinking and introduced to McDonald's adult customers in 1996.

The Irrelevant Duck Walk

If it looks like a duck, walks like a duck, and quacks like a duck, it must be a duck. Arch Deluxe™ looked like a hamburger. Smelled like one. Tasted like one. It must be a hamburger. One question: How did the Arch Deluxe™ differ from the burgers being grilled at Wendy's and Burger King down the street? McDonald's couldn't answer the question. Or, how did it differ from hamburgers already on the McDonald's menu, like the Big Mac® or Quarter Pounder®? McDonald's scratched its head on that question, too. The Arch Deluxe™ was irrelevant. There was no surging adult need for another hamburger patty with lettuce and tomato. It had been done before. Hamburgers are supposed to be part of McDonald's core competency, but not this one.

Initial sales weren't too bad. The Arch Deluxe™ benefited from low promotional pricing. McDonald's desperately wanted to believe in its burger creation, ultimately investing $140 million in advertising to market this ordinary looking hamburger patty.

For some unknown reason, the folly of Arch Deluxe™ was

enhanced with ads "featuring kid-favorite Ronald McDonald telling children they were not old enough to eat the Arch Deluxe™."[4] This alienated the burger chain's core clientele, and adults wondered why this gregarious kid-like clown was trying to sell them a hamburger.

The Arch Deluxe™ price was moved to a more expensive, non-promotional level. Interest and sales quickly faded. After spending massive marketing dollars to make this irrelevant hamburger patty relevant to adults, the Arch Deluxe™ was pulled from McDonald's menus.

The Arch Deluxe™ was developed at McDonald's corporate headquarters, yet many of the restaurant's successful menu items—think Egg McMuffin® and Filet O' Fish® as examples—came from franchise owners who spent every day trying to meet the needs of McDonald's customers.

Who had a better perspective on the biorhythms of customers—the corporate whiz kids with the MBAs or the franchisees? One of the reasons why the Japanese produce better cars than Detroit is the heavy use of dealer networks for styling and design ideas. These are the guys in the trenches talking to the customers, just like the franchise owners in the McDonald's system.

Consumer research suggested there was a need for an adult burger. "After conducting masses of marketing research, it emerged that people would love to eat a burger designed specifically for adults."[5] However, since nobody showed up to buy it, it made one wonder about the marketing research initially done at McDonald's. This represented another good reason to listen more closely to the franchise owners who deal with the "hamburger crowd" on a daily basis. The Arch Deluxe™ was put on the mantle alongside another hamburger fiasco: the McLean Deluxe™, a seaweed-derivative, healthy burger that flopped in the '80s.

It is not unreasonable for McDonald's to want more business from grown-ups, but its adult food image required a better logic structure than the Arch Deluxe™. Recently McDonald's has used product innovation more skillfully in targeting adults. Salads and premium-priced coffee have become successful menu items for its adult customers.

These menu options resonate with the grown-ups rather than baffle them, like the so-called adult hamburger did.

Lessons Learned

Do not innovate products for markets that do not exist. Who drove the innovation agenda? McDonald's needed the Arch Deluxe™ more than its customers did. Customers decide what is an innovation and what is not. Every company pays lip service to being customer-centric. Few do it well.

Case #3 Insignificant Positioning: Bayer® Women's

The Market

Aspirin is a paradoxical product. A German chemist invented it at the end of the nineteenth century. If aspirin were presented to the FDA today, the agency would not approve it due to its side effect of gastrointestinal bleeding. Many Americans are unaware of the risk associated with heavy aspirin consumption. Aspirin benefits from a grandfather clause that allows it to be sold over the counter.

About thirty-five years ago, an unheralded Bristol-Myers scientist started preaching about the therapeutic value of aspirin in heart disease, but it took the slow-moving medical community about two decades to finally accept the role of aspirin in cardiac therapy.

It has been approved for preventing second heart attacks and strokes as well as treating heart attacks as they occur. As pointed out earlier, Bayer®, a well-known aspirin brand, has aggressively touted these benefits in its advertising, bringing new life to a tired, old brand.

Many Americans prefer not to wait around for the first heart attack. About 26 million American adults are already on daily aspirin therapy, and it is estimated that over 100 million Americans may benefit from the regimen. This has created a lucrative marketplace for aspirin, destined to grow as the Baby Boomer segment grows older.

They tend to be a health-oriented crowd, with the entitled expectation that there must be a cure for every disease associated with chronic aging. This development has fallen into Bayer®'s lap. It wanted all the daily aspirin therapy action, but its sandbox was about to be invaded by a new competitor.

An Old Pal Returns

Many Baby Boomers fondly remember their mothers giving them orange St. Joseph® baby aspirin for fevers, colds, headaches, and other assorted illnesses. It was truly "mother's little helper" in a bygone era.

Consumers who popped aspirin every day had propelled aspirin sales to a level beyond $800 million. Johnson & Johnson wanted a piece of that pie. It acquired the venerable St. Joseph® brand, with the intention of relaunching it nationally as an 81 mg aspirin tablet for adults—part of a doctor-recommended regimen to reduce the risks of heart attacks and strokes.

Bayer® executives went ballistic upon hearing the news. How could they put the "big hurt" on Johnson & Johnson? Their first line of attack focused on an advertising issue. There was a spirited dispute about St. Joseph®'s advertising: Was 81 mg the optimum dosage level for daily aspirin therapy?

Bayer® insisted that 325 mg was the dosage level most often recommended by cardiologists for daily therapy. Therefore, Bayer® contended that its entire aspirin line was denigrated by the St. Joseph® ads. The lawyers from Bayer® and Johnson & Johnson got involved in this advertising issue, and the involved parties spent long days in courtrooms arguing about advertising claims. Bayer® did not have a strong position in this controversy, and St. Joseph® continued running its 81 mg aspirin ads.

But wait! Bayer® had a secret weapon up its sleeve—an innovation initiative to trump Johnson & Johnson.

The Aspirin War Intensifies

Aspirin was not the only daily therapy that had caught consumer attention. Women were also taking daily calcium supplements to fight the ravages of osteoporosis. Johnson & Johnson had taken an interest in aging bones through the acquisition of Viactiv®, a caramel candy snack fortified with calcium and vitamins D and K, from a Bristol-Myers Squibb subsidiary. Calcium tablets are like horse pills, hard to swallow. Viactiv® was an easy way for women to get their calcium—two chews provide 100 percent of the daily calcium requirement.

In a moment of not very divine inspiration, Bayer® management reasoned as follows: If Johnson & Johnson could take the aspirin business away from us, we'll take some calcium business from them. They introduced Bayer® Women's—a combination aspirin and calcium tablet. One way to generate a new product concept is through a marriage of benefits from two different products—an example is a shampoo and conditioner in a single product—but it didn't work this time.

Bayer® even had the courage to advertise its hybrid on network television. Women were bewildered. What was it? The product came across as neither fish nor fowl. Women still needed to get three-fourths of their daily calcium requirements from other sources. Why would one take this product for calcium without the presence of body aches and pain or headaches?

The new product attempted to straddle two segments—pain relief and calcium—creating a major identity crisis. What Bayer® had on its hands was a short-lived line extension with insignificant product positioning. But it did learn from the experience: Bayer® added an 81 mg aspirin tablet to its product line. If you can't beat them, then the next best strategy became joining them.

Lessons Learned

In both poker and marketing, always check emotions at the door before putting any chips on the table. An emotional response to competitive strategies often results in counter strategies that are poorly thought out, which is a charitable way of saying: "It can lead to very dumb innovation initiatives."

Antidotes for Insignificant Positioning

If you cannot produce a significant position for your product or service, you may be in a battle you cannot win or a war you should not fight.

Marketers who try to invade new markets have not been very successful with the head-on attack of heavy advertising investments and massive campaigns. This was the approach Procter & Gamble tried with Citrus Hill™. Established brand habits are not easily given up, especially in situations where consumers have emotionally bonded with the brand. Why give up a good thing for exploration with a replacement product?

Established brand habits are a formidable barrier to overcome. It clearly points out the need for real differentiation in positioning a product or service. Underpositioning never works and should always be avoided in the innovation game.

CONFUSED POSITIONING: CONSUMERS DO NOT UNDERSTAND WHAT YOU ARE TRYING TO SELL

Case History #1 Confused Positioning: Crest® Rejuvenating Effects

The Market

Colgate's Total® toothpaste knocked Crest® off its perch after it had dominated the market for three decades. It was a sad day at Procter & Gamble headquarters, but there's no truth to the rumor that the Procter & Gamble flag was lowered to half-mast. The company simply reloaded its bazookas and took aim at Colgate, its archrival.

Two new products surfaced from the oral hygiene renaissance at Procter& Gamble. One, Crest Whitestrips®, was a huge success. The company reconceptualized teeth whitening—the hot trend in oral hygiene—with bleaching trays that were form-fitted around the teeth. The other, Crest® Rejuvenating Effects, was more marketing hustle than substance—toothpaste positioned especially for women, with no truly female-specific ingredients. In reality, anybody can use it, because there aren't any differences between men's teeth and women's.

The genesis for the idea came from work done on Olay® Total Effects antiwrinkle cream. In group sessions, some women remarked they would like a toothpaste that "worked like the restoration products available in skin care."[6] These comments caught Procter & Gamble's attention. One way to generate new product ideas is through transference—take a new product success in one category and apply the same basic principles to another category. This became the path that Procter & Gamble went down: a cosmetic-oriented toothpaste. The ingredients in the tube were about the same as regular Crest®, making the brand more a triumph of marketing than science.

However, there was a trap in the thinking process. Women can see skin deterioration on a daily basis—dry, flaky, sagging, and wrinkles. They slap some lotion on, and they see their skin rejuvenated. Toothpaste benefits are less visible. How do we know our gums are protected from gingivitis, or we will have fewer cavities at our next checkup? There is no daily reinforcement. We simply brush and hope for the best.

The research behind Crest® Rejuvenating Effects appeared to be very "touchy, feely" and primarily qualitative in its orientation. This may have been a mistake. Colgate® also researched the women's toothpaste idea in a quantitative concept test, and it could not find a strong viable target segment for the idea. The target segment selected for Rejuvenating Effects was women aged thirty to forty-four. It was introduced to them with a $75 million ad budget using Vanessa Williams as the spokesperson. It was the toothpaste for the "nip and tuck" generation.

The product's feminine touches included a shimmery package, cinnamon vanilla flavor, and the notion of rejuvenation, but the brand didn't exactly want to close the door on men using it. So, it was important to not make it too "girly-girly." They didn't want to alienate men if Rejuvenating Effects became the only toothpaste in the medicine cabinet, but what they really wanted was "his and hers" tubes of toothpaste in the bathrooms of America. No more unisex toothpaste, and that's a big challenge, even for a masterful marketer like Procter & Gamble.

What Does Remineralize Mean?

The positioning was structured around three benefits:

- **Remineralize**: strengthens tooth enamel

- **Refresh**: freshens breath for hours with a unique flavor

- **Restore**: polishes away surface stains

Women understood refreshment and polishing away stains, but most toothpaste brands made those promises already. So where was the uniqueness? What they didn't understand was the concept of remineralization. It sounded like something straight out of a chemistry textbook. How did one look into the bathroom mirror and determine whether her teeth had been remineralized?

Benefits work best when they are understandable and our senses are reinforced (sight, touch, smell, etc.). Why didn't Crest® Rejuvenating Effects simply say, "We strengthen tooth enamel"? Everybody understands that.

A Procter & Gamble marketer said, "This is one of the few categories in personal care where there are no products marketed to women."[7] And maybe there was a reason for this. Gender positioning is difficult to pull off. It works best when there is imagery—think Virginia Slims (women's rights, chick power, etc.) or Marlboro (outdoors, blue skies, cowboys, etc.). There was not a lot of opportunity for imagery in a functional, straightforward category like toothpaste. This made it more difficult for Crest®'s positioning to succeed.

Crest® Rejuvenating Effects was fake innovation. It was basically the same old Crest® with a few superficial flourishes. Its best feature was the cinnamon vanilla flavor. Success is all in the eyes of the beholder. The success of the cinnamon vanilla flavor triggered Procter & Gamble to aggressively pursue its flavor strategy for Whitening Expressions®. The company received a lot of PR from the women's positioning. Chick power had come to Procter & Gamble with the product and the marketing team, composed of three talented women in its marketing department.

Procter & Gamble may someday topple Colgate from its toothpaste perch, but it will not do it with "marketing gimmicks" like Rejuvenating Effects. Reflecting a lack of that famous Rice Krispies® "snap, crackle, and pop," the brand encountered a subdued marketplace reception, and the "two tubes in the bathroom" strategy remained the impossible dream.

Lessons Learned

Procter & Gamble forgot how to speak English. Not all differences are meaningful or worthwhile. While the "remineralize" concept is distinctive, it is not important, communicable, or preemptive. Touting that toothpaste strengthens tooth enamel tells consumers what they need to know in a way that "remineralize" doesn't.

Case History #2 Confused Positioning: Medipren®

The Market

Tylenol® dominated the over-the-counter analgesic market for a decade with its brilliant positioning as a strong, yet gentle pain reliever. Tylenol®'s dominance and tranquility was shattered with the introduction of Advil® (containing ibuprofen, a nonasprin pain medication) from a division of American Home Products (AHP, now Wyeth Healthcare).

AHP was typically criticized for not supporting its over-the-counter brands with appropriate marketing budgets. This was not to be the case with Advil®; the brand received massive advertising and promotional support behind its positioning as "a new advancement in pain relief."

This was a switch from prescription to over-the-counter, where a brand was sold to consumers over the counter in a reduced dosage without a doctor's prescription. Advil®'s active ingredient, ibuprofen, was previously found in a prescription drug, Motrin®, and it provided longer lasting pain relief than Tylenol®. This benefit, along with the brand's prescription heritage, gave Tylenol® a migraine headache. Advil®'s sales surged, and a significant portion of that sales volume came from Tylenol®, the dominant brand accounting for about one-third of the total category sales.

An Expensive Exercise in Consumer Confusion

Johnson & Johnson decided it needed an ibuprofen brand, and its entry was dubbed Medipren®. However, the company confronted a critical positioning decision. It could adopt Gillette's innovation strategy—attack yourself—which meant that Medipren® would be positioned to relieve headaches, the mainstream symptom in the category. This was also Tylenol®'s turf, and such a strategy would require courage. Few marketers are comfortable attacking one of their own brands, especially a money machine like Tylenol®. The decision was made to position Medipren® for body aches and pain rather than headaches.

On the surface, the strategy appeared plausible. This kept Medipren® away from Tylenol®'s marketing turf. The flagship brand was protected from cannibalization because each brand had a different and distinctive positioning. This was the battle plan drawn up to counter the Advil® sales surge.

Our company, Rainbow Consulting, was working with Richardson-Vick in the pain reliever category on Aleve® when Medipren® was launched. Aleve® was another prescription pain reliever that was reformulated for over-the-counter purchase, and our assignment was to find a positioning for it. This would not be easy, because Aleve® had no clinical data demonstrating competitive superiority, despite its prescription heritage.

In the quest to find a positioning for Aleve®, we showed users of second-generation pain relievers like Tylenol® and Advil® advertising for current brands, including Medipren®. This turned out to be a very revealing exercise for Medipren® and Aleve®. Despite the initial logic of Medipren®'s positioning strategy as a reliever of body aches and pains, and a hefty $40 million advertising campaign, consumers were very confused about the brand.

Many consumers thought Medipren® was for menstrual pain even with the advertising right in front of them. The brand name and red packaging reinforced this perception. No self-respecting male was going to walk through the supermarket checkout clutching a bottle of Medipren® for menstrual pain, even if he thought it would cure his backache. Men were lost by default as customers. Moreover, many women thought Advil® was just fine for their menstrual cramps and pain as well as their headaches. What we didn't hear was any indication that Medipren® was great for body aches and pain.

Johnson & Johnson's attempt to derail Advil® with its own ibuprofen brand was not successful, and Advil® became the number two brand in the over-the-counter pain reliever market. Medipren® was inevitably withdrawn from the market as a victim of its own confused positioning. Rather than trying to finesse Medipren® with a confusing positioning, it would have been better to position it for headaches and accept the inevitable cut into Tylenol®'s market. This is what Gillette would have done in the same situation. It was better for Tylenol® to lose the business to a sister medication like Medipren® than to a competitor like Advil®. This would have at least kept the business in the Johnson & Johnson family.

Life After Medipren®

Johnson & Johnson still needed an ibuprofen brand in its product portfolio, and it obtained it by swapping brands with Upjohn. Motrin IB®, acquired in the swap, became a companion brand to Tylenol®. The brand was reasonably successful, riding the coattails of Advil®, which had established the ibuprofen beachhead. Upjohn did not want to continue playing the expensive, high-stakes marketing game, which was absolutely essential in order to survive in the competitive over-the-counter pain reliever market.

Motrin IB® was viewed as a potentially strong global brand within Johnson & Johnson, but there remained the same issue that confronted Medipren®—how to position Motrin IB® in a way that protected Tylenol®'s flanks. The company understandably wanted to keep the milk flowing from the cash cow. This time Johnson & Johnson did some very good homework.

A segmentation study of the pain relief market revealed a segment of women who medicated aggressively. Very importantly, Tylenol® was not heavily represented in the segment. This became Motrin IB®'s target segment, and its initial "kick butt" advertising campaign worked brilliantly with these aggressive medicators while minimizing Tylenol® cannibalization. It is possible to "have your cake and eat it too" with smart positioning.

Score another one for David Ogilvy. Positioning is one of marketing's most important decisions. It is always out there in the marketplace, ready to perform miracles.

Lessons Learned

Don't be a marketing wimp. Have the courage to attack yourself if that's what is needed, and avoid the Medipren® syndrome. Keep the cash register ringing in your own family of products. Less is more. Don't try to be too clever. If pain relievers are used primarily to treat headaches, find a good headache niche positioning, like Motrin IB®'s kick butt strategy.

Case History #3 Confused Positioning: Michelob®

The Market

The Anheuser-Busch website informed us that super-premium Michelob® was developed in 1896 as a draught beer for connoisseurs, and drinking it was a very special experience. It wasn't just another beer: it was, to borrow a phrase from a competitor's advertising campaign, the "champagne of beers."

The only thing constant in marketing is change. Imported beers like Heineken® and Corona® arrived on the scene, invading Michelob®'s premium beer sandbox. It was time for Michelob® to fight back and protect its turf. What Michelob® needed was positioning power. Here's a chilling statistic: From 1980 to 1998 Michelob® lost almost 80 percent of its volume (from 8.1 million barrels down to 1.7 million barrels).[8] What happened to premium Michelob® during this period of imported beers flexing their muscles?

Searching for Positioning Success in All the Wrong Places

The brand became a victim of positioning inconsistency. For almost two decades, Michelob®'s heritage was diluted by a steady stream of positioning strategies that confused beer drinkers. Michelob®'s positioning waltz, as reflected in the examples below, illustrate the brand's core problem during this critical period:[9]

- Weekends were made for Michelob®.
- Put a little weekend in your life.
- The night belongs to Michelob®.
- Some days are better than others.
- A special day requires a special beer.
- Some days were made for Michelob®.
- Where you're going, it's Michelob®.

The stewards of the Michelob® brand had ants in their pants. They ricocheted from positioning to positioning, violating a prime tenet of good positioning strategy, which is maintaining consistency.

Beer drinkers were totally confused about why and when to drink Michelob®. Weekends are made for Michelob®. Does that mean, "Please don't drink our beer the rest of the week, we don't want your business"? Why imply that Michelob® is only for special days? Doesn't Anheuser-Busch want its Michelob® customers to drink it every day? This positioning is a self-limiting approach. Another positioning suggested Michelob® was only for nighttime consumption. Does that mean one shouldn't drink it in the daytime after cutting the lawn or playing softball, two thirst-inducing activities?

These were very narrow occasion positionings with the focus constantly shifting on which occasion was best suited for drinking Michelob®. No brand can defend its turf with this kind of inconsistency. A once proud premium beer slipped into positioning oblivion. Meanwhile, beer drinkers had no problem figuring out when was the right occasion to drink Heineken® or Beck's®.

Dr. Atkins to the Rescue

The Atkins diet was reincarnated in 1997 with a new book that stayed on the best seller list for four hundred weeks. The high-fat dieting craze inspired low-carb everything, including beer. Anheuser-Busch was first out of the starting gate with what? You guessed it. Enter Michelob® Ultra. It used the respected, established Michelob® name as the launching pad for its low-carb beer. Anheuser-Busch understood the power of the Michelob® brand name, while at the same time diluting its brand equity over a period of twenty years. They were more than willing to do it again.

The success of low-carb beers had the beer barons foaming at their mouths in a state of mind that approached ecstasy. But there were two issues Anheuser-Busch chose to ignore. First, it walked into the line extension trap. The low-carb sales surge looked good on the surface, except when the source of business was examined. Anheuser-Busch didn't mind that almost half of Ultra's business came from other Budweiser® brands, including poor old Michelob®. The company got a premium price for Ultra, justifying the pillaging of its other brands.

Was low-carb beer a fad, or did it have lasting power? It was predictably a fad that would not last, but Anheuser-Busch preferred to live on Fantasy Island. It rolled the dice, desperate for sales in a stagnant beer market. The company had chased mirage segments before, such as nonalcoholic beer, dry beer, ice beer, malternatives (malt beverages), and low-alcohol beer. None of these opportunities turned into an oasis of long-term, sustained growth. Low-carb beer joined this distinguished list of "boom and bust" failures—here today and gone tomorrow. All so-called diet trends will die out, and a smart company like Anheuser-Busch should have known that.

Were the beer bellies at the corner pub—the heavy beer drinkers— really concerned about carbs as they hoisted a brew and munched on an artery-clogging cheeseburger and a plate of greasy french fries? Heavy beer drinkers accounted for 80 percent of the beer volume. Many compared low-carb beers to diet sodas; there was something missing when it came to taste. They wanted the real thing.

This left Michelob® Ultra with the "Gucci Pucci crowd," notorious for drifting from one fad to the next. About half of Michelob® Ultra's users were individuals on low-carb diets. Once they departed to chase their new passion, Michelob® Ultra was left with a depleted customer base. Where did that leave Michelob®? Answer: Still searching for its former glory.

Today Michelob® sells a little over a million barrels a year. The Michelob® saga might have had a different ending if Anheuser-Busch had done its positioning homework or, better yet, sent out an SOS signal for David Ogilvy to work on the brand's advertising positioning.

Lessons Learned

Once you have found a strong positioning, stick with it. No wonder Michelob®'s volume declined. Michelob® couldn't make up its mind and decide what it wanted to stand for, and it ended up standing for nothing.

Agencies and senior management often get bored with the status quo. They want to tamper with a solid positioning simply for the sake of change. It's a sign of progress. BMW has used the same positioning—the ultimate driving machine—for three decades. Never walk away from a good positioning. A bird in the hand is worth two in the bush. Otherwise, brands end up undifferentiated, like Michelob®.

Case History #4 Confused Positioning: Kmart

The Market

Both Wal-Mart and Kmart opened their first stores in 1962. For a quarter of a century, Kmart had the upper hand, primarily because it was spawned from an established retail company, S. S. Kresge Co. However, with the arrival of the millennium, Wal-Mart left Kmart choking in its dust.

A Positioning Waltz

As Kmart waltzed its way to bankruptcy, critical positioning mistakes were made in the competitive world of discounters. On the way to the forum, Kmart lost its positioning bearings, much like Michelob®.

Let's review discount positioning:

- What does Wal-Mart stand for? Everyday low prices. Always.

- What's Target's positioning? Chic, cool, trendy, and cheap.

- What does Kohl's signify? Department store brands at low prices.

- Now the $64,000 question. What's Kmart's positioning? Who knows? Or, isn't that the store we pass on the way to Target and Wal-Mart?

Kmart never communicated a reason for shoppers to go there and go there often. The store's positioning was constantly shifting, confusing shoppers and leaving them clueless in terms of strong reasons to shop at Kmart.

Kmart tried a low price positioning, and then Wal-Mart lowered its prices even more. If you are going to have everyday low prices, you also better have everyday low costs. Kmart's operating costs were 50 percent higher than those of Wal-Mart. This positioning battle was lost.

Military history tells us never to attack the enemy's core strength. One of the primary reasons for Wal-Mart's low overhead was the company's management information system, the best in the business world, allowing it to squeeze every last penny out of its operation. And Wal-Mart pressured its suppliers and vendors to upgrade their technology. The minute a Barbie Doll was sold at Wal-Mart, it showed up in the computers at both Mattel, the makers of Barbie, and Wal-Mart. It took Kmart years to get its information processing systems up to speed.

A consultant discovered that "Kmart had a twenty-six-week supply of snow shovels at a time when they really should have only a four-week supply."[10] That was supply chain management Kmart style. While Sam Walton could be notoriously frugal, he had no qualms about investing money in technology and IT talent.

In a desperate attempt at retro marketing, Kmart brought back the cheesy blue light special as its positioning cornerstone. It was exactly what it didn't need—a fire sale of junk merchandise. Times had changed. The blue light special no longer had cachet.

Kmart had its positioning right under its nose in the form of Martha Stewart but failed to seize the opportunity. "Consumers adored her, and Kmart had her exclusively."[11] Martha was cool, chic, and definitely the high-priced spread. It was exactly what dull, drab, dowdy Kmart needed, but it never leveraged her in a consistent positioning strategy.

Martha had the chic associated with Target. Martha had the department store quality that worked for Kohl's. Martha could have provided a potent positioning to parlay in a rough contest with formidable competition. It might even have saved Kmart from bankruptcy.

It has been speculated by retail consultants that Target watched the Martha Stewart experience with great interest. After seeing what Martha's Everyday line did for dumpy Kmart, Target pounced upon the opportunity to initiate partnerships with top designers like Kathy Ireland, Michael Graves, and Thalia. No retailer today does designer partnerships better than Target, but perhaps they got the idea from Kmart's Martha Stewart partnership.

Rather than go with the obvious, Kmart climbed on a positioning "merry-go-around," changing, shifting, and looking for the magic positioning potion, but the magic was already there with Martha Stewart. Alas! It was not to be, as long as Kmart's "positioning per month" strategy took precedence over marketing logic.

Lessons Learned

Find a position and stick with it, or suffer the consequences of customer confusion.

A Perfect Fit Revisited

There have been changes for Kmart and Martha Stewart. On Kmart's ledger, its purchase of Sears Roebuck for $11 billion created the nation's third-largest retailer behind Wal-Mart and Home Depot. There are many complex decisions to be made about how to integrate these two companies into a unified whole.

One thing has not changed: namely, Kmart's positioning. It still has none, and it is a rare shopper who can utter Kmart's "reason for being." It remains the store passed by on the way to Wal-Mart or Target—two competitors with very clear positionings.

Now, let's swing back to Martha Stewart. She still represents a brand with tremendous equity, despite her short history of legal problems. Her merchandise is still flying out of Kmart stores. Her products in Kmart were, in fact, the only part of Martha's empire not adversely affected by her legal woes. The Stewart design team is the best in the business. Martha Stewart–designed homes are moving briskly for $400,000 and more. There is a deal with Macy's to sell Martha-inspired products, which should be worrisome to Kmart.

Martha is back—a bit more subdued, but definitely a power brand when the fit is right. There still might be merit in Kmart structuring its positioning around Martha. Shoppers would notice her. She provides the relevance that Kmart has lacked for decades.

Antidotes for Confused Positioning

There are four fundamental steps in building a strong brand:

1. Own a Position: Determine what position you want. There are only a few leaders in every industry; everyone else marches in their shadows. Go for a clearly differentiated position that will enable you to market from your core strength. Have a Strategy: A position establishes a base for the offensive, just like: "Everyday low prices. Always" does for Wal-Mart. Be Tactical: The position focuses on natural strengths that provide the benefit bundle that customers are seeking. We "own" a position because of perceived strength—the perception is indeed the reality.

2. Determine Your Market: Who will be your target customers? Know who your potential customers are and who they are not. People accept only that which is consistent with what they already know as they add to their perceptions about the position of a product or service.

3. Be the Best: Determine how you are going to meet the needs of those customers better than anyone else. Focus your strengths on the needs of your customers. All positions are in the mind, and entry to the mind is through emotions, not logic. Logic sounds convincing to marketers, but it is emotions that conquer all. Premier positions are earned by organizations that listen to

their customers. They focus resources on meeting or exceeding needs in a manner that delights them. The idea is to make customers so happy that not only do they purchase your product, but they also choose not to purchase from anyone else.

4. Never Be Satisfied: Get better and better. The more secure your position seems, the greater can be the danger. It is when you feel the most secure that you are the most vulnerable to surprise.

MISMATCHED POSITIONING: A GAP BETWEEN PRODUCT PERFORMANCE AND POSITIONING PROMISE

Case #1 Mismatched Positioning: Keebler's Sweet Spots™

The Market

Keebler's Sweet Spots™, a big chocolate dollop on a bite-sized short-bread cookie, won the prestigious Edison Award from the American Marketing Association for innovation excellence. And well it should have. In the mid-1990s, *Advertising Age* ranked Sweet Spots™ second in new product dollar sales relative to all new products sold in grocery stores. Sweet Spots™ recorded a sales level of about $45 million in the brand's introductory year. But two years later, Sweet Spots™ had disappeared.

What happened? It's a case of mismatched positioning. The product and its positioning were out of sync.

A Chocolate Transfusion for the Cookie Market

Here's how Sweet Spots™ went sour. The cookie market is comprised of four key segments:

- Chocoholics: These people are addicted to chocolate. They will eat anything put in front of them that is brown.

- Chocolate Lovers: Equally addicted, they resist their chocolate cravings. Their most extreme strategy is to not bring chocolate into the house in any form. They might have a little chocolate in the car, but that doesn't count, they say. They often buy chocolate chip cookies from vending machines for portion control.

- Crunch Lovers and Sensible Eaters: These two segments prefer cookies with crunchy textures or those perceived to be more health oriented, like Nabisco's Fig Newtons®, to chocolate.

Sweet Spots™ targeted the Chocoholic and Chocolate Lover segments.

The product was launched, and first-year sales were very respectable. The positioning was working. Chocolate devotees were trying the product. However, chocolate addicts were disappointed, because Keebler used the wax-type chocolate typifying less expensive commercial cookies, and this was a major mistake on Keebler's part. Chocolate addicts seek an indulgent chocolate rush; Sweet Spots™ did not deliver. There was a gap between consumer expectation and product performance.

In the early development of Sweet Spots™, Keebler was urged to use a Hershey-type chocolate as the centerpiece for the shortbread cookie or perhaps even consider partnering with Hershey. This would position Sweet Spots™ above Nabisco, but slightly below the more premium Pepperidge Farm.

Keebler resisted the marketing advice of its consultants because the company was desperate for a new product hit. Nabisco was cleaning its clock, riding the cresting wave of Snackwell's® reduced-fat cookies, whereas Keebler had completely missed this trend. The company mantra became "clear the decks and get this product into the marketplace fast. No marketing logic please! It might confuse us."

The marketing group at Keebler was a carousel. Bodies were

coming and going in a game of marketing musical chairs, and there was no transitional stability on the Sweet Spots™ project. Nobody really understood the enabling strategy behind its development. In discussing Sweet Spots™' demise, a Keebler market researcher commented to me, "I never knew about the enablers built into the product."

The Role of Enablers in Marketing

Sweet Spots™ was developed around the marketing theory of enablers. When buying indulgent products like cookies or candy, people feel they are going beyond what they should be doing. Thus, they seek something that enables them to engage in behavior that makes them feel a bit uncomfortable. In the marketing game, there are three types of enablers: product, packaging, and attitudinal, often expressed within the strategic context of "buy our product because you're worth it," or "you've earned it." Sweet Spots™ used product and packaging as its enablers.

The filter on a cigarette is a product enabler. It makes smokers feel like they are smoking a healthier cigarette while engaging in risky behavior. Sweet Spots™ tried to hook the chocolate lover, because the product had automatically seduced the chocoholic by default. The reality of Sweet Spots™, a shortbread cookie with a big hunk of chocolate in the middle, was that the product was more candy than cookie. Because cookies are perceived to be more nutritious and less indulgent than candy, the chocolate became more acceptable in cookie form. The cookie component became the key product enabler that made chocolate lovers fall limp into the waiting arms of Sweet Spots™. They were eating a cookie, not a big chunk of chocolate candy.

In researching lovers of sweet snacks, it had been found that many eat indulgent products in units. For example, "I'll have three Milano cookies. No more." Who are they kidding! Sweet Spots™ had seventeen inner trays, each containing four cookies. This was a key packaging enabler. If the chocolate lover saw seventy-two cookies tumbling out of the package, he or she would be terrified. These inner packs helped the sweet lovers feel in control, no matter how many times they reached for the Sweet Spots™ package to munch down another inner pack. While chocolate lovers might devour seven inner trays of cookies at a single sitting, the packaging enabler made them feel like they had control over the product, rather than the cookie controlling them. Chocolate lovers could now comfortably join the chocoholics in their quest for a chocolate rush without feeling guilty.

The inner trays also had another marketing advantage. Consumer research indicated that slightly more than 80 percent of all cookie-eating occasions were in the home, often accompanied by a beverage, like a glass of milk. The inner trays made cookies portable, expanding the usage occasions beyond the home. They could be put in a purse, kept in a pocket, or tossed in the front seat of the car. The inner trays could even be packaged separately for convenience store consumption at a profitable thirty cents per pack. On the surface, Sweet Spots™ represented a cookie with a nice bundle of assets.

Au Revoir, Sweet Spots™

A fatal finale was inevitable. Keebler did not understand the critical link between the positioning and the essential need to use a rich indulgent chocolate. After cuddling up with Sweet Spots™ for one or two purchases, chocolate addicts drifted away to alternative products in their never-ceasing quest for a chocolate high.

Lessons Learned

Match product performance with customer expectations. Assess positioning promise and product delivery early in the development process. It was too late to change by the time Sweet Spots™ were on the grocery shelf, disappointing chocolate addicts. Understand the role of enablers. They can contribute to success in innovation scenarios where consumers feel uncomfortable about their behavior.

The Resurrection of Sweet Spots™

Sweet Spots™ was a strong product idea, but execution was the key to making it work. In wandering down the cookie aisle of a supermarket, I was not necessarily surprised to see Sweet Spots™ revisited sitting on the shelf. It had a new name, Sandies® Fudge Drops, but it was the Sweet Spots™ format—a shortbread cookie with a dollop of chocolate in the middle. I bought Fudge Drops, since my wife is a chocolate lover.

She eagerly grabbed the package that evening watching television and started munching. The grimace on her face said it all, but I verified her displeasure by personally eating a couple of Fudge Drops.

It was the same old problem the original Sweet Spots™ had. Fudge Drops tasted very artificial—almost medicinal. Keebler once again used the waxy commercial chocolate that typifies shelf stable cookies. There was no compelling reason for chocolate lovers to have an affair with Fudge Drops; the chocolate rush simply isn't there. Our package stagnated in the pantry until we finally threw it in the trashcan.

Case #2 Mismatched Positioning: Rogaine®

The Market

Fifty million American men experience male-pattern baldness. In 1996, they received some very good news. The Food and Drug Administration cleared Rogaine®, a topical 2 percent minoxidil solution, as an over-the-counter hair regrowth drug for men and women with common hair loss. Hallelujah! Men suffering from hair loss often experienced "anxiety, loss of self-confidence and even depression."[12] Rogaine® gave hair-challenged men a dual benefit—a full head of hair and the restoration of self-esteem.

Rogaine® had a natural contagion, because the preliminary buzz purported it to be nothing short of a miracle. As a result, it had an avalanche of positive publicity prior to its market introduction. Wall Street was especially euphoric about Rogaine®'s prospects, and its parent company, Upjohn (now Johnson & Johnson), did nothing to temper the financial cheerfulness coming from the street. In this situation, Rogaine®'s positive buzz turned out to be destructive rather than helpful. Here's why.

Great Expectations

Balding males naively believed their departed hair follicles would return instantly by rubbing Rogaine® into their scalps twice a day for a month or so. Rogaine® initially attracted the most extreme cases of male-pattern baldness, primarily older males in their fifties and sixties desperately grasping for their youth. Rogaine® could not deliver for these extreme cases. There was a deep ravine between positioning expectations and product delivery.

Rogaine® is a complex product, as explained to me by a Pfizer marketing executive. It is only effective in about 40 percent of the cases. It can take eight months to see the best results. The product is not particularly effective in cases of frontal baldness or receding hairlines. Compliance is essential to see any results. It must be used twice a day. If treatment is stopped, reversal occurs, losing any benefits from treatment. The application process—rubbing it into the scalp twice a day—is awkward. Rogaine® later attempted to make it easier with an aerosol foam version.

Since many of the initial users represented extreme cases and a desire for instant gratification, they dropped out; their perceived expectations—"where's my new hair?"—weren't instantly achieved. The buzz-worthy product was still talked about, but the talk turned negative from a large segment of disappointed men, dampening Rogaine®'s prospects for marketplace success. The Rogaine® rap became: "This stuff doesn't work like I thought it would."

In hair restoration, the early bird gets the worm. It is best to start using Rogaine® at the first signs of thinning hair. This means targeting younger men who have a general thinning of hair on the top of the scalp, rather than old guys with a couple of strands of hair combed over for the sake of vanity. Rogaine® currently does target younger men with a more forthright approach that the product works for a certain type of male-pattern baldness, but it is not a panacea for every conceivable case of male baldness.

The makers of Rogaine® made two major mistakes:

1. Rogaine® made no attempt to dismantle the early perceptions that it was a miracle product. This set an unrealistic level of expectation with respect to its product performance with the brand's early bird customers.

2. Rogaine® required an extensive educational process to help men understand its strengths and limitations; this was never acted upon.

The net result was a wide gap between positioning expectations and product performance.

Lessons Learned

The product must be able to deliver on the positioning's benefit promise, or there will be inevitable consumer backlash. It's hard to get the toothpaste back in the tube. That's why marketers must get the positioning strategy right the first time out of the starting gate. Second chances are very rare. Rogaine® never lived up to its potential, because the initial positioning and target segment were wrong from day one.

Case #3 Mismatched Positioning: Clearly Canadian®

The Market

Snapple, provider of teas and fruit drinks, and Clearly Canadian®, a brand of flavored bottled water, were pioneering beverages. In the early '90s, a new segment of new-age beverages surfaced in the soft drink industry, typified by Snapple and Clearly Canadian®. Both reflected the emerging trend to noncarbonated beverages among consumers who would normally drink Coke®, Pepsi®, Sprite®, Mountain Dew®, or other carbonated soft drinks.

Canadian Duplicity

While consumers never used the term new-age beverage in asking for Snapple® or Clearly Canadian®, sales for both drinks were brisk. Clearly Canadian® turned out to be a sprinter, not a marathon runner, in the world of new-age beverages. It was destined to flameout due to a mismatched positioning.

There were several keys to Clearly Canadian®'s initial success. The packaging and name resonated with its users. The unique package design and bottle shape connoted a drop of water with a blue tint, signifying the clarity of water. Canadian fruits, which have a hearty and robust flavor, were the basis for the six flavors in the Clearly Canadian® line.

These brand assets were coupled with the equity of Canada, invoking wilderness, bubbling springs, minimal pollution, soaring mountains, clean lines, and grassy plains. Only this type of environment could spawn a bottled water devoid of impurities like cool refreshing Clearly Canadian®.

With an image of Canadian goodness, Clearly Canadian® junkies assumed they were drinking "a good for you" beverage, pure water from the mountains of Canada with a subtle hint of flavor.

Clearly Canadian® wasn't any healthier than the carbonated soft drinks that had been abandoned for Canadian purity. Customers were surprised to read the label and find out their bottled water had 160 calories, since they assumed it had no calories. How could it have calories? It was water. Clearly Canadian® used the same artificial flavors and preservatives that typified carbonated soft drinks. In reality, it was positioning hustle, not a healthier alternative.

Clearly Canadian® sales plummeted when consumers realized they had been duped. The brand's positioning was misleading; this disappointment caused its customer base to drift away to the greener pastures of other beverage alternatives. Clearly Canadian® became a sinking Canadian sunset. The company never recovered from the fiasco as the muscle guys—Coke, Pepsi, and Nestlé—rushed into the bottled water market.

Americans now buy about eight billion gallons of water annually at supermarkets, convenience stores, and other outlets. One way to survive in this hotly competitive market is to provide enhanced bottled waters. This genre is characterized by the addition of flavors or nutraceuticals to the basic product—think VitaminWater® or Aquafina Essentials® as examples. So, the Clearly Canadian® strategy—put something in the bottled water—bounced back. But the originator of the strategy watched the action on the sidelines because of positioning duplicity. Consumers in the early days of bottled water preferred a basic product with no frills or embellishments. They felt betrayed by Clearly Canadian®.

Times have changed, but not for Clearly Canadian®, the brand that pioneered enhanced bottled water years before it became fashionable to do so.

Lessons Learned

Don't create a positioning that will leave users feeling betrayed. Consumers are smart. They will eventually figure out the deception, and now with the power of the Internet, the lies and deceptions are even more vulnerable to detection.

Antidotes for Mismatch Positioning

Positioning and product are partners in the innovation process, but only if they are well matched.

- Mission Impossible: Good positioning can't compensate for a bad product. The two must always be in sync to achieve a harmonious partnership.

• The Lesson Plan: Homework is the key to achieving a value-added partnership between positioning and product.

NOTES

1. Al Ries and Jack Trout, *Positioning: The Battle for Your Mind* (New York: Warner Books Edition, 1982), p. 2.

2. Leon G. Schiffman and Leslie Lazar Kanuk, *Consumer Behavior Eighth Edition* (Upper Saddle River, NJ: Pearson Education, 2004), pp. 157–58.

3. "Counterintuitive Marketing: Hall of Shame 2002 Inductees," January 10, 2003, http://www.counterintuitivemarketing.com/hall of shame.htm (accessed January 20, 2004).

4. Matt Haig, *Brand Failures: The Truth About the 100 Biggest Branding Mistakes of All Time* (London: Kogan Page Ltd, 2003), p. 31.

5. Ibid., p. 32.

6. Sarah Ellison, "P&G's Latest Growth Strategy: His and Hers Toothpaste," *Wall Street Journal*, September 5, 2002, p. B5.

7. Jack Neff, "Crest Spinoff Targets Women," *Advertising Age* (June 3, 2002): 53.

8. Kevin Lane Keller, "The Brand Report Card," *Harvard Business Review* (January–February, 2000): 147–57.

9. Ibid.

10. John Gaffney, "Kmart's Marketing Miscues," March 3, 2002, http://www.business2.com/articles.htm (accessed March 3, 2002).

11. Ibid.

12. Matt Krumrie, "Male Hair Loss: Answers and Options," March 31, 2003, http://www.sharpman.com/articles.htm (accessed March 31, 2003).

$$4$$

[THE PERILS OF
DEAD-ON-ARRIVAL PRODUCTS]

In musing on the topic of innovation, Thomas Edison remarked: "Opportunity is missed by most people because it's dressed in overalls and looks like work." The overalls are hung in the closet. The dirt of doing is replaced with the innovation team's unbridled enthusiasm to move forward. The creators of dead-on-arrival new products are madly in love with their creations, but all too often, their love is blind.

These flawed products should never see the light of day, but they unfortunately greet the sunrise with unwarranted enthusiasm. In pushing flawed innovation initiatives forward, the hoops and hurdles in the development process are sometimes circumvented or ignored. The politics of senior management's whims may propel shaky new ventures into the marketplace. Financial considerations may be the fuel that drives the innovation engine toward impending disaster.

Innovation must be planned with an awareness of reality. In the euphoric rush to implement a new idea, an objective or thorough assessment is often ignored. These flawed new products should never end up in our garages, medicine cabinets, or pantries, but they do. The core reasons for this are discussed in this chapter.

Case #1 Dead-On-Arrival Products: Cox-2 Inhibitor Prescription Brands

The Market

For a long period in the '90s, pharmaceutical stocks were the poster children of Wall Street. Investors flocked to them for several reasons.

- Earnings of drug companies were growing faster than the profits for the S&P 500 as a whole.

- Dividends were rising more rapidly for drug companies than other stocks.

"There were only 58 companies in the S&P 500 that have increased their dividend payments every year for 26 years."[1] Five of these high flyers were drug companies.

Although investors found big pharmaceuticals irresistible, all that glittered was not gold. Many of the blockbuster drugs cheered by Wall Street—Claritin®, Nexium®, Vioxx®, and Celebrex®—were marginal advancements in pharmacology. Big pharm was picking the low-hanging fruit from the trees while innovation challenges, such as Alzheimer's or Parkinson's diseases, remained untouched. The days of double-digit growth for pharmaceutical companies have disappeared, perhaps never to be seen again.

Based on a *New York Times* article, two of the hyped drugs, Celebrex® and Vioxx®, appeared to meet a need for a certain type of patient as indicated below:

Researchers at the Stanford University Medical School and elsewhere who had long monitored arthritis and rheumatism patient records noted that thousands of patients were dying annually from bleeding ulcers and other problems caused by widely used pain killers like ibuprofen.[2]

There existed a definite need for pain relievers that were kinder and gentler to the patient's stomach. This paved the way for a new class of drug, COX-2 inhibitors that presumably reduced the rate of gastrointestinal bleeding in older patients. The FDA put both Celebrex® and Vioxx® on a fast track for approval, and this came in a mere six months based on the FDA's belief that they would drastically reduce stomach bleeding.

Madison Avenue Meets Big Pharm

In 1997, the FDA sanctioned drug advertising on television and in newspapers and magazines with the restriction that there be fair balance, which meant the benefits and side effects of advertised drugs had to be proportionately presented in commercials and print ads. This was a bonanza for Madison Avenue, much needed after the demise of "dot com" companies with bloated advertising budgets. DTC (Direct to Consumer) advertising immediately soared to a lofty $2.8 billion in agency billings. These were happy days on Madison Avenue.

A *New York Times* article described DTC advertising as "the confluence of medicine and marketing turning hope into hype."[3] Vioxx® and Celebrex® had lush ad budgets just a shade under $100 million, and their advertising executions reflected cheerful optimism about how much better life could be with the use of the pain relievers. But it was also imperative that the information and implications in the DTC ads be truthful.

Vioxx® advertising used middle-aged Dorothy Hamill, the 1976 Olympic figure skating gold medalist, as its spokesperson. In ad after ad, she could be seen gliding across the ice smiling, full of vim and vigor and pain-free. Aging baby boomers identified with her charisma, celebrity, and energetic personality. Patients walked into their doctors' offices asking for the pill that Dorothy Hamill used. Doctors often resented the request, but usually complied. It was better to acquiesce than to lose patients.

Celebrex® took a completely different approach. Its ads showed middle-aged baby boomers engaged in high-energy activities such as "softball, cycling and tai chi to the strains of the song 'Celebrate' from a '70s band, Three Dog Night."[4] The implication was to celebrate a pain-free life with Celebrex®.

Both of these prescription pain relievers were sold like gum drops, reinforced with heavy doses of beguiling ads and aggressive detailing of doctors by Merck and Pfizer sales reps.

Marketing Deception?

Older people aged sixty-five and over with arthritis were the original target audiences for Vioxx® and Celebrex®. The high priests of marketing at Merck and Pfizer ignored the intended target segment and targeted aging baby boomers starting to experience body pain. The ads never featured older people. Merck and Pfizer advertised the drugs to a mass audience, driving up awareness, interest, and demand as they moved beyond the core group that benefited most from these COX-2 pain inhibitors. The FDA, the regulating agency for drug ads, allowed both companies to reconfigure the target segment without a whimper.

The *New York Times* carried a story focused on the marketing practices of pharmaceutical companies. One drug cited in the article was Bextra®, a COX-2 inhibitor pain reliever similar to Vioxx® and Celebrex®, inherited by Pfizer when it acquired the company Pharmacia.

"Pharmacia (now Pfizer) hired Scirex, a clinical testing company owned in part by Omnicom, one of the major advertising holding companies in the US, to evaluate Bextra® for uses in cases of acute pain caused by impacted molars."[5] The study's findings were presented in the highly regarded *Journal of the American Dental Association*. The new study presented in a prestigious professional journal triggered a 60 percent increase in Bextra® sales within the dental community. Pfizer had found a way to make Bextra® look different from Celebrex®.

The only problem was that the FDA had rejected the article's conclusion six months earlier when Pharmacia sought permission from the agency to approve the drug for chronic pain following dental surgery. Bextra® did not have approval from the FDA for this indication, but the journal article never mentioned this. It was a parity pain reliever, approved by the FDA for chronic pain associated with arthritis, osteoporosis, and menstruation, but nothing else. It was no better than its sister drugs, Vioxx® and Celebrex®. Dentists reading the journal article did not know this, and their prescription behavior was manipulated. What Pharmacia did was certainly legal, but was it ethical? Federal law prohibits the promotion of drugs for indications not approved by the FDA. The deceptive journal article violated the spirit of the law. However, there was a loophole. Published research, such as the Bextra® article and medical education, are exempted from the legislation. Pharmacia (now Pfizer) took advantage of the loophole to market Bextra® for a nonapproved use.

Conclusion

The article was advertising masquerading as scientific evidence. It is an example of how pharmaceutical companies decided to sell and market this new class of painkillers.

Hope or Hype?

Some in the medical profession viewed Vioxx® and Celebrex® as much ado about nothing. Dr. Marcia Angell, former editor of the well-respected *New England Journal of Medicine*, assessed their marginal status in a December 2004 *New York Times* article: "There never was much reason for these drugs. So one should accept virtually zero side effects from Vioxx® and Celebrex®."[6] Since these new painkillers cost $2 to $3 per tablet versus a medication like ibuprofen or naproxen, which cost pennies per dosage, Kaiser Permanente, one of the nation's largest HMOs, adopted a scoring system for Vioxx® and Celebrex® developed by researchers at Stanford University based on factors like patient age, prior medical history, and risk of stomach bleeding. The Kaiser scoring system revealed that only 5 percent of its patients needed the COX-2 inhibitor painkillers. The less expensive alternatives were perfectly suitable and appropriate for the majority of patients.[7]

Celebrex® became the largest-selling COX-2 inhibitor painkiller through big bang marketing, but as noted in an article in the *New York Times*, Celebrex® "never received approval from the FDA for a claim that the drug significantly reduced stomach bleeding, which was suppose[d] to be the reason for this new class of pain killers."[8]

Conclusion

The new COX-2 inhibitor pain relievers were more a triumph of marketing guile than breakthrough medical science.

The COX-2 Implosion

As far back as 1996, almost three years before Vioxx® was introduced, there was internal uneasiness at Merck about the safety profile for the drug. For months after its introduction, there were rumblings among doctors about Vioxx®'s safety, including my own cardiologist. It was time for dodge ball.

Inside the halls of Merck, questions were developed about potential objections doctors might raise about prescribing Vioxx®. Merck sales reps were drilled in daylong meetings on handling and answering the questions. The exercise was called "dodge ball" internally.[9] Merck sales reps dressed in power suits hit the streets to persuade doctors to continue prescribing Vioxx®. Meanwhile, Dorothy Hamill kept smiling and selling in the Vioxx® ads.

Research studies for the COX-2 inhibitor class of drugs were initiated to explore their efficacy for cancer prevention. Several studies focused on healthy people who had polyps removed to see if taking a COX-2 inhibitor drug prevented the formation of polyps again. In these studies, participants taking Vioxx® and Celebrex® had a higher incidence of heart attacks and strokes than did those taking a placebo tablet. In the beginning, Merck and Pfizer aggressively defended their brands. There were denials, press releases, and interviews with the companies' CEOs passionately defending the marketing of the COX-2 inhibitor drugs as responsible and appropriate. They defended the indefensible, because the evidence was pretty damning.

The news got worse. Two new studies strongly suggested that Bextra® boosted heart problems in patients with bypass surgery. The denials and defensive posturing from Merck and Pfizer were unfortunately typical of how companies respond to a product crisis. The initial instincts tend to be very bottom-line oriented. Proctor & Gamble became very defensive when the Centers for Disease Control in Atlanta initiated an investigation into the potential link between toxic shock syndrome and their Rely tampons brand.

It is better for companies to "bite the bullet" in product crises, like Johnson & Johnson did with the Tylenol® poisoning episode in 1982. The company recalled every bottle of Tylenol® in America. Its quick response and handling of the incident was praised in public forums as a template for crisis management.

In the aftermath of Vioxx®'s withdrawal from the marketplace, Representative Henry Waxman stated at Vioxx® congressional hearings that "health risks were viewed as obstacles the sales force was instructed to surmount."[10] He cited a cardiovascular card that Merck sales reps used stating that Vioxx® was eight to eleven times safer than comparable pain relievers, but the claim was not based on the latest clinical data. Merck denied this.

Societal Marketing Concept

The societal marketing concept calls on marketers to balance three considerations in devising marketing strategies for brands:

- Company profits

- Consumer wants

- Society's interest

On the surface, it is easy to feel comfortable with the tenets of the societal marketing concept, but the implementation may not always be easy. Wall Street wanted good numbers from Merck and Pfizer. Both companies were focused squarely on short-term profits in an effort to please investors. The societal marketing concept may be a bit too Pollyanna as articulated in marketing textbooks within the context of everyday reality.

The unholy alliance with Wall Street puts great pressure on company performance and measurement. And that pressure is not going away. So accommodating society's interest and Wall Street's voracious appetite for earnings is a delicate high wire act, and many will fall off the trapeze. US companies are first and foremost focused on profit. A study conducted with senior corporate executives indicated that a CEO's top priority was making the financial numbers. This does not bode well for the implementation of the societal marketing concept in corporate America when the numbers (sales and profits) are the fuel that drives the engine. This was the dilemma that trapped Merck and Pfizer.

Lessons Learned

New products must be marketed with appropriate advertising support to create consumer awareness. The innovation game is not a contest for penny pinchers. Big pharm showed the rest of the marketing world how to do it by pumping millions into high-powered ads.

Advertising on television still works when carefully crafted. The Vioxx® and Celebrex® campaigns hit the consumer's sweet spot—the place in the minds of aging baby boomers where active lifestyles are connected with a miraculous new class of painkillers that could keep them going like the Energizer bunny. Never mind that less expensive pain relievers like Advil® and Aleve® could provide comparable relief.

Honesty is the best policy. Ethical issues inevitably can surface when the marketing id goes unchecked.

Life after Vioxx® and Bextra®

Bextra® and Vioxx® were withdrawn from the marketplace because of safety risks. Vioxx® became a lawyer's paradise, and the lawsuits against Merck mounted into the thousands. Merck made a vow to fight each lawsuit individually; the company is very busy these days in the courts. Merck has another COX-2 drug innovation, Arcoxia®, currently approved in fifty-four countries, and they want to market it in the United States. The FDA is understandably very cautious about drug innovations from Merck—especially in the area of pain management—and the agency has raised the hurdle for COX-2 approvals to a much higher level.

Merck initiated an advertising campaign structured around the theme, "patients come first." Some of the ads featured Merck's CEO, Richard Clark, a not-so-subtle signal that Merck was concerned about the company's image and reputation after the Vioxx®'s debacle, which continues to show up after the results of each lawsuit are thoroughly reviewed in the mainstream media. Merck needed to regain the confidence of investors and the general public. And indeed the Merck stock has moved up from its all-time low because of innovations like Gardasil®, a cervical cancer vaccine, and Januvia, a diabetes drug. HIV drug Isentress is also likely to get FDA approval.

Pfizer put Celebrex® advertising in mothballs, although its ad agency continued to work on new advertising campaigns for the brand. Discretion is the better part of valor in this case. After more than two years of advertising exile, Celebrex® returned to the tube with an unconventional two-and-a-half-minute commercial, rather than the usual thirty seconds. Celebrex® now carries a stringent warning label on the package based on an FDA edict. The *New York Times* reported that Pfizer would fund a large clinical study conducted by researchers at the Cleveland Clinic to assess the cardiovascular risks associated with COX-2 inhibitors. The study will include twenty thousand arthritis patients and could cost Pfizer $100 million to complete.[11] Pfizer's stock, unlike Merck's, dropped because its innovation cupboard was bare, and Celebrex®'s status is uncertain. Wall Street does not like uncertainty.

Despite the controversial nature of COX-2 inhibitor pain relievers, several other pharmaceutical companies are investing millions to prove the safety of this class of drug. Two compelling forces drive their interest.

1. There is a need for pain relievers with a better safety profile for an older population with chronic pain. Even low-dose aspirin therapy carries a risk for gastrointestinal bleeding.

2. Pharmaceutical companies have to fish where the fish are. There are 78 million baby boomers in America morphing into the "aches and pains generation." Many are potential candidates for chronic pain and daily aspirin therapy. It represents a major opportunity, and, hopefully, the drugs that surface from the efforts are safe and effective, unlike those such as Bextra® and Vioxx®.

Case History #2 Dead-on-Arrival Products: Olestra

Loose Stools Foil Fake Fat

The Market

Procter & Gamble's pantry of brands was showing its age as the company moved into the 1990s. Tide® had gone through the "new and improved" routine over seventy times. Pampers® had become an adult, hitting the forty plus age mark. Ivory® was great-grandma's brand. The company's venerable brands were ready for Social Security. The last big start-from-scratch innovation for Procter & Gamble had been disposable diapers in the late '60s.

This plodding, methodical, secretive, conservative, and sometimes even paranoid company had to become more hip and energetic in all aspects of its marketing mix, including product innovation. Competitors no longer trembled at the mere mention of Procter & Gamble's name.

Lots of Fire Power

Over the years, Procter & Gamble brimmed with pride over its vast research and development staff. In profiling the company's research and development prowess, a *Fortune* article noted that Procter & Gamble had "1,250 PhD scientists; more than the combined science departments of Harvard, MIT, Stanford, Tokyo University and London's Imperial College."[12] The company had a treasure chest of 3,000 active patents, protecting 250 proprietary technologies that continued to grow with each passing year.

Where's the Action?

Despite all the patent activity, very few big marketplace hits had surfaced from this beehive of scientific capability. The Procter & Gamble scientists were very busy and extremely powerful within the company hierarchy. However, their innovation had been focused on relatively minor product improvements.

An article in *Advertising Age* noted that a Procter & Gamble scientist bragged about the patents awarded to him. His office wall was adorned with almost three dozen plaques and awards commemorating his scientific achievements. When a general manager asked him about how many new products had surfaced from his patent activity, he hesitated before answering "none."[13]

Procter & Gamble played small ball, pursuing little ideas. Where were the grand slam home runs that made the company famous? The focus on the little ideas unfortunately took time and resources away from discovering the big ones. Procter & Gamble's innovation process required an aggressive tune-up. The company stayed afloat in this period through buying brands like Olay® and Nyquil®, rather than creating new brands from scratch.

The Big Discovery

Within the catacombs of the research and development lab, there was a perhaps promising innovation lurking on the horizon, the development of which the company had poured about $500 million into. However, if opportunity costs were cranked into the equation, the real cost was close to a billion dollars or perhaps even more. Only the Procter & Gamble accountants knew the true cost.

The promising innovation was a nonfattening fat called Olestra. It would be marketed under the brand name Olean®. Senior management speculated that this could be a huge opportunity, as big as NutraSweet®. *Fortune* portrayed the magic of Olestra this way: "The ingredient looks like fat, tastes like fat, and fries like fat, but it does not, under any circumstances, digest like fat."[14]

Olestra moved through the body's digestive system with no side trips to any other parts of the human anatomy. It was also a case of scientific serendipity. The company scientists were really looking for digestible fat "that would help premature babies gain weight."[15] The scientific discovery was described as follows:

> What they found was a fat-like compound so chemically chunky that it passed through the body—all the way through the body and out the other end—unabsorbed. It imparted no calories. But it did have an unfortunate side effect, an oleaginous exudate that showed up on people's underwear, a phenomenon Procter & Gamble scientists obviously forgot to consult their colleagues in marketing for a euphemism—anal leakage.[16]

It was back to the drawing board. Anal leakage was not a desirable consumer benefit. Scientists laboring in the Procter & Gamble vineyards fixed the drainage problem and other things as well. Olestra still passed through the body, but the elimination was now in solid rather than liquid form. Goodbye soiled underwear. During the scientific fine-tuning, Procter & Gamble prepared the reams of documentation required for FDA approval. The company visualized Olestra being used in a variety of food products, with salty snacks selected as the initial category to attack. The category selection was influenced by the fact that Procter & Gamble already had a salty snack, Pringles®.

Salty snacks are loaded with grams of fat. The ability to pig out on potato chips with absolutely zero calories represented a compelling proposition. Snack addicts could go bonkers on a diet of Olestra-laced chips. For the first time, they now had psychological permission for unlimited indulgence without feeling depressed about their depraved snacking behavior. This truly represented a snacking nirvana.

The FDA Serves Up a Curveball

The big day arrived, and the FDA approved the use of Olestra in salty snacks but with a huge caveat. The agency required Procter & Gamble to enrich the ingredient with vitamins, because Olestra tended to suck up fat-soluble nutrients as it moved through the system. But there was even more devastating news for the fat substitute. The FDA required a very graphic warning statement for all products containing Olestra. The advisory citation was to read as follows:

> This product contains Olestra. Olestra may cause abdominal cramping and loose stools. Olestra inhibits the absorption of some vitamins and nutrients. Vitamins A, D, E, and K have been added.

End of warning label. This represented a huge burden for any product containing Olestra. It made olestra sound like a laxative rather than a fat substitute.

Procter & Gamble's first customer for Olestra was marketing-savvy Frito-Lay. The company had exclusive rights to the ingredient for salty snacks until mid-1999. The launch of the company's WOW!™ chip line, including Ruffles®, Doritos®, and Tostitos®, represented one of the biggest launches in Frito-Lay's storied marketing history. This was confusing, since the products were already available under the Frito-Lay banner.

Frito-Lay estimated that Olean®-laced chips sold under the brand name WOW!™ would be at least a $400 million business. So there were great expectations for WOW!™ The company already had over a 70 percent share of the salty snack market, so it should have passed on the Olestra adventure. Why not let Procter & Gamble be the first guinea pig? Procter & Gamble needed Frito-Lay more than it needed Procter & Gamble.

Not surprising, the less than appetizing warning label was problematic for WOW!™ Was WOW!™ really Ex-Lax® in a new form, or simply a great tasting, fat-free salty snack? Only trips to the bathroom could answer this $64,000 question. The ominous warning label was a barrier in attracting users. Who would want to risk gastrointestinal distress? The marketing of WOW!™ was surprisingly inept, including greedily pricing the brand at a 40 percent premium for the potential benefit of gastrointestinal backlash. But, not even great marketing and advertising could save this dead-on-arrival product.

A Public Relations Disaster

Frito-Lay and Procter & Gamble ramped up their Olestra ventures. Health concerns about the ingredient refused to abate within the scientific community. The nonprofit Center for Science in the Public Interest pushed the FDA for an even stronger warning label. Consumer complaints about Olestra got inordinate visibility in the media. Typical of the negative buzz, a CNN news flash about a woman in Pennsylvania who ate a bag of WOW!™ chips and immediately departed for the hospital emergency room, where doctors gave her intravenous morphine for pain described by the victim as worse than childbirth. The media loves this kind of stuff, and the newspapers and airwaves became addicted to negative buzz about Olestra.

The news about Olestra got worse when the risk of cancer surfaced as a new health concern "linked to the way Olestra passes through the body without being digested."[17] WOW!™ advertising was criticized as misleading by the Center for Science in the Public Interest (CSPI), because the ads did not discuss side effects. It had become mandatory for direct-to-consumer advertising from pharmaceutical companies to mention side effects so the public was fully informed about benefits and risks. This was the fair balance rule, which consumer advocates like CSPI demanded also be applied to WOW!™'s advertising. Olestra's health issues were the kind typically associated with a drug, not a food product. This was alien territory for Frito-Lay and Procter & Gamble.

The Knockout Punch

The final nail was hammered into Olestra's coffin with news from Canada. Health Canada rejected the use of Olestra in that country. The decree was a crushing blow to Olestra's fortunes. Lynn LeSage, a spokesperson for Health Canada, provided the rationale for the decision by saying: "Procter & Gamble did not provide enough data to prove Olestra safe for consumers."[18]

Olestra was toast. There was no opportunity for it to be a global business as Procter & Gamble once had dreamed. The only available market was the United States, where a multiplicity of health issues and controversy were a burden.

Sales for WOW!™ and fat-free Pringles® (Procter & Gamble's snack product) became wobbly very fast. The initial sales projections for WOW!™ to be a $400 million brand went into a precipitous free-fall. Frito-Lay poured plenty of marketing muscle into the WOW!™ launch, including $35 million in media, a broad-scale consumer-sampling program to counter suspicion about the taste of fat-free products, and dollar-off coupons. Nothing worked, and WOW!™ became a drag on Frito-Lay's profit projections. Frito-Lay scaled back the marketing support, and Procter & Gamble ultimately announced the sale of its Olestra plant. The chip sales had become stale.

Olestra was at the end of a long, circuitous journey. The company had poured over a billion dollars and a quarter of a century into the venture and Olestra became a Jay Leno joke, not to mention a frivolous use of shareholders' money.

The End of the Trend

Procter & Gamble was caught with its trend trousers drooping at its ankles as the sun sank in the west on Olestra. By the time WOW!™ and Pringles® hit the marketplace with their fat-free miracle snacks, the era of fat-free or reduced-fat food products was over. Indulgence was fashionably back, because consumers with bulging waistlines had spent over a decade stuffing themselves with food products like Snackwell's® fat-free cookies that compromised taste for fewer calories. They now wanted a big bowl of Häagen-Daz® ice cream. The problem for Procter & Gamble was that its scientists had formed an emotional bond to Olestra. They failed to understand that the fat-free trend had passed them by. They had become like Rip Van Winkle in their passion for the technology.

An Innovation Revival

Companies can be trendsetters or trend followers. Procter & Gamble was a follower of the fat-free trend with Olestra, but a few years later, they reconceptualized how to mop kitchen floors with Swiffer®. Procter & Gamble instantly became a trendsetter again.

Procter & Gamble had a power shift problem in the development process. The research and development group had become very powerful in terms of assessing marketplace opportunities to pursue and very narrow in its refusal to be receptive to innovation opportunities from the outside. Marketing should evaluate the marketplace opportunity for innovation-shaping technology, not starry-eyed scientists. For example, the scientists at Bell Laboratories came up with a forecast that AT&T might be able to sell a million cell phones. But they underestimated marketing's ability to push the merchandise.

The same group of cerebral PhDs who spent twenty-five years chasing Olestra also came up with Citrus Hill™, that better-tasting orange juice that failed; Encaprin™, a coated analgesic that flopped; Rely, a tampon that introduced America's women to a new disease called toxic shock syndrome; Pringles®, the wood chip that pretended to be a potato chip; and Soft Batch® cookies, which have disappeared from grocery shelves. The bottom line: A research and development effort without a marketing focus is a recipe for disaster.

Under the stewardship of a new CEO, A. G. Laffley, Procter & Gamble's innovation machine picked up momentum. The company has given more say to marketing over research and development recently in assessing what category-shaping innovations the company would pursue. Research and development's arrogant, not-invented-here attitude has become a thing of the past.

About one half of the innovation ideas at Procter & Gamble now come from outside sources as a result of a Laffley mandate—as an example, SpinBrush® became a category killer after Procter & Gamble bought the toothbrush concept from a start-up entrepreneurial company in Cleveland and later sold it to Church & Dwight after acquiring Oral B in the Gillette acquisition.

From an article in *Time* magazine, here was the good news for shareholders when product innovation was clicking on all eight cylinders: "This kind of innovation has sent Procter & Gamble's profits into double digit growth and made the company the best performer on the Dow Jones this year [2002], rising 14% to nearly $90 a share."[19]

Innovation creates shareholder value, and there are several valuable lessons to be learned from the Olestra experience.

Lessons Learned

Public relations has historically been a stepchild in the marketing mix. It is underutilized. Negative buzz put Procter & Gamble on the defensive. The company should have had a savvy public relations company on board before the launch, as part of the innovation team, to temper the inevitable negative hype the media eventually feasted upon.

When in Rome, do as the Romans do. In its quarter-century pursuit of Olestra, Procter & Gamble misplaced its knitting needles. The company moved beyond its core competency; it was never a leader in food products. In dealing with government bureaucracy and the scientific community, Procter & Gamble should have viewed Olestra as a drug product rather than a food ingredient. Romance the entire scientific community, not just the FDA.

Moreover, the scientific community wanted to see more traditional clinical data on human subjects, which the company did not have. And yet Procter & Gamble had a pharmaceutical division that could have provided guidance in dealing with the scientific issues. Large corporations tend to live in their own silos with no cross-fertilization or communication between the many facets of a company.

Be alert to balance-of-power shifts in the innovation equation. Who steers the innovation vessel? Is it marketing or research and development's Svengali-like spell over the environment based on an obsession with technical grandeur?

It is just as important to know when a trend is over as it is to identify the trend before anyone else does. Make trend analysis a component of the innovation process. Target and Hallmark take trend analysis and detection very seriously. In both companies, senior managers are responsible for supervising trend teams that tease out the key developments that have marketplace significance. The choice is ours. Trends can work for us or against us. A formal system makes trends a valuable ally in the game of innovation roulette.

Case History #3 Dead-on-Arrival Products: Cheap Jaguar®s

The Market

Jaguar®s had an iconic, mystic quality about them as a result of the styling genius of Sir William Lyons. In 1989 Ford acquired this illustrious brand for $2.5 billion, integrating it into the company's Premier Automotive Group, along with Aston Martin®, Volvo®, and later Land Rover®. It was a vanity purchase for the Ford family, and they paid too much for it. Life would never be the same for this iconic brand; the decline of Jaguar® had begun.

Ford, at the time of purchase, made all the correct statements about protecting and nurturing the heritage of the brand. Company officials insisted they understood the brand and would never do anything to destroy its aristocratic image. They then shuffled the brand off to the MBA crowd, and Jaguar® was destined to bleed an endless stream of strategic miscues and red ink.

The Cheap Jag Strategy

The MBA crowd running Jaguar® noticed that BMW and Mercedes had stretched downward with less expensive versions of their prestigious luxury cars. The executive mantra became "why not Jaguar®?" There was nothing wrong with this innovation strategy that good execution couldn't handle, but Ford's execution was blemished. Mercedes and BMW retained the styling heritage of the parent brands in stretching downward. This was the kind of smart execution that escaped Ford's grasp.

Ford made the decision to drive Jaguar®'s fortunes toward the "near luxury" segment: consumers who didn't quite have $50,000 or $60,000 to pay for a top-shelf Jaguar®. It was surmised that a cheaper Jaguar® was exactly what the doctor ordered for these less affluent souls. The strategy moved Jaguar® from its well-defined niche status to a mass offering; this was a huge mistake, reflecting Ford's deep misunderstanding of Jaguar®'s brand equity.

Ford alerted its dealers to get ready for Jaguar®'s explosive expansion. Many Jaguar® dealers expanded their facilities in anticipation of crowded showrooms. They later regretted the expansion decision as they desperately discounted the near luxury Jaguars® that nobody wanted to buy.

The shunned vehicle that dealers had to discount was the Jaguar® X-Type, which looked like a Ford Taurus®. The only thing about the X-Type that remotely resembled the Jaguar® was the universally recognized hood ornament—the leaping Jaguar®. Jaguar®s should devour the road with power and elegant styling; this ugly duckling limped down the highway. This Jaguar® was dead the day it rolled off the assembly line.

The high-volume vehicle was built on a midlevel Mondeo® platform (the Ford Contour® in the US) and had an anemic six cylinder motor. "Why not borrow a chassis from Volvo®,"[20] suggested one critic of Ford's Jaguar®-lite execution. The interior was a cheap-looking plastic showcase out of alignment with the feline grace and styling of its ancestors. An insider at Ford remarked, "If they spent 200 bucks on the interior, they could get some results."[21] The exterior styling was drab and dowdy.

Affluent Jaguar® owners became incensed about the cheap Jag strategy. Jaguar®'s brand loyalty plummeted. Owners of expensive Jaguars® believed the car had lost its aristocratic status every time they saw the cheap imitation. They felt betrayed. This was a perfect example of how Ford didn't understand the brand or its target segment.

The Death of an Icon Brand

The only way the X-Type could move off dealer lots was through deep discounting, because the vehicle was not ready for prime time. The ultimate humiliation for Jaguar®-lite was a $199 per month lease; dealers played a game of "the price is right." Lease or buy: We got a deal for you. This cheapened Jaguar®'s image, and it transitioned from visual opulence, grace, performance, exclusivity, and oh so very British to a perception of everyday bland. The morbid styling issue eventually transcended the entire line, as reflected in a *Business Week* article:

> Its design studio has to style cars with the sinuous, feline grace that
> defines the brand, while making sure that new offerings look fresh.
> Sales of the revamped XJ, Jag's flagship model, are suffering,

because it looked too much like the old one; buyers who shell out $70,000 want everyone to see that they have a new Jag.[22]

To be successful again, Jaguar® had to regain its styling and design gravitas, but the brand also had to discover its positioning power. Jaguars® are an alternative to BMW and Mercedes. Why had this obvious fact been so difficult for Ford's MBA crowd to grasp?

BMW has used the same positioning—"The Ultimate Driving Machine"—for three decades. The Lexus positioning—"The Relentless Pursuit of Perfection"—was leveraged for almost two decades. These are power positionings, and BMW and Lexus had the products to deliver on the benefits promised. It was difficult to position Jaguar®-lite this way by any stretch of the imagination.

In the musical *South Pacific*, the male lead sings, "Once you have found it, never let it go." While the lyrics refer to love, the same applies to positioning. BMW and Lexus found durable positionings. Consumers understood what these two luxury brands stood for, while Jaguar®'s positioning had changed more often than the transmission fluid in an old Ford. Jaguar® desperately needed a positioning consistency that truly reflected the dimensionality of the iconic Jaguar® brand.

What was astonishing about Jaguar®'s demise was that Ford had the solution in its grasp but walked away from it for the ill-fated cheap Jag strategy. Peter DeLorenzo noted, "Ford almost snatched victory from the jaws of defeat several years ago when it stunned the Detroit auto show with its F-Type Concept. It captured the essence of the Jaguar® brand, and it was definitely on the right track, but they didn't have the courage to build it, instead hinging the success of the brand on the ill-fated X-Type, and thus losing their grip on Jaguar® altogether."[23]

The Jaguar® debacle crystallized Ford's incompetence. No wonder the Asian connection pulverized the company in the marketplace. Rumor now has it that Jaguar® is on the auction block. Wonder what Toyota could do with it?

Lessons Learned

Damage to a brand can be irreversible when its brand equity is not well understood. In acquiring Jaguar®, the first thing Ford executives should have done was spend lots of time with Jaguar® owners to understand their affection for the brand even though it had major quality problems at that point.

Ford fixed the quality problems, but the company never got to know the brand. The cheap Jag strategy never would have surfaced had Ford done its brand equity homework. Brands have limits. Ford should have understood this.

Case History #4 Dead-on-Arrival Product: Mobile ESPN

The Market

On September 7, 1979, ESPN was launched by Scott Rasmussen and his father, Bill Rasmussen. Now recognized as the leader in sports, ESPN became one of the most powerful and influential media companies in America. What started as a novel idea—sports on television—has morphed into a powerful broadcasting entity that constantly seeks ways to tap into the ravenous appetite for sports that can be found not only in America but across the world.

ESPN properties include radio, television, and restaurants. With these, ESPN had become a brand, and the stewards of the brand were always looking for ways to extend the brand's tentacles. This involved using the ESPN name to launch an innovation in a new business category under the ESPN banner. An example of the brand franchise extension strategy was the ESPN Zone-themed dining and entertainment restaurants located in several cities. At the same time, there were risks associated with brand extensions, and ESPN found this out.

The Business Proposition

ESPN had lots of sports content. So why not provide the content over special ESPN cell phones? It was an innovation initiative that looked good on paper—delivering programming and content directly to customers. It was a daring idea, not a proposition for the faint-hearted. ESPN decided to go it alone, even though it already provided content to wireless carriers.

ESPN planned to make money on the hardware and incur savings by not paying wireless carriers to run ESPN content on their networks, eventually coming into its own on Sprint®'s Nextel network.

ESPN stoked the interest in the venture through house ads on its flagship station. It did this to the tune of $40 million—lots of reach and frequency, since ESPN reaches almost 80 percent of the homes in America with television.

Cell Phone Users

Although cell phone carriers relentlessly advertise the reliability of their networks, that's not the primary interest of their customers. They look for the latest in cool phones with features galore at the best prices. This was not what Mobile ESPN was selling. Its phone was ugly looking—black and red, clunky, and generally very pedestrian. It had none of the cool, "gotta have" features of competitive cell phones. And another problem: The rather unremarkable Sanyo® phone carried an initial price tag of $199. None of this fit the paradise cell phone users preferred to live in.

Subscribers to Mobile ESPN paid anywhere from $65 to $225 for monthly service. ESPN also pressured potential subscribers to switch carriers and give up their family plans. Consumers balked at the high prices and arm-twisting pressure tactics.

The Experience

Mobile ESPN gambled that sports fanatics had no other life, but they do. There was work, family responsibilities, and the requisite eight hours of sleep. First and foremost, people wanted to talk on their cell phones, and delivered content had to be more than just sports. Four hours of baseball was not good for battery life. There were also visual limitations. You kind of saw the soccer or baseball game on the cell phone's small screen, but it wasn't as good as viewing the same event at the neighborhood bar or at home.

The Result

Mobile ESPN needed five hundred thousand subscribers to break even. ESPN went into the venture with its confidence flag flying high, supremely positive that "there were plenty of people out there willing to pay for the privilege of getting sports all the time, whether at the grocery store, the kid's soccer game, or waiting for the bus."[24]

Boy, were they wrong. Maybe it was hubris, but it never happened. After launching the service on Super Bowl Sunday 2006, it was discontinued in a mere seven months, with only thirty thousand subscribers and a cost of $150 million.[25]

Lessons Learned

ESPN should have spent more time hanging out with cell phone users. The company didn't seem to understand the basic dynamics that impact a cell phone user's thought process—the little things, like penalties for terminating an existing contract with a wireless carrier, were important to them. ESPN suffered from brand arrogance. It naively assumed that anything sports-related was its turf.

Marketers must understand their core competency. ESPN got into a business that was beyond its core strength. The attempt to become a MVNO (Mobile Virtual Network Operator) was an innovation idea that should have stayed in the conference room. ESPN is about sports, not telecommunications. It was as nonsensical as McDonald's wanting to get into the solar energy business.

Brand names have limits. Choices must be made. A brand can't be everything to everyone, and ESPN did not understand this. Brand franchise extensions work best when there is a logical fit. Nobody would eat Alpo® baked beans. In the same way, cell phone users didn't rush to sign up for Mobile ESPN; there was no fit.

Case History #5 Dead-on-Arrival Products: Excedrin® Quick Tabs™

A Nightmare of Problems

The Market

Excedrin® was born in the 1960s and became famous for advertising that touted the brand's efficacy for attacking heavy-duty headaches. The marketplace position for Excedrin® was severely eroded with the arrival of megabrands like Tylenol® and Advil®. These second-generation brands benefited from a prescription heritage that made Excedrin® look like yesterday's news.

The brand settled into a comfortable number three position in the over-the-counter pain-reliever market, and Excedrin® became a strong niche brand with $400 million in sales. It had a core of loyal users, but nothing that Bristol-Myers Squibb did could energize the brand beyond its core constituency. Excedrin® was the first over-the-counter pain reliever approved by the FDA for treating migraine headaches. Despite widely advertising the news to consumers, there was no appreciable lift in Excedrin®'s sales. Excedrin®'s curse was a flat trend line for almost two decades.

A New Division

Bristol-Myers Squibb wanted to dispose of noncore products and focus on prescription drugs to prevent and treat diseases. Since several important drugs were coming off patent, the company wanted cash and a neat, antiseptic reorganization that reflected its strategic interest in becoming a pure pharmaceutical company with no low–profit margin consumer brands hanging around in the closet.

A major step in this strategy was to sell Clairol® to Procter & Gamble. It was a great fit with Procter & Gamble's portfolio, but Bristol-Myers Squibb lost its sales force in the transaction. The company was left with the Excedrin® product line and a few "cat and dog brands," like Keri® lotion and Comtrex®. It was decided to create a new division, the Consumer Medicines Group, for these nomad brands. The key positions in the group were staffed with new people, including a division president.

Excedrin®'s Salvation

The company had been working on an Excedrin® line extension before the Clairol® sale, and the people in the new division inherited it. A former BMS executive summarized the situation as follows: "We were told to see what could be done with the product."

It just might have been the panacea that the stagnated Excedrin® line needed. The product was Excedrin® Quick Tabs™, a fast-dissolving, pleasant-tasting tablet that would deliver pain relief without the need for water to wash it down. The division desperately needed a bump in sales, and it was a gamble worth taking. The cat and dog brands weren't going to provide any sales spark. The challenge was clearly on Excedrin®'s shoulders.

The idea had been evaluated in a test market simulation model commonly used in assessing innovation initiatives in consumer goods companies. These approaches involve basic consumer research and modeling. The reliability of these models depends upon client assumptions about marketing issues like consumer awareness and trade support. This became a key factor in Excedrin® Quick Tabs™' ultimate fate.

Excedrin® Quick Tabs™ performed reasonably well in the simulation model. Consumer research also indicated that most consumers experienced their headaches when they were not at home or didn't have easy access to water. The information appeared to support the need for headache relief anytime, anywhere, and without water.

Test Market

The division assembled a management team that had no sales force. It was decided to put Quick Tabs™ into a lead market to gain experience with it as the management team was forming.

Excedrin® Quick Tabs™ was dumped into a single, controlled store test market in Pittsfield, Massachusetts. The decision about success or failure would come from an evaluation of store sales, a household-diary data-tracking trial, and repeat purchases of over-the-counter pain relievers, including Excedrin® Quick Tabs™. The distribution was forced; this meant Excedrin® Quick Tabs™ was put on the grocery shelves automatically, without a sales force persuading the grocery or drug trade to carry it in their stores. The market researchers wanted two lead test markets, but the financially strapped division could not afford it. One would have to do, but this made the diary tracking data less reliable because of a smaller sample size.

The decision was made to introduce Excedrin® Quick Tabs™ nationally after only eight months in testing. Remember, the test market for original Excedrin® took almost three years. There was not enough information about the repeat purchase pattern for the Excedrin® line extension, but the division was anxious for sales. It was the old story of living by the numbers. They rolled the dice.

The Floating Assumptions

As pointed out earlier, the favorable test market simulation sales estimates for Excedrin® Quick Tabs™ were based on assumptions. These assumptions started to change—always a dangerous sign.

- The price for Excedrin® Quick Tabs™ was increased from what had been tested in the initial simulation model.

- A broker sales force was used to sell the product to the trade, because the division no longer had a sales force. A company sales force always does a better job of selling-in a new product. Broker sales forces typically sell many different products with loyalty to none of them. The trade support assumption in the marketing model was considerably less robust in the national introduction because of the broker sales force. This made the distribution and trade support assumptions used in the model invalid.

- The advertising lacked a strong efficacy message that impacted the brand awareness assumption used to calibrate the sales volume estimate. The brand awareness came in lower than anticipated because of this.

The disintegration of these assumptions made Excedrin® Quick Tabs™ a dead-on-arrival product.

Other Issues

Consumers were confused about how to use the product; they chewed the tablet rather than letting it dissolve on the tongue. Chewing it was not a pleasant taste experience, even with peppermint- or spearmint-flavored tablets. There were no directions on the package about how to use the product, nor did the advertising explain it.

The advertising was weak, focusing on the convenience of Excedrin® Quick Tabs™. There was no mention of how well the product worked; this was a major communications issue. Convenience is fine, but relieving headache pain is what consumers wanted from Quick Tabs™.

The retailers were very excited about a melt-in-your-mouth pain reliever; this had news value in a stagnant product category, but a melt-down loomed on the horizon. In manufacturing the product, an ingredient was in short supply, thus delaying the launch. Prominent retailers had been holding space in their analgesic section of the over-the-counter drug aisles, waiting for Excedrin® Quick Tab's four SKUs to show up. The retailer mood turned from impatient to nasty, which negatively impacted the trade support.

Arrivederci Excedrin®

There were too many problems with Excedrin® Quick Tabs™ to make it viable; it would not be Excedrin®'s salvation. The venerable Excedrin® brand had run out of luck and time in a company environment that wanted to focus solely on the higher return from prescription drugs. Excedrin® and the "cat and dog" brands were put up for sale. Another pharmaceutical company, Novartis, bought them. One company's poison is another company's feast.

Lessons Learned

Doing the required homework costs money. Don't be stingy. Skipping steps never illuminates the darkness. The Excedrin® innovation team should have known that consumers would be confused about how to use Quick Tabs™.

Never move out of testing too prematurely. There is likely to be critical information that has not yet surfaced. For example, will customers buy the product again? Never go into a national launch with an advertising campaign that is flawed. Line extensions are more difficult to introduce for brands with low market shares.

Case #6 Dead-on-Arrival Product:
The Mountain Dew® Assassins

The Market

For years, Coke watched the growth of Mountain Dew® with envy. Pepsi took this quirky, hillbilly regional brand and made it into a marketing powerhouse. The early Dew ads featured outhouses and cornball copy, like "It'll tickle your innards." The successful repositioning of Dew became so famous that it morphed into a Harvard Business School case study. How did Pepsi get teen boys and blue-collar workers to guzzle the Dew with gusto?

Advertising was an important part of Dew's success. Taking a page from the sports apparel industry, Mountain Dew® sold a lifestyle. The high-energy ads showed action sports like sky surfing, skateboarding, BMX, and snowboarding. Teens embraced the fun and irreverence in the ads. Dew's advertising ventured outside the mainstream establishment, and it represented the nonconformity that so many teens devour.

Pepsi worked with ESPN to invent the summer and winter action games. Young Dew drinkers wanted to be like the daring athletes in the action games. These Tony Hawk–type athletes became Mountain Dew® ambassadors. It made the teens want to join the Mountain Dew® tribe.

The Dew ads fit the high-octane image of the drink. Even blue-collar males liked the in-your-face ads. While they might not engage in the activities depicted in the Dew ads, they fantasized, reminiscing about their own wild and rebellious days as youths.

Beat the Dew Up

Coke tried to counter with a rival—Mello Yello®, a citrus-based drink sold primarily in the Southeast. Ads featured teens in action sports, but they were viewed as diluted Mountain Dew® rip-offs. The Dew already wore a coolness mantle with teens. Other Mello Yello® campaigns were equally unsuccessful in getting teens to abandon their Dew preference.

Packaging graphic changes were implemented for Mello Yello®, but committed Dew drinkers even rejected the brand when a can was "on deal" for the ridiculously low price of thirty-five cents.

Coke thought Mello Yello® and Mountain Dew® were interchangeable soft drinks; they were not. Dew users wanted no part of the Mello Yello® taste. The brand came across as weaker or slightly different from the robust, high-octane taste of Mountain Dew®. Nothing worked for Mello Yello®, and Mountain Dew® rolled on, racking up impressive sales gains. It was not Coke's answer for stopping the Dew juggernaut. What to do about the Dew?

Join the Dew

Can't beat them? Then why not join them? Coke soon introduced Surge®, a fully loaded citrus soda with a bright green color. Surge® was a Mountain Dew® wannabe. The targeting, positioning, and ads were identical to Mountain Dew®. Was Pepsi nervous? Nah!

Surge® struggled to find a target audience. It finally settled on pre-teens—the idea was to grab them before they became Dew addicts. In the conference room it sounded wonderful, but Coke did not understand a key dynamic, as pointed out in an *Advertising Age* article: "Kids that age don't have a lot of discretionary income. They are too young to have any buying power. It was a dumb idea."[26]

There was an additional problem for Surge®, because it was high in caffeine. Mothers were concerned their preteens would get too wired from this caffeine-laced drink. The perceptions of mothers were reinforced by Surge® advertising that showed teens climbing over one another to get their Surge® charge. Surge® had no place to go with the preteen strategy because:

- Preteens didn't have the pocket change to buy it.
- As gatekeepers, mothers wouldn't let it in the house.

Coke should have understood these consumer dynamics, but it was again the last one to show up for the party. Surge®, the Dew killer, fizzled. The brand was discontinued. Coke was forced to rethink its Mountain Dew® strategy.

Lesson Learned

Have a solid reason and strategy for entering the category sandbox. Strategy on the run never works. It is a sign of desperation. Surge® brought no new benefit to the carbonated soft drink category. Therefore, it had no reason for being.

The single most dominant characteristic of successful new brands and businesses is the ability to bring a new benefit to an existing category.

- Mach 3® brought superior performance to shaving.
- Healthy Choice® brought health (low fat) and good taste to food products.
- Apple and Microsoft brought simplicity to computing.
- Starbucks brought high quality and variety to away-from-home coffee.
- Quaker® Rice Cakes brought "crunch" to healthy snacking.
- Snapple brought great taste and all-natural flavors to iced tea refreshment.

What did Surge® bring to the party? Nothing! You get the picture.

Life After Surge®

Although attacking and joining did not work, Coke decided to do both in its next Mountain Dew® adventure. Its new "attack dog" was Vault®—a hybrid citrus-flavored soda that came across like a combination Mountain Dew® and energy drink, like Red Bull®. The brand was really Surge® revisited with a bit more of an octane kick.

The neither-fish-nor-fowl beverage strategy disappointed both in -

tended segments. It didn't have the energy kick of Red Bull® or Monster Energy®. Nor did it taste like Mountain Dew®. In assessing Vault®'s prospects, Tom Pirko, president of Bev-Mark, a beverage consultancy, said, "Imitating can be an expensive waste of time. Isn't it time for [Coke] to come out with new things rather than copy competitors?"[27]

Vault® was an imposter—a fake Mountain Dew®. Teens placed their trust in Mountain Dew®, because it brought an irreverent authenticity to their world that Vault® or Surge® did not. Teens can tell a fake like Vault® from the real thing.

In the Surge® period, the brand did develop a cult following that remains today. An expired can of Surge® sells for $150 to $200 on eBay. SaveSurge.com is lobbying Wal-Mart, Coke's biggest customer, to bring it back. Since Vault® didn't seem to have much going for it, maybe Coke should have named it Surge® II. That would at least have brought it some built-in customers.

Coca-Cola lavished millions of dollars in introducing teens to Vault®, but Mountain Dew® defended its turf aggressively. Dew had the best year in the brand's history, selling a billion cases in 2006, while Vault® limped along. Vault®'s weak sales made it a minor brand somewhere near Barq's® Root Beer. Mountain Dew® retained its position as the fourth-best-selling soft drink in America. Coke still had that age-old problem. What to do about the Dew? It was back to the drawing board.

Pepsi Sings the Blues

Coke and Pepsi had created a monster. The youth market is their heavy user; teens drink on average eleven cans of soda a week. Young people have become attuned to attention from marketers: They thrive on it, but they also become fickle and easily bored. They expect exciting new ads that dazzle their senses. They want new packaging. They want new games and contests. Their taste buds are bored. They want new drinks. The cola connoisseurs try to accommodate the whimsical youth culture with a litany of "new." It might be new ads, new drinks, new packaging graphics, or new something else, but it better be new.

Enter Pepsi Blue®

The hot segment was flavors. Coke and Pepsi watched their cola franchises disintegrate at the edges as the youth market moved to fun and funky flavors from Snapple, Mystic™, and others. What could be done to stem the tide?

The Pepsi strategy was to drive youth to their cola franchise with a funky flavor: Pepsi Blue®, a fusion of berry and cola, surfaced in an attempt to stop the hemorrhaging. A key target segment was inner-city youth, because research showed African American consumers preferred flavors, especially grape.

The haughty folks at Coke viewed the drink as a knee-jerk reaction to their temporary success with Vanilla Coke®, which was destined to disappear because it tasted like cough medicine. This was obviously delusional on Coke's part. The fact remained that Pepsi needed some news to feed the ravenous appetite of the youth market. Why not a blue cola, even if it did look like a toilet bowl cleaner?

In a 2002 marketing class I taught, I asked thirty students if they had ever purchased Pepsi Blue®. Twenty hands shot up in the air. How many drank it more than once? One lonely hand flapped in the air. Pepsi Blue® attracted the youth market, but only once.

The novelty of the blue color worked to induce trial purchases. Adults found it repulsive, but they were not the target consumers, anyway. The potential for repeat purchases was diminished by the product's taste, as reflected in the remark of one teen in my marketing class, who said, "This is one nasty tasting dude." It didn't look like Pepsi®. It didn't taste like Pepsi®. When the Pepsi® name is put on a beverage, there is a taste and image expectation. There was a wide gap between expectation and product delivery. Surprise, surprise!

Adios to Pepsi Blue®, the "nastiest" soda ever tasted. In press releases, Pepsi claimed the product was tested with thousands of teens. Pepsi either did the wrong research or the teens lied to them.

Lessons Learned

Colas should be brown, and Pepsi should have known this. Pepsi Blue®
had no long-term sustainable competitive advantage. New products
structured around novelty never have staying power. The Pepsi® brand
should be viewed as a bank account. The name should not be
exploited. The new product should make a deposit in the bank account,
not a withdrawal. Pepsi Blue® was a withdrawal, and too many with-
drawals can destroy brand equity.

The Magic of Lemon

In its quest for new products, Coke and Pepsi became enamored with
lemon-flavored colas, in both diet and regular varieties. Pepsi
attempted four times to sell a lemon-flavored cola without success.
Pepsi had forgotten that past behavior is the best predictor of future
success.

An Irresistible Beverage

It is true. There is nothing more refreshing than a Coke® or Pepsi®
spiced-up with a fresh wedge of lemon. In seeking taste variety, cola
users often dropped a lemon wedge into their cola. This common consumer behavior drove the cola connoisseur's passion for lemon-
flavored sodas.

Pepsi Twist® was introduced with a flourish of big-bang marketing. A Super Bowl ad featuring Ozzy Osbourne kicked off a pool
of commercials starring celebrities, including Pepsi's pricey teen pop
princess of the moment, Britney Spears. It was vintage Pepsi big-bang
marketing. Pepsi's ad agency knew how to advertise the brand, and the
Twist® ads received rave reviews, but the product had no mojo. Award-
winning advertising can't sell a bad product.

It's the Taste, Stupid

It was a formulation issue. Pepsi Twist® couldn't deliver the *real* fresh lemon taste, which was the consumer expectation. What it did deliver was a stale, artificial taste. One consumer described the Twist® taste as similar to "drinking expired cough syrup." Pepsi's lemon-flavored cola still tasted artificial the third time and fourth time around.

How did Pepsi evaluate and test Twist®? The gold standard was a fresh lemon wedge squeezed into cola. This was the only valid benchmark. If Pepsi did not test Twist® against the best benchmark, this was a flaw in their taste testing. Twist® might have tested better against earlier formulations. However, this is not an acceptable benchmark. Only the real thing was acceptable to consumers.

Pepsi Twist® went down for the count for the fourth and final time. Give Pepsi an "A" for effort. However, paraphrasing from a competitor's advertising campaign, the problem for Pepsi Twist® is simple—it wasn't the real thing. This was a mismatched positioning; the benefit promised and product performance were not in alignment.

Coke experienced a similar problem when it introduced Coke with lime. The consumer taste buds didn't care for it, either. Coke couldn't emulate the taste of a fresh wedge of lime squeezed into a cola. Once again, it was not the real thing.

Lesson Learned

In developing the product, always test against the best standard or benchmark. Twist must equal fresh lemon wedges in taste testing. Otherwise, you are undertaking an impossible crusade.

Innovation Scorecard

Both Coke and Pepsi emulate one another in terms of new product efforts, just in case the archrival might have a potential winner. Both cola connoisseurs tried lemon- and lime-flavored colas, vanilla cola, and low-carb cola, which was really a midcalorie beverage that had failed several times before.

Both pursued the spaghetti strategy—throw a lot of spaghetti (new products) against the wall and perhaps something will stick. Each was betting that a few of its multiple initiatives would achieve a scale that could accommodate their expensive overhead and infrastructure. Both companies have to sell millions of cases of a brand to make it worthwhile. While this may seem wasteful, neither manufacturer has a choice.

Coke has become a cobweb of confusion. Currently, more than a dozen different colas carry the Coke® brand name. This is choice morphed into madness. These days it is relatively easy to select the wrong Coke®, because the differentiation is not good between some of the items in the ever-expanding Coke® line. This is the spaghetti strategy in full bloom. Which Coke® is the real thing? Could someone please provide the answer?

There are also risks associated with the "many Coke®s" innovation strategy. Coca-Cola's name is the most valuable asset the company has. A strong brand name can't carry a weak, marginal product. It's the impossible dream. Brands must be careful about the company they keep. If a brand associates itself with too many losers, brand equity (the stored value of a brand) may dissolve into brand liability.

Coke's latest losing innovation initiative has been Coca-Cola Blak®, a carbonated, artificially sweetened beverage touted as a fusion of Coca-Cola® effervescence and coffee essence. Pepsi's dominant Starbucks Frappuccino® drink need not worry about the infiltration of a new coffee beverage. One Blak® drinker described the experience as similar to drinking sludge. Blak® made Vanilla Coke® taste like a chocolate sundae.

Coke spent a massive amount of trade money to get Blak® on the shelves; it basically bought the distribution. And because repeat purchases have been abysmal, a massive inventory has been left languishing on store shelves and the backrooms of supermarkets, much of it expired, leaving Blak® with major product quality issues. This loser didn't help enhance Coke's brand equity or impress Wall Street.

Coke may have used Blak® as a learning experience or an in-market laboratory that could help it prepare for the next generation of coffee-based beverages coming down the innovation pike, notably from strategic soft drink alliances with companies such as Cinnabon® and Godiva®. It was an expensive way to learn, but Coke had a lot of shareholder money to throw around. It definitely didn't have the luxury of standing around watching Starbucks dominate the coffee segment. That strategy was in play for far too long. Good luck, Coke. Starbucks has become one of the most powerful brands in America, and Pepsi has the partnership with Starbucks.

In the innovation war, Pepsi trumped Coke in two important ways. Pepsi's partnerships with companies like Lipton and Starbucks were superior to Coke's partnership with Nestlé. Pepsi did not hesitate to buy brands, notably Gatorade® and SoBe®. Coke unsuccessfully attempted to pursue a start-from-scratch strategy, with a notable string of failures the likes of Fruitopia®, KO Soda®, Blak®, and many others. On the other hand, Pepsi has to keep its three power brands—Gatorade®, Lipton®, and Starbucks®—aligned with wellness trends.

Advertising Age noted that consumers "once drank because they were thirsty. Now they drink to hydrate, boost energy, relax, refresh, or beautify."[28] These are called need states, and beverage innovation must tap into this new consumer mind-set. The major functional drink innovation has come primarily from smaller, more nimble companies like Red Bull®, Arizona®, and VitaminWater®, which move very fast.

This has not gone unnoticed by Coke and Pepsi in a category that is expected to grow globally to be $175 billon in the next four years. Moreover, the functional drinks are siphoning off business from the venerable carbonated brands of both companies. Pepsi is launching a number of new initiatives—Gatorade A.M.®, Tropicana Essentials® with Omega 3, Aquafina Alive®, and several others—to satisfy the varied need states of consumers. These innovation initiatives should further establish Pepsi's health and wellness lead over archrival Coke.[29]

Coke bottlers, weary from waiting for Coke to innovate, decided to take matters into their own hands. Coca-Cola Consolidated, the number two bottler in the Coke distribution system, signed a deal with Brain Twist to market a Cinnabon® coffee beverage. Consolidated wanted to refresh its product portfolio right away, rather than waiting for another uninspiring new product from Coke like Vault® or Coca-Cola Blak®.[30]

Coca-Cola must revitalize its own product portfolio just like Consolidated did, since the company completely missed the noncarbonated beverage trend. It recently paid $4.2 billion in cash to buy Glaceau®, the maker of VitaminWater®, a vitamin-fortified water offered in flavors. Coca-Cola is also rumored to be interested in buying Snapple and Arizona Iced Tea. Coke has been forced to buy innovation from others in the wake of its dismal innovation track record, but better late than never.

Lessons Learned

Category trends require a nimble response. There are on-trends and up-trends. On-trend are those trends a company has discovered along with everybody else. An up-trend is discovered by a company before its competitors can get their hands on it.

He who hesitates is lost in fast-moving categories. Innovate now or lose your fizz, like Coke did. Don't have an innovation menu comprised of copycat new products.

The second important lesson learned is that defending one's turf against an interloper can be more than just a defensive response. It may build market share, because brands tend to become complacent. Mountain Dew® had its best sales year ever when it defended its brand franchise against Vault®'s expensive but failed attempt to dance with the Dew.

Product Case #7 Dead-on-Arrival: Funky Fries®

Introducing the Lemming Syndrome

What do movies, television, and marketing of today have in common? They lack original thinking. A successful action movie or television series spawns an inevitable chain of imitations. Marketers have a similar affliction. They can't resist chasing another company's perceived success rather than coming up with one of their own. A whole industry may jump off the cliff, like the beer barons did in chasing ice beer and malternatives. This is the lemming syndrome.

The Market

America's favorite vegetable snack is the french fry—great with ketchup, but also an artery-clogging death wish. According to *USA Today*, the typical American eats twenty-eight pounds of french fries each year. About 90 percent of french fry–eating occasions occur at fast-food restaurants.

The Department of Agriculture reported bad news in 2002. French fry consumption was down. A major problem was the slowdown in fast-food restaurant expansion. There is "a fast-food something" in every nook, cranny, and crevice of America. McDonald's, known for its fries, was dethroned by Subway in the race for the most fast-food outlets. This was not a good development for french fries, because Subway doesn't sell them.

What the french fry funk needed was a dose of innovation. H. J. Heinz was ready to oblige.

Color Me Blue

H. J. Heinz has a pantheon of brands, but the largest is ketchup. Heinz also dominates the frozen potato market. For every dollar spent on tater tots, french fries, and the like in grocery stores, about fifty-four cents goes to Heinz.

Heinz temporarily rejuvenated the ketchup category by developing an easy-grip package for kids and offering the venerable condiment in colors such as green and purple. Technicolor ketchup was a huge, but temporary, hit with kids. They could express themselves creatively at meals by making happy faces on their hamburger buns. What do you put ketchup on? Hamburgers? French fries? Was there a connection between the condiment and the products it was used on? There was for Heinz.

Ore-Ida®, a division of Heinz, introduced America to Funky Fries®. They came in unorthodox shapes flavored with chocolate, sugar, and cinnamon. One of the Funky Fries® items was "Kool Blue," a french fry with a radical sky-blue color. But fries were already kid friendly. They didn't need a blood transfusion via gimmicks. Heinz had hoped that some of the items might be used at breakfast. Wake up, Heinz! America doesn't eat a sit-down breakfast anymore. Would the average guy or gal jump out of bed at seven o' clock in the morning to cook up a batch of cinnamon and sugar french fries? What is the rationale for a weird concoction like chocolate french fries? Is this dessert?

Here is what Heinz really forgot. The apparent success of green or purple ketchup was the novelty of its entertainment value. Kids could doodle with it at mealtime, playing tic-tac-toe or making smiley faces on their hamburger patties. Blue fries, on the other hand, just lie on the plate staring at you.

The other thing that Heinz overlooked was that even green and purple ketchup had limited staying power. Kids tired of it, being the fickle little devils that they are. And moms got tired of seeing two or three half-finished ketchup bottles hanging around in the fridge. Technicolor ketchup was a temporary phenomenon destined to drop off the map. Novelty-oriented food products like blue fries or green ketchup have short life cycles.

Heinz's sales were disappointing. Earnings and profits were off, primarily due to the Funky Fries® debacle. Both good and bad innovations impact the bottom line. Shareholders should have asked Heinz to put the innovation cap in their back pocket if blue french fries represented the best they could do. Heinz shareholders need a secure sanctuary from marketing gimmicks like chocolate or blue french fries—it is called a board of directors with gumption.

Lessons Learned

If it ain't broke, don't fix it. Stay away from new products that are novelty based. Repetition of this mantra is obviously necessary, since marketers insist on repeating this mistake.

The Aftermath of Blue Fries

The lemming syndrome came storming out of the starting gate after purple ketchup and blue french fries. Food manufacturers viewed color as the next great innovation wave. There was hot-pink and electric-blue margarine. There was a line of neon-colored salad dressings. Mickey's Magix® Cereal turned the milk in the bowl blue. Oreos® appeared on grocery shelves with a "spring yellow filling." Smiley-face potatoes and "kool-blue" fries surfaced from McCain. Kid Quisine, the TV dinners for kids, featured shapes and colors. The beat went on.

This was reproductive thinking—jump off the cliff with everybody else. None of these "color-oriented products" survived. The lemming syndrome also surfaced in the '90s, but by then the fad was clear, color-less products. There was clear toothpaste, mouthwash, soda, dishwashing detergent, and liquid soap. There was even a clear beer from Miller. The clear products went down for the count. They now romp in the pasture of failure along with blue french fries and technicolor ketchup.

Chasing an Illusive Mirage

The lemming syndrome is never dormant: it can strike food and beverage marketers unannounced. The entire food industry went bonkers over low-carb products in 2002. There were even low-carb wines and low-carb colas from Coke and Pepsi. The carb rage predictably disappeared in two years as not-so-smart companies shipped their excess inventories of low-carb food products to the hungry and needy.

The food industry has more recently been seduced by the organic fad. Organic makes more sense for fruit and produce than for shelf-stable products like spaghetti sauce, ketchup, and macaroni. Yes, it is true. Heinz is once again chasing the latest fad with organic ketchup. The company learned nothing from its ill-fated flirtation with colored ketchup and blue french fries.

The "organic" label just doesn't help sales of most self-stable food products. Organic spaghetti sauce, for example, is twice as expensive as the nonorganic version. Consumers aren't going to pay the premium. Do kids chowing down their macaroni and cheese really detect a difference between organic macaroni and the regular stuff? Will the meatloaf taste better smothered with Heinz organic ketchup?

Smart companies chase these fads because so many product categories are stagnant, but they have only themselves to blame for their dire straits. An editorial in *Advertising Age* cried out that food marketers need a new recipe, and it's called real innovation rather than chasing every fad that appears on the horizon:

> Rather than chasing after fleeting trends, smart marketers must have the guts to invest in research aimed at identifying the next big thing. They also must be willing to pay for creative minds and skilled research and development executives who can bring new business-building ideas to fruition. They must have the fortitude to break down silos and banish old ways of thinking. They must fund entrepreneurial ventures and spread seed money among creative-thinking savvy employees.[31]

The *Advertising Age* equation made a clarion call to build foundations that trigger real innovation. Swiffer® reconceptualized how consumers mop kitchen floors. iPod® revolutionized how people listen to music. Mach 3® brought a new dimension to shaving. Red Bull® created the energy drink market. Häagen-Daz® ice cream redefined indulgence. This was real innovation. Blue french fries or organic macaroni represented fads from creativity-starved marketers. Innovation lite never crushes archrivals.

Lesson Learned

Don't try to lead a market to water when it is not ready to drink. Act on current trends while they are actionable. Remember: If it goes up too fast like colored, low-carb, or clear products, it's a fad. Trends take a long time to develop. It took about two decades for the Jeep® to morph into the SUV.

NOTES

1. Paul J. Lim, "Pfizer's Plunge Will Have Side Effects for Investor," *New York Times*, December 19, 2004, p. BU9.

2. Barry Meier, "Medicine Fueled by Marketing Intensified Trouble for Pain Pills," *New York Times*, December 19, 2004, p. 1.

3. Ibid, p. 38.

4. Ibid.

5. Melody Petersen, "Madison Avenue Has Growing Role in the Business of Drug Research," *New York Times*, November 22, 2002, p. C4.

6. Alex Benson, "Ban or No Ban Celebrex Sales Will Dwindle," *New York Times*, December 21, 2004, p. C1.

7. Meier, "Medicine Fueled by Marketers Intensified Trouble for Pain Pills," p. 38.

8. Ibid.

9. Mike Adams, "Merck Caught in Scandal to Bury Vioxx Heart Attack Risks. Intimidate Scientists and Keep Pushing Dangerous Drugs," NewsTarget.com, http://www.newstarget.com (accessed November 6, 2004).

10. Julie Appelby, "Merck's Marketing of Vioxx Called Misleading," *USA Today*, May 6, 2005, p. 6B.

11. "Cleveland Clinic to Lead Large Study on Safety, Efficacy of COX-2 Inhibitors, OTC Painkillers," *Medical News Today*, http://www.medicalnewstoday.com (December 15, 2005).

12. Ronald Henkoff, "Procter & Gamble New and Improved," *Fortune*, October 14, 1996, p. 152.

13. Jack Nerr, "R&D Marketing," *Advertising Age* (March 25, 2002): 27.

14. Ibid, p. 154.

15. Ibid.

16. Ibid.

17. Eugenia Halsey, "Consumer Group Renews Assault on Olestra," June 10, 1998, http://www.cnn.com/HEALTH/9806/10/olestra.htm (accessed March 12, 2002).

18. Cliff Peale, "Canadian Ban Adds to Woes for Procter & Gamble's Olestra," *Cincinnati Enquirer*, June 23, 2000, http://www.equirer.com/editions/2000/06/23.htm (accessed April 12, 2002).

19. Daniel Eisenberg, "Healthy Gamble," *Time*, September 16, 2002, p. 46.

20. Kathleen Kerwin, "The Care and Feeding of Jaguar," *Business Week*, October 4, 2004, p. 38.

21. Ibid.

22. Ibid.

23. Peter M. DeLorenzo, "Saving Jaguar," *Autoextremist*, August 9, 2006, http://www.freerepublic.com/focus/f-news1680613/posts.htm (accessed October 25, 2006).

24. Tom Lowry, "ESPN's Cell-Phone Fumble," *Business Week*, October 30, 2006, p. 26.

25. Ibid.

26. Hillary Chura, "Coke Shifts Strategy as Surge Fizzles," *Advertising Age* (February 12, 2002): E32.

27. Kate MacArthur, "Coke Tries a Dew Me-Too Again," *Advertising Age* (May 2, 2005): 8.

28. Kate MacArthur, "Pepsi, Coke: We Satisfy Your Need States," *Advertising Age* (November 27, 2006): 3.

29. Ibid.

30. Ken Hein, "Key Coke, Pepsi Bottlers Refresh Own Portfolios," *Brandweek* (January 30, 2006): 8.

31. Editorial, "Food Marketers Need New Recipe," *Advertising Age* (August 15, 2005): 13.

⑤

[COMPETITIVE DELUSION]

The best-laid plans of mice and men have the potential to crumple in the innovation game. After months of meticulous planning, the innovation initiative is ready to leap out of the starting gate and vanquish an unsuspecting foe. Wait! Has any consideration been given to the competitive response of the unsuspecting foe?

Innovation teams often make the blithe assumption that competition will do little or nothing, that they'll simply stand around watching the invasion of their category sandbox. Look out! Competitive delusion is ready and eagerly waiting to chew up this naive assumption. In the game of innovation roulette, the contest is not over until the great marketplace judge has made it a success and the innovation team is in the shower lathering up with a bar of Irish Spring® soap.

INNOVATION PARTY POOPERS

Innovation initiatives should expect ruthless competition in confrontations with high-powered testosterone brands. These feisty competitors have two common traits:

- They are corporate cash cows.

- They also may be sentimental brands—an important part of the corporation's heritage. Think Band-Aid® or Colgate® toothpaste as examples.

This also means that fire-engine red CEOs are likely to get involved in preserving the company's sentimental, or cash cow, businesses. The combination is a sure recipe for a competitive response, with the potential for total annihilation.

There are various competitive responses that can be pursued. One is lowering prices. This probably is least palatable, because it is more like a variable cost. However, there are no guarantees in the innovation game. Both Minute Maid and Tropicana dropped their prices in response to Citrus Hill™ and successfully knocked the brand out of the orange juice category. There are many ways to "skin a cat," and testosterone brands will pull out all their weapons to make life for the new entry profoundly difficult.

Case #1 Competitive Delusion: Purify™ Denture Cleanser

The Market

Johnson & Johnson was in a state of euphoria as it was about to enter the denture cleanser market. On the surface, its internal glee appeared to be justified. Denture wearers preferred Johnson & Johnson's product, Purify™, to the category leader, Efferdent®, in blind product testing. Moreover, the Purify™ win was a decisive one, suggesting that

Efferdent® was highly vulnerable to the new entry. The Purify™ innovation team didn't know it yet, but they were about to encounter a classic unfriendly response from a very powerful testosterone brand.

The Competitive Response

Efferdent® rolled out its guns of Navarone in a brutal competitive response.

- Efferdent® hung samples on the doorknobs of almost every household in the two test markets before Purify™ started its advertising. This took denture wearers out of the category for a considerable period of time. Why buy Purify™ when Efferdent® samples were sitting in the medicine cabinet? Since less than one-fifth of the population wears full dentures, the sampling was an expensive, roll-of-the-dice response, but testosterone brands are noted for taking no prisoners—complete and total defeat of the enemy is the sole objective.

- The aggressive sampling program was further supplemented with increased media weight—the equivalent of a $20 million advertising campaign—for a brand that had seldom been advertised.

Purify™ wilted when confronted with this competitive blitzkrieg; the test markets were shut down. However, Johnson & Johnson should not have been surprised by Efferdent®'s hardball tactics. Efferdent® had done this before to every new entry that tried to invade its sandbox. By choosing to ignore this, Johnson & Johnson suffered the consequences.

It should be pointed out that consumers also lost in this scenario, because both the option of choice and the opportunity to try a better product were squandered.

Lessons Learned

Don't live on Fantasy Island just because your new product is superior to the category leader. The sledgehammer of competitive response can smash an innovation initiative into a thousand little pieces. Anticipate! Anticipate! Anticipate!

Case #2 Competitive Delusion: Total® Instant Oatmeal

The Market

General Mill's Total® cereal had a compelling positioning premise: It was the only ready-to-eat cereal that contained 100 percent of twelve vitamins and minerals essential for a healthy diet. This "fortification premise" gave Total® a strong competitive advantage over rival cereal brands.

Although Total® was introduced in the 1970s, it really leaped off the launching pad in the '80s with advertising claiming, "You'll need this many bowls of your regular cereal to match Total®." Stacks of bowls filled with "the other stuff" reinforced the positioning message. Each stack represented a competitive brand—for example, Special K®—that lacked the 100 percent level of a specific vitamin or mineral found in Total®. "Say it and show it" became an effective format for Total®'s competitive superiority message.

The grass is always greener in the conference room. Total® was healthy, wholesome nourishment. So was oatmeal. Why not Total® Instant Oatmeal? On a cold winter morning, what could be better than a warm, tummy-filling bowl of Total® Oatmeal? In the friendly confines of the conference room, it appeared to be a marriage made in heaven.

General Mills had no illusions about the toughness of the principle oatmeal competitor, Quaker® Oats. The Total® innovation team did not want to make a Purify™-type mistake. They introduced the product nationally rather than dumping it into two or three test markets. The strategy was to use a massive piece of geography—the entire United

States—thus making Quaker®'s potential retaliation more difficult and expensive.

A Critical Information Gap

Quaker threw everything at Total® Instant Oatmeal, including the kitchen sink. Not surprisingly, Quaker ramped up the advertising for its product line, but this was minor compared to what was lurking in the shadows. General Mills had an information gap—it did not understand the dynamics of the oatmeal category. Oatmeal was a business with a seasonal and regional skew; the business cycle peaked in the fall and winter, while ready-to-eat cereal had no seasonal trends. These highly significant category dynamics passed by General Mills like ships in the dark of night.

Ready-to-eat cereals were a year-round business, but in a seasonal business like oatmeal, the brand that gets to the supermarket trade first with promotional dollars wins. In the past, General Mills could load up the trade with its new cereal brands, but not this time around. Money speaks volumes when it comes to the retail trade. Retailers really don't care about the new product; their interest is very parochial. The trade's focus is on the real estate that they own and the promotional dollars they can get for it. The grocery stores were asking, what's in it for us? Quaker had greased retailers' palms with silver first, well in advance of any promotional effort from Total®. The early deals consummated between Quaker and the supermarket chains made it almost impossible for Total® to get any trade support for its new entry.

General Mills was shell-shocked. It could not believe Quaker®'s low prices and massive in-store displays along with its own inability to get distribution in grocery stores for Total®'s five flavors. Total® was a power brand; General Mills never had trouble getting shelf space before. But testosterone brands can always trump power brands with an array of clever, skillful tactics, especially when the newcomer is afflicted with competitive delusion.

Quaker® Oats had hidden in the weeds with a better game plan, just waiting for General Mills to attack. Both companies purchased rolled oats from the same vendors. Quaker's loyal vendor partners alerted them that General Mills was making inordinately large purchases of rolled oats, far beyond what was needed to make granola bars and cereals. Quaker then verified that General Mills planned on invading the oatmeal category. The company correctly speculated that General Mills would market its oatmeal under the Total® banner. This important piece of competitive intelligence allowed Quaker to prepare a battle plan focused on destroying the new competing venture.

There was still another issue associated with this innovation debacle that escaped General Mills' attention. Total®'s powerful positioning, reinforced with advertising that visualized the competitive difference, was not transferable to the oatmeal category. So Total® was simply a parity brand with no sustainable competitive advantage. The product was doomed to sit on the grocery store shelves of America gathering dust without the benefit of Total®'s positioning and advertising magic. Total® Instant Oatmeal limped into the second winter season and finally disappeared from the marketing landscape.

Lessons Learned

As improbable as it seems, some companies do not understand their successes. The Total® innovation team did not realize that the brand's brilliant positioning and advertising strategy was not transferable to the oatmeal category. Extending a brand into a new category requires understanding its assets and the leverage it offers, or fails to offer, in a new environment.

Anticipate the worst. Quaker's competitive response was very predictable. It is difficult to take business away from a company that is oatmeal personified. Quaker® Oats was the first trademarked breakfast cereal in America and remains one of the few consumer products still around after 125 years. Quaker® Oats is an authentic icon in American culture.

Every product category has key dynamics that drive its marketplace rhythms. General Mills should have understood the differences between the ready-to-eat cereal and oatmeal categories. In entering a new category segment, always do a SWOT analysis—one scrutinizes strengths, weaknesses, opportunities, and threats. A carefully conducted SWOT analysis should reveal any dangerous red flags.

Case #3 Competitive Delusion: The Scotch-Brite® Soap Pad

The Market

In 1917 Ed Cox, a pot and pan peddler, invented S.O.S® soap pads while his creative wife came up with the name, S.O.S®, meaning "Save Our Saucepans." S.O.S® became a venerable brand name comfortably residing in the sleepy, unexciting soap pad category. General Foods wanted to unload the yawn-producing S.O.S® business, and it found a sucker in Miles Laboratories (now Bayer®).

The brand was acquired in an effort to build a household products division leveraging the S.O.S® name. The logic behind this decision remains mysterious to this day. Why would a pharmaceutical company want to enter the household products business? This was not its core competency. This is the same stick to the knitting mistake that Nabisco made in its attempt to get into salty snacks.

The company was never able to extend the S.O.S® name to other household product categories. It lacked the people resources, especially in research and development, for product categories like bathroom cleaners. Competitors like Procter & Gamble had deep pockets for product development and massive advertising campaigns.

What remained after many years of trying was a faded dream. S.O.S® was a reasonably well-known brand name in an invisible household products division. It became a big fish in a very small pond that would never become an ocean.

Miles Laboratories's household products division was S.O.S®, and that was about it. So S.O.S® sales and profits were extremely important to the division. The company needed to defend the brand in the marketplace to keep the division afloat.

And then there was the sentimental factor. Senior management at Miles Laboratories could never admit that acquiring S.O.S® was a mistake, or that the fit had never been there in the first place. It was hard to cut the umbilical cord. The emotional attachment was powerful, but rationality was absent. These dynamics were the cornerstone for how S.O.S® responded to a new product entry from 3M.

Let the Games Begin

In a discussion with 3M marketing managers about competitive response, we heard the following: "That's exactly what happened to us." They were referring to their nifty but ill-fated new product Scotch-Brite® Never Rust Soap Pads. The 3M® scouring pad had excellent cleaning efficacy, with the additional benefits of not rusting or splintering. It was a nice bundle of assets that made the 3M® soap pad superior to S.O.S®.

If the competitor is a strong product with killer instincts, product superiority is not worth much. S.O.S®'s competitive rebuttal was savage, completely catching the gentle midwesterners from 3M off guard. S.O.S® flooded Sunday newspapers with coupons. Since Americans clip almost four billion coupons annually, it was a potent way for S.O.S® to defend its turf. It also ratcheted its advertising, beefing up the S.O.S® media by a five to one ratio over Scotch-Brite®—a favorite tactic for testosterone brands.

3M expected to compete in a sleepy category with minimal marketing expenditures. S.O.S® changed the rules, and 3M's blood flowed through the supermarket aisles. The company licked its wounds as it limped out of the category, another victim of competitive delusion.

The tentacles of competitive delusion directly impacted consumers once again. In the 3M scenario, consumers lost the opportunity to benefit from a superior scouring pad. Competitive response may chalk up a win for the testosterone brand, but it can also be a defeat for consumers; they lose the option of choosing a better alternative.

Lessons Learned

Be prepared. Incumbent brands prefer to fight the innovation war with high levels of advertising and other forms of promotional support. These fixed costs give high-share brands economies of scale that category interlopers might find hard to match. 3M should have understood this dynamic. Such understanding might have prompted it to reconsider entering the category at all or, better yet, license the Scotch-Brite® brand to a testosterone brand—like maybe S.O.S®.

Case #4 Competitive Delusion: Datril® Pain Reliever

The Market

Johnson & Johnson inherited the Tylenol® brand when acquiring McNeil Pharmaceuticals. After the acquisition, the company continued to detail Tylenol® to doctors and healthcare specialists without any advertising or promotional support. The brand was priced 50 percent higher than regular aspirin, with a modest marketing budget. Johnson & Johnson had stumbled upon a money machine. The plan for Tylenol® was to maintain the status quo—detail healthcare professionals with no advertising support and continue to count the money.

Each year Tylenol®'s sales increased without significant marketing support such as network advertising. It was difficult to maintain a low profile among competitors under these conditions. One such competitor was Bristol-Myers (now Bristol-Myers Squibb).

The Datril® Strategy

Because its over-the-counter pain relief brands, Excedrin® and Bufferin®, were experiencing sales erosion, Bristol-Myers introduced Datril®, a lower price point Tylenol®-type pain reliever with the same active ingredient and a comparable safety profile. The core of Datril®'s strategy was the assumption that a parsimonious Johnson & Johnson would not lower Tylenol®'s price—a classic case of competitive delusion in operation.

In fact, Bristol-Myers was so confident in Johnson & Johnson's resistance to tinkering with its money machine that it openly tested Datril®'s lower price strategy in Albany, New York. This was a big mistake. All the world saw its intentions, including Johnson & Johnson.

The One Tough Hombre Strategy

The Datril® strategy was about to encounter the fire-engine red Johnson & Johnson CEO, James E. Burke. Underneath his beguiling smile, there lurked a killer instinct. The Johnson & Johnson CEO came from the "take no prisoners" school of marketing. He made his mark at the company with the bold strategy of convincing adults to buy baby products like shampoo and powder for their personal use. This success gave him corporate visibility and, ultimately, CEO status.

Burke possessed the wisdom of Benjamin Franklin; the strategic cunning of General George S. Patton; and the charm, charisma, and smarts of John F. Kennedy. It was quite a combination, and his leadership skills were legendary. His feats include leading his company through two episodes in which Tylenol® had been laced with poison. In discussing Burke's leadership capabilities, a former colleague said, "Jim could lead a barracuda to law school." Datril® didn't know it yet, but the brand was about to take a one-way trip to Hades.

Burke organized a war room team at company headquarters in New Brunswick, New Jersey. The team evaluated strategic scenarios, crunched numbers, and debated strategy. Burke finally made the unthinkable decision that Bristol-Myers was convinced he would never make: bottom line be damned. Burke sent an armada into the field to make sure Tylenol® was priced competitively with Datril® in 165,000 retail outlets. Johnson & Johnson even issued credit memorandums to reduce Tylenol®'s price on existing stock in stores and warehouses.

Burke delivered a knockout punch; Datril® had no strategy. It could no longer advertise that it was cheaper than Tylenol®. Moreover, because of Burke's spirited leadership, Tylenol® remained a cash cow for Johnson & Johnson, and it still does to this day.

Burke transferred the Tylenol® business to the stewardship of Wayne Nelson, an executive with a strong consumer marketing background. Although Nelson sometimes rankled contemporaries with his unorthodox management style, Burke realized that Tylenol® had to take on the trappings of a conventional consumer brand, and Nelson was the right choice for the job. He did not disappoint Burke.

Tylenol®'s positioning is a work of genius—the pain reliever that is both strong and gentle. Normally, one would expect these two elements to clash. A medication can't be strong and gentle simultaneously. Tylenol® managed the high-wire act because of its endorsement heritage from hospitals and physicians. There are very few brands in any category that have successfully "owned" these benefits in a single product. The original Tylenol® was gentle, but the next-generation product, Extra Strength, was stronger. However, advertising managed to fuse strong and gentle for both regular strength and extra strength. The only other packaged goods brand to ever achieve this was Secret® deodorant—"strong enough for a man, but made for a woman."

Tylenol® went on to claim one-third of the over-the-counter pain-reliever market. In a way, Bristol-Myers pushed Tylenol® into its orbit of success. Who knows when Tylenol® would have come out of the closet without the competitive delusion from Datril®?

Lessons Learned

A new product strategy based on a lower price is self-limiting. Best advice—don't play the innovation game if that's all you have. Know who you are dealing with, and try to understand the leadership styles of CEOs, because they shape the culture of their companies.

Case #5 Competitive Delusion: Hershey's Chocolate Bar Flavor Puddings

The Market

America has a sweet tooth, and Hershey has been satisfying it for decades, ever since Milton Hershey constructed a chocolate plant in 1903 in an area that would become Hershey, Pennsylvania. The Hershey® bar became an American icon, and the company sub - sequently expanded its product line far beyond the original Hershey®'s chocolate bar. But there's one market it missed out on, surrendering the turf to Jell-O®. America was slow to respond to dairy-based desserts, which had widespread popularity in Europe. Dairy-based desserts had a nice bundle of assets—tasty, fresh, and ready-to-eat. Swiss Miss® pioneered the market in this country, but it would be General Foods (now Kraft) that would blow it open.

Jell-O®, the quintessential American dessert, moved to ready-to-eat cups to capitalize on the convenience trend. It was so successful that Jell-O® decided to extend the brand into pudding snacks. General Foods used Jell-O®'s brand equity and product quality to carve out a large merchandising area in the refrigerated sections of supermarkets. The company suddenly had a $150 million business on its hands with Jell-O® pudding snacks.

Follow the Leader

Hershey could not help but notice the marketplace success of Jell-O® pudding snacks. The new category seemed to fit the company's chocolate equity. Hershey subsequently moved into the northeast region with Hershey®'s Chocolate Bar Flavor Puddings. They were sold in six-cup cartons with a strategic focus on the company's popular candies: chocolate bars, chocolate bars with almonds, York® peppermint patties, and chocolate and vanilla Hershey's Kisses®. The company had astutely leveraged its icon flavors, and the venture looked promising as Hershey's garnered about a 25 percent market share in the refrigerated pudding category. Not a bad marketplace performance for a late entry.

Cheapskate Strategy

Consumer research with mothers indicated that they wanted pudding to be all-natural. Neither Hershey nor Jell-O® could make an all-natural claim, but Hershey debated the feasibility of doing so, which would give the company a competitive advantage. It would take Jell-O® six months or longer to convert its pudding line to all-natural status.

The all-natural positioning would cost Hershey's a penny more per cup, so the company decided not to move forward with it. It speculated that Jell-O® would never do it because of the increased cost of goods it would require. So, why should Hershey? Case closed.

About four months later, Jell-O® had all-natural puddings in the supermarkets of America. It now had a strong competitive advantage in delivering what mothers had requested, and Hershey had been trumped with its line of still-unnatural puddings.

Every innovation team needs a champion or sponsor further up the line. These sponsors are not directly involved with innovation initiatives on a daily basis, but they provide internal support and encouragement for the new venture. Savvy team leaders periodically have informal chat sessions with sponsors to let them know the state of their project's progress. These sponsors acquired various informal titles like rabbi, cardinal, or monsignor.

Hershey eventually dropped out of the category because the project lost its rabbi. The rabbi's successor felt that the pudding margins were unacceptable in comparison to the company's dry, stable products—goodbye Hershey® puddings, despite an impressive marketplace performance. Too bad the rabbi was not there, because Hershey may have walked away from a promising marketplace opportunity.

Lesson Learned

Never give away a competitive advantage for the sake of a penny.

Case #6 Competitive Delusion: Clorox® Laundry Detergent

The Market

Clorox® is a little fish in a big pond. In the laundry detergent market, it dominated the bleach niche for decades. But the major player is Procter & Gamble, with a current line of eight different laundry detergent brands.

The major Procter & Gamble brand is Tide®, accounting for about two-thirds of the company's laundry detergent sales. Tide® was a remarkable technical achievement—a heavy-duty detergent that really worked on heavily soiled clothes for the first time. Historically, it was such an instant success in its Ohio test market that stores had to ration it, because Procter & Gamble could not manufacture enough product. The marketplace demand was so high in the Ohio test that it took Procter & Gamble three years before Tide® could be introduced nationally.[1]

After 1946, the brand became a cash machine for Procter & Gamble's massive expansion, leading the company into many other product categories. This testosterone brand still provides the funds for many of the company's innovation initiatives. The eyes of Procter & Gamble executives moisten when they think about their cash cow brand.

The Big Mistake

Procter & Gamble had let Clorox® play its bleach game unmolested. The company's disinterest in Clorox®'s core franchise also kept antitrust considerations on the back burner. But Clorox® aspired to greater glory in the household laundry detergent market; it wanted to play with the big boys. Clorox® did the unthinkable, introducing a laundry detergent product to the homemakers of America under the equity of the Clorox® brand name, known for bleach. It was a good concept idea, but not a smart move.

Proctor & Gamble's disinterest in this niche brand turned angry. Clorox® must be punished! The company "rolled out Tide® with Bleach before Clorox® even got its laundry detergent" out of the starting gate.[2] The testosterone brand Tide® responded in typical Procter & Gamble style with a massive promotional effort. Clorox® limped out of the category sandbox badly bruised and nursing a loss of $50 million—another victim of competitive retaliation.[3]

Lesson Learned

Never attack the core strength of a superior foe.

COMPETITIVE DELUSION PRESCRIPTIVES

No Brand Is an Island

When Schick introduced its four-bladed wet shaving system, Quattro®, Gillette already knew about it, having tested ten Quattro® cartridges for patent infringement. How did Gillette get Quattro® cartridges before they were on the store shelves?

The typical business chain deals with customers, suppliers, vendors, and resellers. Each is a potential source of information. Schick gave Quattro® samples to reporters and prospective customers who signed confidentiality agreements. There was a leak, and some of the cartridges ended up at Gillette headquarters in Boston. Gillette sued for patent infringement after inspecting the merchandise; both companies ended up in a court battle, but Gillette lost the case. Schick continued to wonder who gave Gillette the cartridges?

Listerine PocketPaks® encountered the same problem. The makers showed prototypes to Wal-Mart, CVS, and Walgreen's in order to accommodate the long lead times for retailers. All three instantly recognized Pfizer had a tiger by the tail. Wal-Mart and Walgreen's immediately contacted contract manufacturers to see if they could make a private label version of Listerine PocketPaks®. Walgreen's had a breath strip in its stores nine months before Listerine PocketPaks® hit the market. It was an inferior product, but it negatively impacted Listerine®'s trial. Consumers said, "We tried this before. It didn't work." Listerine® had to overcome Walgreen's rush to the marketplace with a bad product.

There are no secrets out there, and smart companies prepare regardless of whether they are the innovator or the defender. There are two things innovation teams should do to minimize the surprise of competitive retaliation:

1. Obtain competitive intelligence
2. Conduct scenario planning

Competitive Intelligence

The innovation game is a war, and like any war, the enemy must be studied. In the desert of Africa in World War II, Montgomery studied Rommel, and vice versa. It is essential to understand the opponent in war and marketing. Remember the lesson learned from the Datril® experience: Know who you are dealing with and try to understand the competition.

The first step—don't assume anything. The "new kid on the block" can discover large amounts of information about testosterone brands through the dirt and grime of intelligence spadework. An entire industry has sprung up around competitive intelligence devoted to finding information for clients about competition.

Make a Phone Call

The simplest intelligence tactic is to pick up the phone. A senior account executive at Wells Rich Greene advertising agency tracked down a former Gillette employee with a phone call. The agency's client, Bic, was bringing its disposable razors from Europe to the US market. He wanted an opinion about Gillette's competitive response to Bic's invasion. The former Gillette executive correctly speculated that Gillette would also market a disposable razor, even though the margins were inferior to nondisposable blades. The agency executive got good competitive intelligence with a five-minute phone call. There would be no competitive delusion on Bic's part; it knew what to expect— Gillette would enter the disposable segment.

Hire the Pros

"The Society of Competitive Intelligence Professionals (an industry trade group) estimates that the market for business intelligence amounts to $2 billion annually."[4] These professionals maintain they are conducting legitimate marketing research, not spying or industrial espionage, "but they leave no stone unturned—even searching through the garbage of a competitor."[5]

Intelligence gems surface from unlikely sources. Among the professionals who gather information for clients, a choice morsel for intelligence is building security guards, who work late at night. They tend to be naturally gregarious, always bored and willing to talk, and a few probing questions can open up a great deal of insight and information. A reasonably accurate profit and loss assessment can be estimated for almost any brand with a bit of spadework—tracking down former employees, suppliers, and vendors. This exercise can pinpoint the cash cow brands by exposing their weaknesses.

Competitive intelligence sets the framework for what to expect, but it doesn't tell which tactical response is best. This is best accomplished in the next step: scenario planning.

Scenario Planning

There is always a war being fought in marketing. Coke and Pepsi are engaged in a cola war. Burger King and McDonald's fight the burger war.

Gillette and Schick are combatants in the razor war. Gillette, for years, let Schick survive, driven by antitrust concerns. However, Schick became a more formidable competitor when it was bought by Energizer. It trumped Gillette's Mach 3® with the four-bladed Quattro®, reflecting a new muscular vitality that took Gillette by surprise. Schick suddenly had innovation spunk after being dormant for years.

Gillette bounced back with the launch of its Fusion™ razors with five blades, but Schick was not intimidated. While Gillette's pricey "more blades strategy" may be tired and frayed at the edges, Schick astutely defended its turf, leaving Gillette a victim of competitive retaliation.

- "Schick suppressed demand" for Gillette's new razor in advance with a heavy free sampling program for Quattro® before Fusion™ was launched.[6] The move took wet shavers out of the market. It was hard to resist a free Quattro® razor.

- As Fusion™ hit the market, Schick quit going after the male segment, and its marketing focus switched to heavy consumer and trade promotion for Schick's women's razors—Quattro® for Women and Intuition®. Gillette ignored the women's market as it ramped up the dollars for Fusion™ in the male market segment. This had always been Gillette's strategy: win the hearts and minds of the men first and later move on to women, launching a similar product featuring feminine touches. Schick understood that the female turf was uncontested, and it went for it.

- Then Schick subsequently launched Quattro® Titanium, with the positioning that it was "smoother shave than the leading men's razor."[7] Fusion™ had high visibility stemming from a massive advertising campaign, so the perceived implication was that the leading razor must be Fusion™. But "the leading men's razor" really referred to Gillette's earlier generation Mach 3®. It was a clever piece of advertising maneuvering on Schick's part, but perfectly valid.

Now, let's switch gears to Pepcid® AC. The Pepcid® AC innovation team was disappointed, since an FDA advisory panel had recommended against allowing the Johnson & Johnson-Merck partnership to market Pepcid® AC, a reduced dosage version of Merck's prescription ulcer drug Pepcid®.

The stakes were high. The potential dominance of a new segment of over-the-counter stomach remedies called acid blockers hung in the balance. These drugs had a slow onset, but once activated they blocked the secretion of stomach acid for ten to twelve hours. Conventional antacids, like Tums® and Rolaids®, temporarily neutralize acid, but the heartburn or acid indigestion could be back in twenty minutes. Acid blockers had a strong competitive advantage.

The Pepcid® innovation team created a war room, much like the one James Burke established for the Datril® episode. What should they do? It could have been dangerous to move forward without FDA approval. There was, however, the possibility of gathering more data to pacify the FDA advisory panel about Pepcid®'s preventive positioning. This would slow down Pepcid AC®'s launch.

Management believed the market share battle in the acid blocker segment was destined to be short-lived with four new, but very similar, stomach remedy products surfacing at the same time. One of the four brands, Axid®, was viewed by senior management as a nonthreat. Tagamet HB 200® and Zantac® were the two largest-selling prescription brands; Pepcid®'s prescription sales were minor in comparison. Two issues were paramount in the minds of the Pepcid® innovation team. Could the two leading prescription brands be trumped? What was the most viable strategy that could achieve this objective?

Scenario planning involves envisioning the alternative competitive responses that might occur in an attempt dampen the fortunes of an innovation initiative. "It is a derivation of a technique first developed by the Royal Dutch/Shell Group to deal with oil reduction and price shocks."[8] In innovation initiatives, scenario planning is a good way to understand the dynamics of competitive response. It is a game of chess that puts the innovation team into the shoes of competitors.

This was the approach that Johnson & Johnson's Merck took in the war room. Members of the innovation team assumed the roles of major competitors Tagamet HB 200® HB, Zantac®, and Axid®. They assembled data and information about each competitor, with a special focus on Tagamet HB 200®, because the parent company, SmithKline Beecham, had consumer marketing expertise with Tums®. The innovation team debated the various strategic scenarios that each competitor could take in its sprint to be first-to-market. Counterstrategies were developed for the competitive scenarios that appeared most viable. The goal was to develop a superior launch plan that would lead to dominance in the acid blocker segment.

Pepcid® AC managed to get there first, and it dominated the acid blocker segment. There are many reasons for the product's success, including a brilliant preventive positioning strategy—treat the symptom before it occurs. A cornerstone of the success equation was a disciplined process that laid out the range of competitive responses Pepcid® AC could encounter and how each one would be handled.

In innovation initiatives, there is always an innovator and defender. Both can use scenario planning to their advantage. The Pepcid® team used it to fine-tune the brand's national launch. As the defender, Schick used it to structure a survival plan against a company with deep pockets. Gillette should have used it to anticipate Schick's countermoves. There might have been fewer surprises for Gillette, but competitive delusion often hampers developing a complete and total battle plan.

Our marketing consulting company first encountered scenario planning at a food company when a marketing director asked us to think about the various obstacles that could be thrown in the path of his new product. We came back in three weeks with six scenarios of competitive responses for his two key competitors, along with counterstrategies. This was a marketer who adhered to the Boy Scouts motto—"Be prepared." He was not going to let competitive retaliation rain on his innovation parade.

Scenario planning is more than a tool for midlevel managers. Even CEOs can use it; Andrew Grove, former chairman of Intel, was a daily practitioner of scenario planning. A *Business Week* article described his passion for it as follows: "He thought about his operational environment like a master chess player, always anticipating what competition might do in response to his moves—and then what he would do in response to that."[9]

As pointed out earlier, Purify™ denture cleanser got pulverized by the unanticipated competitive response from Efferdent®, even though Purify™ was a superior product. If Johnson & Johnson had a better product than Efferdent®, a potential scenario might have been to introduce the brand nationally so Efferdent® lost its strategy—it couldn't hang a sample on every doorknob in America. What could have been Purify™'s counterstrategy when Efferdent® increased its media weight? One possible counterstrategy might have been a regional rollout or a national launch, because media becomes more expensive in larger geographical areas in contrast to smaller test markets with more economical media buys.

Scenario planning lays out the range of predatory moves from competitors and their potential impact on the new venture. What counterstrategies are appropriate for each contemplated move from the competitor? This was a process that Purify™ desperately needed.

Counterstrategies

Many competitive responses are predictable. Large-share entrenched brands prefer to fight with higher levels of advertising and other forms of promotional support, like sampling and cents-off coupons. These are fixed costs that have an economy of scale advantage for large-share brands. Changes in the promotion mix are always good starting points in thinking about competitive response scenarios. It may mean going down a different path than was originally planned.

In the toothpaste war, Crest® Pro-Health™ was an attempt by Procter & Gamble to dislodge Colgate's Total® from the leadership position it took away from Crest® in the 1990s. Colgate did its homework and defended its position very well.

- It ramped up its advertising with a very strong message that Colgate® kills germs for twelve hours. The scientific approach was later replaced with an emotional advertising campaign using Brooke Shields.

- It attempted to block Crest® out of the Internet by tying up key words like "toothpaste" on the major search engines, like Google® and Yahoo!® When consumers searched the word "toothpaste" in any shape or form, they were likely to see an ad for Total® on their computer screen. This tactic would have been unheard of two decades ago. In a technology-enhanced society, blunting key word searches became an important tactical response. The search engine companies simply wanted the money that Colgate paid for keyword searches. It is a revenue stream for them. In turn, Colgate, a feisty competitor, made it difficult for Crest® Pro-Health™ to have an Internet presence. It became a survival stream for Colgate.

- Another tactic Colgate implemented was aggressive promotional programs to trigger "pantry loading." Consumers loaded up their medicine cabinets with Total® just prior to the Crest® Pro-Health™ launch.

These are major tactical weapons that astute competitors like Colgate use, and each one must be assessed in scenario planning.

There are always wild cards that are difficult to anticipate in scenario planning—such as Schick's clever advertising for its Quattro® Titanium razor. Dropping the price is another wild card, but as Peter Doyle points out in *Value Based Marketing*, "The bigger the brand, the more it loses in lowering the price."[10] Pricing can be a very emotional response, as reflected in James Burke's decision to drop Tylenol®'s price. Nobody expected him to do it, but despite uncertainties, every innovation initiative should involve scenario planning.

Scenario planning should be executed early in the innovation process. There is a risk that the execution will be hurried if the process is activated late in the innovation game; the potential benefits and business wisdom may be lost due to time constraints.

Marketing Plans

Scenario planning is not a mere game to be played at an off-campus site. The marketing plan for any new product should have a competitive response section—the potential counterstrategies that any competitors might use. Since every response has a price tag associated with it, the financial implications of counterstrategies should be part of the plan. This is why it is important to implement scenario planning early in the innovation process. Why move forward if the new venture doesn't have the financial resources to stay in the game?

Chief marketing officers should send the plan back to the drawing board if there is no competitive response section in it, because the plan is incomplete. The integration of scenario planning into the marketing plan brings much needed discipline to the innovation process.

NOTES

1. Gerald Michaelson, *Winning the Marketing War* (Knoxville: Pressmark International, 1987), p. 62.

2. Peter Doyle, *Value-Based Marketing* (West Sussex, UK: John Wiley & Sons, 2000), p. 179.

3. Ibid.

4. Justin Pope, "Swiping Rivals' Secrets No Surprise," *Trenton Times*, September 14, 2003, p. D1.

5. Ibid.

6. Jack Neff, "Energizer Sticks It to P&G in Razor War," *Advertising Age* (October 2, 2006): 84.

7. Ibid.

8. David Jones, "Crystal Ball: Scenario-Planning Is Peek at What's to Come," *Marketing News* (February 18, 2002): 6.

9. Jeffrey E. Garten, "Andy Grove Made the Elephant Dance," *Business Week*, April 11, 2005, p. 26.

10. Doyle, *Value-Based Marketing*, p. 179.

(6)

[FATALITY IN FRUGALITY]

In a high-stakes poker game in San Francisco, W. C. Fields remarked to a potential player, "If you want to play, you have to pay. This is no game for pantywaists." New products must be marketed with play-and-pay budgets that are lush enough to have impact. The cheapskate strategy does not work.

Introductory budgets must be bountiful, equaling or perhaps exceeding the threshold spending levels of competitors in the category. Brands in a given category want to inflict pain on interlopers by requiring them to prescribe to a heavy diet of advertising and promotion. The strategic goal is to see the new entry raise the white flag of surrender. Parsimony does not play well in this cutthroat scenario.

Anemic budgets are not the only symptoms of cheapskate marketing. Some try to pinch their pennies in the early stages as the product innovation surfaces from the womb of idea generation, rushing to meet a launch date. Successful new products generally have more time and money spent on them than their failed counterparts.

One study indicated that 75 percent more time and twice as much money is devoted to the early developmental activities of a product, thus separating winning new products from those ending up on the scrap heap. The early life of new product innovation is called the fuzzy front end; it takes a lot of energy, time, and money to bring clarity to the ambiguity often associated with the fuzzy front end.

Case # 1 Fatality in Frugality: Much Ado about Nothing

The Market

Hail! Hail! The gang's all here—Keebler, Nabisco, Procter & Gamble, and Frito-Lay. The heavy artillery is out. Keebler and Nabisco have brought out their bazookas. Procter & Gamble is rolling hand grenades down the aisles of supermarkets. Frito-Lay has its panzer division roaming the stores. What's going on? It's the battle of soft batch cookies.

- Procter & Gamble and Frito-Lay are category interlopers, obsessed with soft batch cookie technology.

- Nabisco and Keebler are forced to defend their positions in the cookie category.

Soft batch cookies are supposed to taste like David's® or Mrs. Field's®. They don't. The misguided combatants have their very expensive blinders on as they pour their marketing dollars down the ever-welcoming new product drainage ditch.

How the Race for Soft Batch Cookie Supremacy Began

Frito-Lay moved into the cookie market through the acquisition of Grandma's®—a revered cookie brand with roots in the Northwest.

Duncan Hines® was a line of shelf-stable cake mixes, competing with that grand old dame from General Mills, Betty Crocker®. Like most food products at Procter & Gamble, Duncan Hines® limped along, dwarfed by the company's plethora of power brands in personal care and detergents.

Both companies stumbled upon technology for soft batch cookies. Frito-Lay viewed soft batch cookies as the springboard to Grandma's® becoming a national power brand. Procter & Gamble saw this new moist and chewy cookie segment as a way to diversify the Duncan Hines® line, revitalizing a stodgy, conservative brand. The company moved into its marketing research mode with typical Procter & Gamble vengeance. Product testing results were extremely promising; 80 percent of the consumers who tested the Duncan Hines Soft Batch® cookies said they would buy them again.

In this product testing environment, did test consumers have a strong commitment, or were they simply being nice because they had been given the cookies to try with no exchange of money? Despite the positive results, the marketing research department recommended further evaluation in the form of sales wave testing. Sales wave testing measured the likelihood that consumers favorably disposed to the Duncan Hines Soft Batch® cookies would continue to buy them with their own money once the cookies were no longer free. The goal was to determine the depth of customer commitment. Can these soft, moist cookies deliver long-term consumer satisfaction? This was a critical issue that determined repeat purchases in the marketplace. However, the marketing group in the end took a contrary point of view, deciding there was no need for further testing.

In Procter & Gamble's history, few products achieved the 80 percent repurchase rate, among the thousands of product tests conducted over the years for a myriad of products. The numbers were simply too good; additional testing was a waste of money. The marketing mantra became "full speed ahead," and the trapdoor of fatal frugality opened. Procter & Gamble applied for a patent, constructed a new bakery, and rolled out its formidable marketing guns, but it was spending its money in all the wrong places.

For a while, all four companies found themselves slashing each other's throats in Kansas City, where their marketing weaponry was of the "shock and awe" mode. Kansas City became cookie crazed, spurred on by heavy advertising, store displays, and high discount coupons, with consumers buying cookies at a rate three times higher than the national average. To escape this market madness, Nabisco went national with its soft batch cookie brand, Almost Home®.

Competitors also moved into larger geographical areas to keep pace with Nabisco. On the surface, the sales of these soft, moist cookies soared. However, as any good marketer knows, it is the behavior behind the sales curve that counts, because sales are only the tip of the iceberg. These soft batch cookies were about to follow the path of the Titanic.

Soft batch cookies were a mismatched positioning. Names like Almost Home® and Grandma's® implied a homemade cookie: one that is warm, moist, and deliciously chewy. Cookie lovers initially gave the new type of cookie the benefit of the doubt, but their passion quickly waned. Taste fatigue set in. Soft batch cookies could never have the aromatic warmth of homemade. Nabisco's CEO, Ross Johnson, described the Frito-Lay cookie as " biting into a hockey puck."[1] His own cookies weren't much better.

The impressive sales curves represented the exuberance of early trial, fueled by extraordinary marketing expenditures. Who wouldn't try soft batch cookies when seduced with a coupon saving $1.00 or $1.50? However, there was no underlying pattern of repurchases. After a few purchases, consumers drifted away, disappointed with these mediocre-tasting soft batch cookies that became as hard as hand grenades when the package was not properly resealed. This was the same problem—a mismatched relationship between the promised benefit and product performance—that plagued Keebler's Sweet Spots™ cookies years later. As pointed out previously, chocolate lovers expected Sweet Spots™ to be a rich, indulgent chocolate experience, but the product performance was disappointing. Thomas Edison remarked that the single most important quality for an executive is "a fine memory." History is a good teacher when we choose to remember it.

How the Race for Soft Batch Cookies Ended

As the smoke from the battlefield cleared, Nabisco won a hollow victory. Neither Frito-Lay nor Procter & Gamble had the production and distribution infrastructure to compete with Nabisco. Both interlopers withdrew from the category sandbox, but Procter & Gamble sued the competition for patent infringement. Litigation involving patent infringement requires proof of commercial damage—evidence that one's sales suffered because of the alleged patent-infringing product. Since the market was declining long before the litigation, Procter & Gamble was awarded a modest sum of money to save face.

The soft batch cookie segment is barely a blip on the radar screen today. It was truly much ado about nothing. The market researchers made the right recommendation. Procter & Gamble should have done the sales wave testing to unearth the taste fatigue problem. It would have meant spending a little more money, but the company would have learned a lot more. This was Procter & Gamble's fatal frugality— spend millions chasing a bad idea, but resist spending a few bucks to avert a disaster.

Lesson Learned

There is no substitute for doing the proper homework. Marketing research is the eyes, ears, and voice of the consumer. Listen to the voice and understand how the consumer's mind works. That's where to find the pay dirt, or the consumer's wants and needs. Soft batch cookies became one of the most expensive concept tests in the history of packaged-goods marketing. That's a hefty price to pay for not listening.

Case #2 Fatality in Frugality: The Nightingale Sings— Cheap, Cheap, Cheap

The evaluation journey for product innovation often begins with alpha testing, which is a fancy word for in-house testing. At the early stages, the product is far from perfect, and product variations are necessary. Each one must have its day in court; in-house testing is an inexpensive way to sort out variations.

Most food companies use test kitchens to sort out taste and texture variables. Wine companies have tasters who search for the best combination of bouquet and taste. Fragrance companies have internal panels of discriminators with sensitive nostrils. Many companies use employee panels that test products on a daily basis. Both Schick and Gillette use workforce panels to shake down their wet shaving systems. However, because consumer needs are complex, in-house testing should never be the final word on the merits of a product. Only real-life customers can provide this insight.

A personal care company (name unidentified to protect the guilty) was testing a new shampoo with its employee panel. The results were spectacular, well above the company's norms for this type of testing, and the marketing director was intrigued by the shampoo's performance. There was an internal fear that a competitor was working on a similar product. The presumably impressive results from in-house testing triggered a decision to move the product into a regional rollout.

The new shampoo sank like a rock. When the slower-moving competitor finally launched its shampoo, it was a huge success. Employee panels may be less expensive, but they are rarely predictors of marketplace outcomes.

Lesson Learned

Testing employees may tell us what we want to hear, but testing with customers tells us what we need to know.

Cutting Corners Can Be Expensive

Frito-Lay decided to branch out beyond salty snacks and get into the cracker business. On the surface, the cracker invasion seemed logical, since both crackers and salty snacks require front-door distribution in grocery stores where salespeople can rotate stock daily for freshness. This appeared to be a perfect fit with Frito-Lay's core competency— it had the best front-door delivery system in consumer packaged goods. No stick to the knitting mistakes here.

Given that good fit, the marketing mavens decided to forego extensive product testing and other marketing research activity. By doing so, they saved a million dollars, money that could have been used for "more productive marketing activity," such as advertising and promotion.

Unfortunately, however, because of poor product quality—a weakness that would have surfaced if stringent product testing had been adhered to—the cracker line went down in flames. The math of destruction was simple. The million dollars the company thought it could save by skipping an essential step—evaluate the product thoroughly—created a $100 million flop.

Things happen in the innovation game. People plan. God laughs. Flawed assumptions about product performance are a fool's folly. Marketing academics Merle Crawford and Anthony DiBenedetto offer two case histories reinforcing the point:

> General Electric took a $450 million pretax charge for a new refrigerator compressor that was never field-tested, because the firm was sure it would work. The impossible happened. Black & Decker once pulled thousands of flashlights off store shelves and stopped shipments on a new line of smoke detectors that carried the Ultralife battery after Kodak discovered an unexpected buildup of material that affected its shelf life. The discovery was made during introductory marketing, not during use testing.[2]

Rather than being cheapskates, Black & Decker and General Electric should have spent more time and money doing their homework.

Lesson Learned

All that glitters is not gold. Saving a few bucks on development is a mirage. Murphy's Law is out there lurking in the shadows. The goal should be a quality product. Fools and money part with certainty when comprehensive product testing is bypassed.

Case #3 Fatality in Frugality: It's a Nine-Inning Ballgame

The innovation game is like a nine-inning game of baseball; each inning must be played with intensity. Marketers have a tendency to front-load their budgets, marketing with impact, but only for a few innings.

It takes a long time for a new product to build a base of committed users. BASES, a company that evaluates new products via test market simulation models, has tested thousands of new products worldwide, and its president, Joe Willke, describes the slow journey toward a stable base of core users:

> Of everybody trying a new product, typically half come back for a second purchase and half do not. Of the people who do repeat their purchase, 65 percent go on to make another purchase—but the other 35 percent don't. Then 75 percent of those make a third repeat—but 25 percent don't. If the product makes it to eight, nine, or ten repeat purchases with a consumer, the chances that they'll make the 11th purchase are high. With these people, you've become an established brand. They are sticking with you.[3]

What are the implications for innovation? The diffusion of product innovation often moves at a glacial pace. The high priests of marketing tend to pour a lot of money into their love child in the first five innings and then pull back. This is fatal frugality, because the repeat sales base has not yet firmed up. If the product innovation is to succeed, the only way to bring more consumers into the tent is with continuous, long-term investment spending.

Vanilla Coke® had reasonably strong first-year sales by the company's own standards. The parent had to make a choice about its future. Coke made the decision to withdraw the brand's support and funnel the money into propping up its ailing bottler operation Coca-Cola

Enterprises and the floundering flagship drink Coca-Cola® Classic. Vanilla Coke® became an orphan, and the second-year sales showed it.

Coke tried to play a nine-inning innovation game in five innings, and it didn't work. Historically, this has been Coke's pattern with line extensions like Vanilla Coke® and Coke® with lime—play three or four innings and then quit the game.

One might argue that Vanilla Coke® never stood a chance for survival because of its taste problem. However, another Coke product, Tab, became a successful diet cola, despite its taste problem. There surfaced a small, but dedicated fringe of Tab buyers who proceeded to drink it with gusto. Who knows what could have happened with Vanilla Coke® had Coke given it decent marketing support?

Yogi Berra said, "It is not over until it's over." He understood that many games are won in the later innings. Like many other marketers, Coke forgot that product innovation is a nine-inning game.

Lesson Learned

Put a lot of logs on the fire. The second-year budget for a new product should at least equal the first in the innovation game. Few marketers, in the United States or globally, understand or act upon this principle. About three-fourths of the product innovations that succeed adhere to the "nine-inning game" principle.

Case #4 Fatality in Frugality: Big Bang Marketing

The Market

Seldane™ was the first nondrowsy allergy medication to provide twenty-four hours of symptom relief. It was a money machine, but then disaster struck; it was pulled off the market because of serious heart and liver side effects.

Not surprisingly, the chemists at Schering Plough recognized the potential of the nondrowsy, twenty-four-hour allergy relief benefit

Seldane™ offered. An intense research and development effort was initiated that resulted in Claritin®, an allergy drug offering Seldane™-type benefits (relief of allergy symptoms) without the drowsiness side effect other brands offered.

Claritin® is a relatively simple drug in composition. Anyone with a chemistry degree could mix it up in his or her bathtub, but it was destined to become a big, bold blockbuster drug, permanently altering the marketing of new drug products in the pharmaceutical industry.

It Was a Very Good Year for Claritin®

In 1997 the FDA sanctioned the growing trend of drug advertising on television with some restrictions. It was determined that these ads must contain "fair balance," meaning that the benefits and side effects of the advertised drugs must be proportionately represented in commercials or print ads. Television was soon inundated with drug advertising, and Claritin® took to the new marketing environment like a duck to water.

Most pharmaceutical brands sound like alphabet soup. There are about forty-five brands that begin with the letter Z. Claritin® broke this mold with a consumer-friendly name, very unusual for a new drug. The name contained most of the word "clarity," implying a clear path to a world free of allergy symptoms. However, this was only the beginning of Claritin®'s journey to runaway success.

Claritin® Covers the Waterfront

Doctors' offices became Claritin® billboards as sales reps dropped massive amounts of signage. The brand was everywhere. The name could be found on tissue boxes, shopping bags, note pads, pens and pencils, calendars, and prescription pads; but its presence was especially prevalent and powerful on television.

In 1998 the Claritin® advertising budget was an obscene $185 million—an ad agency's fantasy. The brand set a precedent for the marketing of drug products employing principles borrowed from consumer packaged goods brands; its consumer-centric advertising messages were cheery, optimistic, and glowing. They featured happy, allergy-free people interacting with the world around them. Allergy sufferers walked into their doctors' offices asking for the pill that Joan Lunden, the brand's sweet, cheerful spokesperson, used. Legions of doctors were seduced by Claritin®'s "big bang marketing" as they became apostles for the brand.

Claritin® cured more than allergy symptoms for twenty-four hours. The brand's marketing model was a classic cure for fatal frugality. It became a $3 billion global brand, accounting for 28 percent of Schering's revenues. It was little wonder that the company tried to get patent extensions for Claritin®, claiming the drug was stuck in the FDA pipeline longer than necessary.

Other new drugs like Celebrex®, Nexium®, and Vioxx® adopted the successful Claritin® model of "big bang marketing." Most of these new drugs represented minor advances in pharmacology, offering only minimal incremental value over already existing medications. For example, many Nexium® users could most likely get comparable relief from its predecessor, Prilosec, now sold over-the-counter at a much lower price. However, the Claritin® model worked for these rather ordinary, non-earth-shattering drugs, turning them into blockbuster money machines.

Don't dismiss Claritin® as simply a collection of many, many television commercials. The force of "big bang marketing" permeated every nook and crevice of Claritin®'s marketing effort. Across the fruited plains of America, more and more doctors' offices became inner sanctums for Claritin® signage. The makers of Claritin® had "feet on the street"—thousands of sales reps persuading doctors to prescribe it. All these elements worked together to create an exceptional financial and marketing success story.

Lesson Learned

Product launches are like a leaky bucket. If you don't keep pouring more water into the bucket, the water level goes down fast. Spend,

spend, spend when it comes to a winning new product. In the cases of drugs like Claritin®, Celebrex®, Nexium®, and Vioxx®, rather ordinary drug products became huge financial successes driven by "big bang marketing" investments.

Case #5 Fatality in Frugality: Is Anybody Out There Listening?

Will the new product's voice be heard in the communications jungle of our everyday lives? Before consumers can try the product, there has to be awareness that leads to interest and evaluation. This makes it possible for the consumers to embark on a maiden voyage with the product.

The marketing effort, especially advertising, is responsible for promoting this maiden voyage. This represents a quantity issue—the advertising budget—and also a quality issue—the nature of the message. This leads to an obvious, but very important, consideration often forgotten by innovation teams: do consumers know you exist?

Market with Impact

The initial budget should be lush, ideally above category threshold levels, for a two-year period. As pointed out, management often wants to pull the support plug after a few months. Sales revenue and frugal budgets are rarely compatible soul mates. Joe Willke, senior executive with BASES, remarked:

> For the brands that succeed, we find that when it comes to spending, Year Two must be Year One all over again. This flies in the face of current industry practice.[4]

Here are examples of the average purchase frequency for a few common consumer packaged goods:[5]

Product:	Once Every:
Coffee	three weeks
Shampoo	eight weeks
Mouthwash	thirteen weeks
All-purpose cleaners	thirty-five weeks
Hair coloring	twelve weeks
Furniture polish	twenty-seven weeks

These are rather long purchase cycles; therefore, it will take time to develop a base of loyal users. It is not going to happen in six months. This means one has to keep stoking the fire. It is not time for frugal budget cutbacks.

Unfortunately, even the most sophisticated packaged-goods companies put out almost all of their budget "upfront," during the first six months of the product's existence, and then they pull back drastically, before consumers can go through multiple purchase cycles. This inevitably leads to the "sophomore slump" phenomenon. New product sales drop anywhere from 30 to 70 percent in the second year, and marketers scratch their heads, wondering what happened.

Sound Bite Communications

The noise level of our daily lives is too high for most of us to bear. We live in a communications blitzkrieg, each of us exposed to five thousand branded messages a day. Our society spends more money on advertising brands than on educating our children. Consumers seek refuge from the noise pollution. Nobody turns on their television to see ads, except on Super Bowl Sunday.

The noise problem is compounded by the reality that most advertising is average. We remember the quacking Aflac duck campaign. It is concrete proof that good advertising works miracles, making an obscure insurance company selling a commodity product famous. The "nonquacking, mediocre ads" pass us by. There are too many bland, boring ads that make us want to hit the television remote.

Many of the commercials we see on television are researched. The process is called advertising research, or copy testing. Agency clients use research as a quality control measure to make sure their brands will be supported by strong advertising messages.

All commercials tested have "scores" based on various evaluative measures. If the "scores" for every commercial tested in the past twenty years were compiled, about 80 percent would fall in the middle of what the statisticians call the bell-shaped curve. This means they are average. The remaining commercials are about equally divided between two extremes: awful and outstanding.

On top of these issues, a new product has an additional burden; it has no prior advertising history—there are no cues, symbols, taglines, or brand equity for support. It must start from scratch, attempting to build a niche in the consumer's mind.

Although an aggressive media plan and budget can partially compensate for average copy, the new brand should seek to find a communications sound bite that has legs—like that of the Aflac duck. In other words, the message has a "talk of the town" quality that transitions the new product into an environment of free media exposure.

What is sound bite communications? By using verbal, visual, and symbolic cues, sound bite communications break through the pollution barrier, touching self-absorbed consumers overburdened with advertising. A good sound bite is short and crisp. It has visual and verbal dimensions, striking with the precision of a laser beam.

With an effective sound bite, consumers retain the marrow of the advertising message; the brand's essence sticks in their minds. A product innovation must find its sound bite. Otherwise, its message may pass like a ship in the night. That's the innovation challenge for those with the heavy responsibility of creating the message.

We live in a sound bite society, because an attention-deficit public surrounds us.

- *USA Today* is the sound bite newspaper for busy people who don't want to pore through many pages of the *New York Times* or *Washington Post*.

• *People* is the sound bite magazine for those who want the vicarious thrill of reading about the lifestyles of the rich and famous in a few short, pithy paragraphs. Throw in some photos, but no essays, please.

• CNN Headline News is the sound bite news channel for those who can't handle *The News Hour* with Jim Lehr.

• Even politicians covet the art of sound bite communications. Want to scare senior citizens? The appropriate "vote-getting" sound bite every election season is the repetition of the opposition's will to take away Social Security benefits if elected. Senior citizens recoil in terror, although the likelihood of this occurring is extremely remote, and the politicians know it.

In the innovation game, good sound bites are both verbal and visual. "Research conducted at Columbia and Harvard indicates that retention increased from 14 to 38 percent when the verbal message is accompanied with effective visuals."[6] Another reason sound bite communications can't be just verbally dependent is "that we are visually oriented from the day of our birth."[7] We move through a world of visual stimulation—television, movies, road signs, video games, and computer monitors are just a few examples of what we encounter every day.

But there is a role for language in sound bite communications. Intel's slogan, "Intel Inside," differentiates the microchip from the chocolate chip. Pfizer created new language, penning "erectile dysfunction" in order to sell drugs for diminished sexual performance. The combination of the new phrase (the verbal) and Bob Dole (the visual) brought the problem out of the closet, paving the way for broader acceptance of this new lifestyle drug. It is the best of all worlds when the visual and the verbal morph into a unified whole.

Here are some examples of good sound bite communications:

• **The milk moustache**: A picture is worth a thousand words, and the milk moustache campaign featuring celebrities in silly situations with milk-stained lips provided compelling evidence of this point. With a modest ad budget compared to beverage powerhouses like Coke and Pepsi, the campaign took a dull, boring product and gave it energy and excitement. And, in the spirit of good sound bite communications, this finely crafted campaign was spoofed all over America on TV shows like *The Tonight Show with Jay Leno*.

• **Joe Camel®**: Camel® cigarettes had morphed into "the old man's brand." Something had to be done to revive this relic. Enter Joe Camel®—a cool, hip cartoon mascot with a phallic face. With his arrival, the teen grapevine vibrated with animated conversation about the new, cool dude peddling Camels®. And suddenly, one-fourth of young smokers aged twelve to seventeen were smoking Camels®. Five-year-olds found him more recognizable than Mickey Mouse, Fred Flintstone, and Ronald McDonald. The transition strategy was a success. Camel®'s sales were up 8,000 percent—that's right, 8,000 percent. *Mad* magazine and *The Simpsons* did parodies of the campaign. Public health advocates complained about the campaign's lewd sexual innuendos and influence on teen smoking behavior. News programs marveled at the wide acceptance of Joe Camel® among the teen population. Teens basked in the glow of Joe's outrageous bravado. Everybody talked about Joe Camel®, aided and abetted by a massive level of free media exposure. However, unfortunately for R. J. Reynolds, the maker of Camel® cigarettes, the Joe Camel® sound bite was too successful. Under pressure from the government and public interest groups, Reynolds voluntarily withdrew Joe Camel®, and his perceived negative impact on young smokers, from the public domain. But what a powerful sound bite it was, while it lasted.

• **Absolut® Vodka**: Here the talkative sound bite is a vodka bottle. Absolut® Vodka created a new "type of advertising that stretched the boundaries between advertising and art."[8] The ad's common

denominator was always "witty variations of a common theme"
—a picture of the Absolut® vodka bottle alongside a two- or
three-word caption always beginning with the word Absolut®.[9]
The first sound bite ad, Absolut® Perfection, appeared in 1980.
This timeless communications gem redefined the advertising of
spirits. The creative approach focusing on the vodka bottle
became a media sensation. People talked about the ads in a way
that one would discuss top movies or TV shows. The ads became
collector's items; people even papered their rooms with Absolut®
ads. There were countless free sound bites in every medium,
including an Absolut® Hunk drink featured on the popular TV
show *Sex and the City*. Although some of the activity was
planned by the Absolut® marketing team, much of the free exposure was spontaneous. That's the way powerful sound bites work.

- **Viagra®**: Pfizer knew that the introduction of Viagra® would generate literally thousands of media mentions. Viagra®'s marketing
team wanted to bring male impotence out into the open in a dis-
crete, tasteful way. The product's message had to avoid the implications of recreational sex or perceptions of a licentious lifestyle.
Pfizer also knew that men were reluctant to visit doctors to discuss medical issues. The company needed to find the right balance—a tasteful, but persuasive sound bite that would generate
noise. One that would bring men out of the closet. Pfizer found
its tasteful cheerleader in the form of an "over the hill" politician,
Bob Dole—a prostate cancer survivor who motivated men to talk
to their doctors about erectile dysfunction. Dole's folksy candid-
ness removed the issue's stigma for many men. Dole was a
classic synergistic communications sound bite. He made a talkative drug even more talkative, elevating Viagra® media mentions
to an even higher level. Dole even gave Pfizer M³—More Media
Mentions per gallon—when he peddled other brands. In a Pepsi
spoof commercial, Dole romped on a beach with a golden
retriever and referred to Pepsi® as his "little blue friend" that

made him "feel like a kid again." While it was a Pepsi® commercial, the media and Internet vibrated with mentions of Viagra® instead of the soft drink. Pfizer should have paid Pepsi for doing the spot.

- **Swift Boat Veterans for Truth**: In America's last race for the oval office, candidates George W. Bush and John Kerry spent an estimated $990 million in advertising, making the 2004 presidential election the most expensive customer acquisition campaign in the history of marketing. Yet, Swift Boat Veterans for the Truth ads attacking John Kerry's war record spent less than $500,000, but generated a massive unprecedented level of free media attention. Almost 70 percent of Americans were familiar with the ads as a result of the free media. The "free media ride" reflected the synergistic power of sound bite communications.

Sound bite communication accomplishes three things. It gets ads noticed, remembered, and talked about. As a result, the advertised products get considerably more bang for their marketing dollars. A survey by consulting agency Schneider Associates indicated "that 56 percent of Americans could not recall any new product introduced in the past 12 months."[10] The survey has been repeated with the same discouraging results. This does not bode well for a new product that must create awareness with its advertising message.

Innovation teams have to think "out of the box" about the structural elements of their advertising messages. Consideration should be given to sound bites that have the potential to be more powerful than the actual media buy. These marketing messages extend well beyond media placement, showing up on Jay Leno's show, CNN, the evening news, talk radio, *Access Hollywood*, and even the conversations of everyday folks. They have the potential to sweep through mass media like a virus.

Patients didn't ask for Vioxx®. They did ask for the sound bite in the advertising—give me the pain pill that Dorothy Hamill talked about as she laced up her skates, ready to glide across the ice. Sound bites create the necessary level of noise that product innovations must have to achieve awareness, interest, and, ultimately, a consumer purchase.

It could even be argued that the insurance company Aflac was a new product. Nobody had heard of it until a duck with a lot of attitude started waddling around in commercials. Brand awareness soared to 91 percent from an anemic 13 percent. Aflac sales moved up 30 percent in a flat insurance market.

The Aflac duck, conceived by the Kaplan Thaler Group, one of America's fastest growing ad agencies, and sound bite communications are perfect together. The visual is the waddling duck, frustrated in its quest for attention. The verbal sound bite is the duck quacking "Aflac." The visual and the verbal merged into an implosion, disrupting the complacency of bored consumers.

Good sound bites "have legs." To date, there have been over thirty Aflac duck commercials, and just like the Energizer bunny, the duck keeps going, going, and going. Aflac stock and earnings jumped dramatically as a result of the duck campaign. The potency of sound bite communications works on many different levels.

In some rare instances, the product innovation itself is the sound bite. Such was the case with Listerine PocketPaks®. When the buyers at Wal-Mart saw the product, they immediately wanted it. The product had a natural contagion that spread like a California brush fire.

The introductory advertising for the brand was bland; most consumers couldn't remember it. This would normally be disastrous for a new product, but Listerine PocketPaks® was an atypical new product. The brand generated its own built-in excitement, because it was truly innovative. The package dispenser was unique. Mouthwash breath freshening became mobile. The flavors were robust. It became a status symbol with young people. Its devoted users spread the gospel about it, offsetting the mediocre advertising. The product buzz swept through networks of young people like a virus. A talked-about product such as PocketPaks is the ultimate in sound bite communications. Since many new products lack this built-in excitement, especially new products with marginal differences, the advertising campaign had better be good. Listerine PocketPaks® survived, and even thrived, despite its rather dull advertising.

Sound bite communications is easy to talk about, but may be hard to do. Remember, most advertising is average. A good sound bite works best when there is also a good budget. It is a matter of quantity and quality holding hands and skipping down the yellow brick road of innovation.

Lessons Learned

If the dog is going to bark, it had better be ready to bite, too. Don't be stingy. New products must be marketed with a big sustained bang. This means an ample nine-inning budget. Tell your ad agency to take risks and find something really different—think the Aflac duck or the milk moustache—as models for finding a synergistic sound bite.

The best place to start is shunning traditional focus groups and surveys. Agency creativity that excels often starts with an original approach to the consumer designed to find fresh insights. An example is the "Got Milk?" campaign:

- Goodby, Silverstine & Partners were the architects of the "Got Milk?" campaign. Their imaginative approach to the consumer research process provided the agency with the insight and inspiration for the campaign.

- In one scenario, they took all the milk out of the agency's three refrigerators and placed small video cameras in each one to record how employees reacted when they found out the milk was gone.

- In another research project, they instructed a group of milk-loving consumers to "swear off" drinking it for two weeks. The group was interviewed to find out if there was life after milk. There wasn't. Their tales of frustration and despair clearly indicated that milk was an important part of their everyday lives.

Their war stories and recollections provided fresh insight that led to the vignettes used in the final "Got Milk?" creative.

If the agency can't find a fresh insight, they haven't looked hard enough.

Not every new product will be talked about like Listerine Pocket-Paks® were. But it needs to have talkative advertising. A *USA Today* headline says it all: "TV ads must be remarkable for impact."[11] Average doesn't cut it anymore, now that "remarkable" is the new standard set for getting messages across in our noisy world.

This has implications for new products attempting to establish a beachhead. There has to be more than a play-and-pay media budget. In launching the new venture, the innovation team—client and agency—should have a formal plan to make the talkative sound bite even more talkative. The overall goal should be to garner free media exposure many, many times over.

The possibilities can be rich and varied:

- There's the usual rip-offs, spoofs, and commentary via the likes of Jay Leno, David Letterman, *Saturday Night Live*, and other broadcast environments.

- Don't forget licensing merchandising rights. Aflac licenses its duck. The "Got Milk?" trademark has appeared on more than a hundred products, including Hot Wheels, cookbooks, teen and baby apparel, and Christmas ornaments, among others.

- Leave no stone unturned. Ducks can be found wading around in a pond in front of Aflac's corporate headquarters. A field in eastern Kansas the size of twelve football fields was shaped in the form of an Absolut® vodka bottle visible only from the air.

- There's a Web site selling "Got Milk?" stuff including watches, toys, cookies, and books. Zippo couldn't keep up with the demand for its Joe Camel® lighters.

Clearly, there are many ways to compound talk, supplementing the media buy.

Finally, it is advisable to bring the ad agency into the innovation process as early as possible. Pharmaceutical companies often bring in their ad agencies two years before a new drug hits the market. When agencies have early residency in the category sandbox, they are more likely to find fresh insights—the cornerstone for talkative advertising. And since talkative advertising is a formidable challenge, drastic measures are required. There should be at least two agency creative teams on the attack perimeter. Best sound bite wins.

NOTES

1. Bryan Burrough and John Helyar, *Barbarians at the Gate* (New York: Harper & Row, 1990), p. 37.

2. Merle Crawford and Anthony D. Benedetto, *New Products Management*, 7th ed. (New York: McGraw-Hill Irvin, 2003), p. 356.

3. Carol Fernsholt, "Product Introduction: Getting It Right. But Some Things Are More Important Than Others," *GMA Forum* (Third Quarter, 2003): 97.

4. Ibid.

5. Crawford and DiBenedetto, *New Products Management*, p. 458.

6. Gerald L. Manning and Barry L. Reece, *Selling Today Creating Customer Value*, 9th ed. (Upper Saddle River, NJ: Pearson Prentice Hall, 2004), p. 254.

7. Ibid. p. 253.

8. "From the Fine Art of Advertising to the Advertising of Fine Art," http://www.Absolutad.com/Absolut_about/history/advertising.htm (accessed December 29, 2005).

9. Ibid.

10. Nat Ives, "56% Fail to Remember Any New Products," *New York Times*, January 14, 2005, p. C5.

11. Theresa Howard "TV Ads Must Be Remarkable for Impact," *USA Today*, December 17, 2005, p. 3B.

(7)

[THE EVILS OF
TIMETABLE TYRANNY]

Speed to market is a competitive advantage. Most industries are seeking ways to reduce the development timeline. Some new cars are developed in a year. In the innovation effort driving the cell phone business, companies such as Motorola and Nokia are cranking out basic models in six months. There are indeed advantages in achieving first-to-market status.

- Being the first to the market has the following advantage: the "early bird product" is likely to gain the dominant share in the product category. The next product that comes into the category will have about half the market share achieved by the first entry.

- Being the first to the market has another advantage: the learning curve works for the pioneering brand. It knows how to manufacture, distribute, and promote the product efficiently.

- And finally, the new entry establishes the rules for playing the game in the category sandbox. For example, if the pioneering entry introduced its brand with a $40 million media budget, this becomes the threshold level for others that move into the category. Anything less than this falls below the essential volume level required to be heard in the marketplace.

Speed to market is reinforced by the reality that innovation initiatives now function in an instant gratification culture. Venture capitalists want a return on their investment yesterday. Supermarket chains give a new product a couple of months to show shelf movement. CEOs scream that the numbers must be met come hell or high water. There is no time to test and evaluate ideas. While the needs of consumers should be inspirational, their input is often disregarded if it means additional homework and refinements that might cause the new venture to slow down.

The dress rehearsal phase of product development—test marketing—is rapidly becoming a dinosaur. Excedrin® stayed in test markets for almost three years as Bristol-Myers fine-tuned it. Lever 2000®, a soap brand, was tested for eighteen months before it hit the shelves. The days of hanging around in test markets are a thing of the past.

The focus on speed still requires that the basic homework be done. Therein lies the problem: speed to market and sloppy homework are never a competitive advantage. In this scenario, calendar innovation directed by the product's launch date takes over and the temptation to skip steps trumps doing the homework necessary to optimize the new product.

This also means the second, and possibly even the third, brand entering the category may be successful because the early bird entry did the groundwork research for the later entries. Competitors read the rhythms of the marketplace, seeing what the first-to-market brand did right and wrong. California Cooler® pioneered the wine cooler market. However, by the time Brown Foreman bought the brand, Gallo Family Vineyards and Seagram's had figured out the flaws in California

Cooler®'s fabric and knocked it off the radar screen. Brown Foreman was left with an impotent wine cooler business on its hands.

Speed to market remains a viable concept, and innovation initiatives should always explore the available options to achieve it (cross functional teams, outsourcing, etc.). But speed and poor execution represent a recipe for failure; the required homework must still be skillfully executed. The tentacles of timetable tyranny can be triggered by any combination of the factors below:

- The introduction date must hold, because the pipeline sales are in the sales forecast. The numbers can't be missed. Nobody wants to show up in the executive suite with bad news about the numbers.

- The venture capitalists want a return on the money they invested now.

- Corporations reward people for activity. The marketer who kills two bad new products is regarded less favorably than the one who moves forward with an unrealistic forecast for another new product that will fail. Activity gets confused with achievement.

- The bonuses of the innovation team depend on making the launch date.

- The annual employee reviews are coming up. The new product launch is one of our MBOs (Management by Objectives).

- Promises have been made to large retailers like Wal-Mart or Kroger.

- Retailers have set aside space for the new product and eagerly await its arrival. It would be suicidal to disappoint important retail accounts.

- Since most innovation initiatives take many months from concept to marketplace before bearing fruit, the probability is high that the innovation team will be moved to a new assignment. In the spirit of unenlightened self-interest, management keeps the launch date in play, but its homework may be a bit sloppy. The next group assigned to the new venture inherits the meltdown.

There is nothing logical about timetable tyranny. The riptide force driving it is largely the flawed dimension of the human condition.

Case#1 Timetable Tyranny: Iridium™

The Market

In 1998 Iridium™ redefined wireless communication with the launch of the first global hand-held telephone service. It combined the worldwide coverage of sixty-six low-earth orbit satellites with land-based cellular networks. Subscribers could send and receive calls anywhere on the globe.

The idea was born in 1985, when a Motorola executive's wife was unable to reach her children on her cellular phone while she was vacationing in the Caribbean. She convinced her husband of the need for worldwide wireless system. Mother knows best, or does she?

The target segment for this elaborate wireless system was an elite group of globetrotting executives with a thirsty penchant for staying connected, whether on safari in Kenya or breaking open the champagne to celebrate a business victory in Paris. Iridium™ was a bold, risky venture promising to revolutionize communications. The company was flooded with four hundred thousand inquiries about the service, reflecting the promise and vision of this new venture. At that point, it looked as though a lot of high-roller executive types wanted to be Iridiumized.

Wall Street analysts released glowing reports about Iridium™'s prospects. It was part of the street's high-tech hype that duped many unsuspecting investors in the '90s. However, even knowledgeable, high-tech pundits became ecstatic about this new mobile communications network. A senior Sprint executive said at the time of Iridium™'s launch, "From a technology point of view, we're more impressed than we ever thought we'd be. Four years ago Sprint had some doubts that the system would work well and get built pretty much on time."[1] The large Iridium™ investors—Motorola, Kyocera, and Lockheed-Martin—were ready to endure hernias carrying the moneybags to the banks.

An Illusive Emerald City

While the Emerald City might have been the final destination, Iridium™'s yellow brick road of innovation began to reveal some major potholes. Iridium™ wandered off course with a broken compass as it moved out to sea. The architects behind it were oblivious to dangerous red flags as they raced to meet an unrealistic deadline. Timetable tyranny hovered on the edges of Iridium™'s development.

Less than two years after the launch, Iridium™'s once ebullient CEO, Ed Staiano, stomped into a conference room populated with Motorola executives and snarled, "Do you really expect the business traveler to carry around all this crap?"[2] He slammed the Iridium™ phone and its attachments down on the conference room table and stalked out of the room. The dream and promise of Iridium™ had crash-landed. The service only managed to attract 50,000 subscribers, but it needed 500,000 for positive cash flow. The forecast of 27 million subscribers by 2007 was pure fantasy.

A Flawed Product

Numerous product flaws were associated with Iridium™. The base cost of the phone was $3,000, but the price could reach $4,000 with all the phone's attachments. Basic cell phones were selling for $100 or less at the time. While Iridium™'s digital technology had some advantages over analog cell phones, the technical grandeur was not worth paying thirty times the price of a cheap cell phone.

Iridium™'s clunky design was a disconnect in a world accustomed to compact, stylish cell phones. And an additional sticker shock—calls initially cost $10 per minute—hurt the service. It was difficult to justify using a system that was substantially more expensive, even to well-heeled, globetrotting executives. Someone in the subscriber's accounting department had to approve the expenses, and they were a hard sell.

A bewildering bag of attachments came with the phone, which subscribers found difficult to understand. It was not possible to use the phone inside buildings or moving cars, because a clear path was required between the handset and the orbiting satellites. It simply wasn't as easy to "reach out and touch someone" as the service promised. Subscribers in remote areas, like the jungles of Vietnam and Cambodia, the outback in Australia, or the African backcountry, could not get the phone to work. Phonecalls were made with the expectation of actually getting through to someone at the other end.

The much-heralded wireless communication system could not live up to the hype. In essence, it had a mismatched positioning; the benefit promised and the product delivery, or lack of delivery, were out of sync.

Motorola and its business partners were unrealistic in anticipating the magnitude of the opportunity. The system's appeal was to people in remote regions, and there weren't enough people in the Sahara Desert or the North Pole making phonecalls.

The Iridium™ project suffered from a bad case of technology hypnosis. The out-of-control Motorola engineers became mesmerized with Iridium™'s technical grandeur. They ventured beyond their expertise and became dominant players in both product development and marketing.

Marketing and common sense were placed on the back burner. The innovation moral here is relatively simple—stay within the realm of one's expertise. Engineers should practice engineering, not marketing. The objectivity wilts when engineers start to make important marketing decisions.

As the days of Iridium™ dwindled, the venture capitalists became impatient; they wanted a return on their investment, despite their knowledge that a fully operational system would take ten years to develop. And then there was Murphy's Law—innovation initiatives never proceed as smoothly as envisioned in the conference room. Technical and marketing issues surfaced:

- There were quality control problems with the handsets that required a prolonged debugging period.[3]

- The phones were unusable inside buildings and cars without adapters, and users had trouble understanding their complexity.

- "Some gateway providers were not ready to offer full service at launch."[4] Consequently, Russia and Japan—two huge markets—were not up and running at the time of launch.

- The phone's sound quality was poor; some subscribers described it as "tinny" sounding. Moreover, there was an avalanche of complaints about the need to recharge the phone two or three times every day.

- Outdoor transmission was faulty, hampered by obstacles such as tall buildings.

- Iridium™'s innovation team wavered over its target segment selection. Its members debated: Maybe it should be government employees, not the executive elite. The financially strapped consortium started to play both segments, but the financial resources were very limited, hampering the chase for multiple segments. The target selection issue should have been crisply defined early in Iridium™'s life.[5]

On top of these problems were the venture capitalists, who were saying, "Show us the money." Iridium™ marketers had a first-to-market itch: "We have to beat every other upstart go-anywhere telecommunication competitor to the market." A September launch was set, but Iridium™ was not ready. Problems with service, product, distribution, and support remained. There was an even bigger problem with sales— the cash register wasn't ringing. Potential subscribers held onto their money, waiting to see if Iridium™ had the sizable customer base necessary for operation.

In the wake of these problems, Iridium™ moved the launch date back by a mere two months. This was a modest and absurd concession, considering the vast problems confronting the project. Yet, the need to start generating revenue to justify the six-billion-dollar investment became the paramount issue, and the service became operational without rectifying any of the problems. This was a formula for madness and, of course, failure. The operation was shut down two years after its launch.

Lessons Learned

Never introduce a product that has not been fully optimized in product testing. Delay is preferable to launching a half-baked product that leaves customers dissatisfied. Iridium™ subscribers should have been able to make a phonecall anytime, anywhere.

The reliance on heavy-duty technology is a risky strategy. Huge expenditures are entailed to develop the technology without knowing whether it meets customer needs and wants.

Innovation initiatives are a collaborative effort, requiring contributions from many disciplines. Projects need team leaders to lead, inspire, energize, and arbitrate differences on issues, but no single discipline should dominate the process like Motorola's engineers did. Marketing should be the province of the marketers, not engineering technocrats blinded by technical grandeur.

Flawed innovation can have a lingering negative impact on the environment. Motorola went into an innovation funk after Iridium™ failed. The innovation spirit and drive was sapped from its never-say-die engineering group. Nokia passed Motorola with superior cell phone technology. The best thing to do after an innovation debacle is throw a postmortem party—understand the reasons for the mistakes, and use this knowledge to climb the next mountain. A postmortem party should be instructional and motivational.

Case #2 Timetable Tyranny: Pontiac Aztek®

General Motors's Savior

General Motors (GM) lost $2.6 billion in 1992—a pittance when compared to future losses on the horizon, but significant enough to end the reign of Robert Stempel as GM chairman after fourteen brief months. He was unceremoniously sacked in a board coup led by John Smale. Stemple could have saved his job by closing plants, which would have reduced the magnitude of General Motors's losses, but he displayed a trait that was unheard of for a chairman. He was actually concerned about the thousands of GM employees who would have been left unemployed because of a "cut and slash" strategy.[6] How rare—a CEO with a conscience.

Smale had sat on the General Motors board for several years; he enjoyed returning to the spotlight by designing a major restructuring program for the ailing car company. Smale had earned his managerial spurs at Procter & Gamble, where he retired as chairman and steered the company to its lofty status as America's dominant premier personal care company.

Smale brought in Jack Smith from Europe to replace Stemple. The mercurial Smith, unlike his predecessor, had no compunction about closing twenty-three plants and laying off seventy-five thousand General Motors employees. Smale and Smith called it "rightsizing," and the company posted a $4.9 billion profit in a mere two years after the board coup.[7]

Detroit threw bouquets at Smale for saving General Motors from the brink of bankruptcy. The feat probably was more significant for Smale than when he obtained the American Dental Association seal of approval for Crest®, considering how critical the auto industry was to the American economy. The ADA endorsement, a significant market - ing accomplishment, made Crest® the top-selling toothpaste in America. But this time around, Smale had saved a company that poured billions of dollars into the US economy, directly and indirectly.

In restructuring General Motors, Smale had two pet projects. In 1929 Camay® was a struggling soap brand at Procter & Gamble, and a young executive was given the task of trying to turn it around. Camay®'s sagging fortunes were miraculously reversed in a few months. The results prompted the Procter & Gamble management to assign managers to each of its brands. It was the beginning of the brand management system in America. Most packaged-goods companies adopted it as the way to manage brands.

Smale reasoned that if it worked for soap flakes, why not cars? General Motors had a stable of brands, just like Procter & Gamble, but the company didn't have a power brand like Tide® or Crest®. Smale believed that assigning brand managers to cars was the way to achieve this. There also would be committees to oversee and review the brand mangers' strategies and decisions. It was a bureaucratic concept that fit the General Motors mentality.

It never worked out, because the innovation environment for cars was more complex than developing a box of soap flakes. The average car has fifteen thousand parts. Personal care products like tubes of toothpaste didn't have this type of manufacturing and design complexity.

There was no appreciable improvement in General Motors cars, but there were several costly flops, including the one discussed in this chapter. GM's vaunted brand management system was finally scrapped in the late 1990s, and General Motors continued to lose significant market share as long as it existed. Smale discovered it was easier to sell tubes of toothpaste when not confronted by anything with the caliber of Toyota or Honda.

Smale's other pet project "sort of worked out." Smale demanded that the development time be reduced for General Motors cars. He wanted the company to be first-to-market with "gotta have cars," with an emphasis on CAD (Computer Assisted Design) as a tool to achieve this. He wanted all of GM's design teams to work with a common program.[8]

Aesthetically Challenged

The first model using this new design approach, the Pontiac Aztek®, rolled off the assembly line in model year 2001. It was the first graduate of Smales's speed to market philosophy. Chairman Smale bristled with pride in pointing out that the vehicle represented the fastest development time in General Motors history.[9] It had reached dealer showrooms in nineteen months.

There was another piece of good news. Methodical, plodding, bureaucratic General Motors was ahead of a trend, and it had been a long time since Detroit had seen that happen. Smales's speed-to-market Aztek® was one of the first crossovers combining the smooth riding performance of a car with the muscular steroid features of an SUV. It arrived before the crossover trend became fashionable in Detroit, and General Motors showed up before the party started.

Now, the bad news. Smales's speed-to-market Pontiac Aztek®'s ugly rear-end design made it the hunchback of Notre Dame among cars. The only thing missing was the disfigured Quasimodo hovering behind the steering wheel. *Mad* magazine called the Aztek® "the ugliest car in America." To paraphrase a General Motors critic, if the US Postal Service made cars, it would make the Aztek®.[10] Speed-to-market and sloppy design are an incompatible equation; the Pontiac Aztek® was destined for a short life cycle of just four years.

The Aztek® team leader was an engineer who suddenly found himself with the brand manager title, symbolic of Smales's newly installed brand management system. He was clueless about marketing issues while learning the discipline on the run. It was a case of the blind leading the blind.

The target segment for the Aztek® was Generation X and its youthful, active lifestyle. General Motors expected to sell fifty thousand to seventy thousand Azteks® annually, making the Pontiac division a crown jewel in GM's tiara. About twenty-five thousand Azteks® were sold the first year, with half of the units going to rental car companies and General Motors executives.[11] These sales were like a government subsidy used to support farm prices. The volume did not reflect the real sales rhythms of the marketplace.

Three explanations had surfaced for the ugly duckling design. GM's penny-pinching bean counters insisted that the Aztek® be built on a minivan platform, which compromised the design. This was a perfect example of fatality in frugality—one of the eight basic mistakes that drive flawed innovation.

Smales's computer-assisted design philosophy was used to speed development, but the Aztek®'s boxy-looking rear end unfortunately never showed up as a problem on the computer screen. The design team moved forward, oblivious to the issue.

Another styling issue was the Pontiac division's reverence for cladding: attaching plastic ribbed paneling on the sides of cars. The design started with the 1985 Grand Am® and followed up with a rapid transition to all the Pontiac models in an effort to achieve styling differentiation. The Aztek® was burdened with an overuse of cladding; the bottom third of the vehicle was grotesque-looking gray cladding. This reinforced the already existing perception of the car's unattractiveness.

Robert Lutz was hired to be General Motors's styling czar based on his success at Chrysler with the PT Cruiser®. He immediately jumped in and performed plastic surgery on the Aztek®. This included minor styling tweaks and a bold move—painting the unpainted body cladding. In a final step of desperation, the cherished body cladding was removed entirely from the vehicle. Nothing worked. Aztek®'s negative buzz continued to spread, and once it gained critical mass nobody wanted an Aztek® in the driveway.

General Motors executives offered a litany of excuses for the fiasco. They liked to talk about the J.D. Power and Associates favorable buyer surveys. There was only one problem: there weren't enough buyers. Almost all major purchases result in cognitive dissonance, meaning there is some inevitable discomfort for the buyer following the purchase. The positive Aztek® owner surveys probably reflected a desire to justify or defend, either consciously or unconsciously, the decision to buy the hunchback.

The interior of the Aztek® had some cool features, such as a removable center console that doubled as a cooler, ideally suited for the target segment Generation X's active, outdoor lifestyle. A cool interior didn't offset Aztek®'s "nerdy exterior." Consumers want cars that reflect their self-concept; styling is critical in creating this emotional bond. The Aztek® could have been a good consumer value if one could accept the inevitable ridicule from fellow motorists. The only way dealers could get Azteks® off their lots was through deep discounting.[12]

In a moment of candor, Robert Lutz joked, "We'd fire the guy who green lighted the Aztek® if we could find anyone willing to admit it."[13] Since the Aztek® was literally designed by committee, it probably was difficult to find that person in the General Motors bureaucracy. He or she was hiding somewhere in the layers of management that typified the company at that point.

The Aztek® debacle represented all that was wrong with the General Motors brand management system and its design process, but it was also a wake-up call. One General Motors executive said, "The Aztek® was a turning point, because it articulated everything that was wrong with the system."[14] He then went on to say that turning the GM system around was exasperatingly difficult—not exactly an inspiring observation for buying General Motors stock.

Lessons Learned

Haste makes waste. Flawed styling negates speed-to-market every time. General Motors identified the crossover trend much earlier than its rivals, but it couldn't bring home the bacon in the form of a well-designed car.

INNOVATION ENVIRONMENTS

Entrepreneurship

Many great companies start out as little acorns—an individual's passion for an idea supported by persistence and perseverance. Sam Walton bought a dollar store in 1962 off the village square in Bentonville, Arkansas. Forty years later, the store had grown into an eight-hundred-pound gorilla—the largest retailer in America.

Entrepreneurs are more likely to give us new-to-the-world products than conventional corporations, because they are risk takers. The emergence of noncarbonated beverages came from unheralded companies like SoBe and Snapple, not Pepsi and Coke. Pepsi recently bought Izzi, a fruit juice sparkling water, from serial entrepreneur John Bello, the same man who sold them SoBe a decade earlier.

In the last century, major innovations like audiotapes, records, airplanes, personal computers, and contact lenses were developed by entrepreneurs. However, as new companies transition into second and third generations, they often lose their entrepreneurial spirit for innovation initiatives.

Formulated Marketing

Success moves the entrepreneur to the next level—formulated marketing. Jim Koch drove up and down the streets of Boston looking for neighborhood bars that might be willing to sell his Samuel Adams® beer. He never drove out of his garage in the early years without a trunk full of Samuel Adams®. Today, his company has a marketing department, television commercials, and all the other accoutrements of success. Jim Koch no longer wanders the streets of Boston looking for customers. He is the CEO of Boston Beer Company, an entity that pioneered the microbrew revolution in America—small and regional breweries producing high-end premium beers with a traditional taste like his own Samuel Adams®. In 1995 the Boston Beer Company went public, but success hasn't spoiled Jim Koch. He still enjoys a round of beer with the same bartenders who first sold Samuel Adams® at his urging.

And, finally, some of the entrepreneurial acorns grow into big, mighty oak trees. The entrepreneurial spirit that drove an innovation initiative to fruition can get lost in "bigness"—think General Motors with its endless layers of bureaucracy. There is a tendency for large corporations to sterilize creativity.

There are countless meetings, committees, and policy manuals devoted to risk avoidance, and this, compounded with politics and impatience, makes thoughtful innovation more difficult. Norman Macrae, an editor of the London *Economist*, once suggested that "successful big corporations should devolve into confederations of entrepreneurs."[15]

"Intrapreneuring"

Large corporations that want to recapture the entrepreneurial spirit advocate "intrapreneuring," a process that promotes innovation within the confines of conventional corporations. The company most notable for this philosophy is 3M; its employees may spend 15 percent of their time pursuing pet projects that are outside the boundaries of their mainstream work. 3M has developed several successful new products this way, but its implementation requires faith, patience, and a willingness to tolerate a lot of quirky ideas in order to hit the big one.

Most corporations take a more conventional approach to new product development, creating new products groups with people, budgets, and priorities. They focus on a common agenda with no latitude for wandering off the ranch. However, there may be an underground of intrapreneurs in these companies lurking in the corners, ready to take risks. These people step outside their job descriptions in an attempt to make things happen. This form of intrapreneuring is very different from 3M's formal endorsement of doodling on the side.

The Virtue of Patience in Innovation

Patience has become a lost art in the innovation game. There is always time to do it wrong, but never time to do it right, as reflected in the high innovation failure rate. Some innovations come from the persistence and perseverance of single individuals with relentless passion for an idea that took years to bear fruit. Here are three examples of how this has happened in corporate America.

Post-it® Notes

William McKnight is the executive responsible for 3M's intrapreneurial culture. As he rose through 3M's ranks to CEO status, his philosophy was to listen to anybody with an idea; McKnight believed in engineering doodling, after seeing several engineers wander off the reservation, following their instincts and returning with new products. McKnight formalized the wanderlust with the company's now famous 15 percent rule—allowing 3M engineers to spend 15 percent of their time "off the books" on projects not formally endorsed by the company. Since 3M never policed the rule, some employees ventured beyond 15 percent, but 3M didn't care as long as their regular work was done.[16]

Spencer Silver was one of the "rule breakers." He had invented a curious adhesive that did not bond very well to surfaces. Silver was intrigued with the science of his discovery; he started wandering the corridors of 3M trying to get someone interested in his strange non-sticking adhesive. Nobody got very excited when Silver pitched it—who wants an adhesive that doesn't bond like iron to a surface?

Silver kept his idea in play and spent five years on it—an inordinate period of time, even by 3M's flexible standards. He accomplished this feat by staying on top of his core assignments, even though he was spending a third of his time peddling the adhesive to 3M colleagues. While Silver was a lousy salesman, his cheerful, optimistic personality made him a tolerable chap—a few colleagues listened to Silver four or five times as he extolled the virtues of his creation.

But time was running out on Silver. After five years of trying, Silver's constant refrain remained: "Surely it must be good for something." Silver's adhesive was a solution to something, but he could not, nor could anyone else at 3M, identify the problem the adhesive solved. 3M colleagues started to run in the opposite direction when they saw Silver approaching them in the corridors. The welcome mat had been yanked out from under him, but the "eureka moment" was ready to occur in the unexpected environment of choir practice.[17]

Another 3M scientist, Art Fry, sang in a church choir during two services on Sundays. He used slips of paper to mark the songs in the hymnal to be sung at each service. By the beginning of the second service, some of the paper markers would fall out, frustrating Fry. In a moment of despair, he remembered Silver's unconventional adhesive, and the lightbulb went on. He thought of putting Silver's adhesive on paper, and it was the "eureka moment" they had been waiting for. Fry went back to the 3M labs and made sticky hymnal markers using Silver's adhesive. They worked, and the solution to the problem had been found. It was the birth of Post-it® Notes.[18]

Innovation initiatives are a culture of collaboration. There were significant contributions from several sources in the development process for Post-it® Notes. Henry Courtney and Roger Merrill invented a coatable paper to make the lightweight adhesive work. Art Fry jumped back into the fray when he was told the manufacturing process for Post-it® Notes was impossible. Although it was not in his job description, he patched together a Rube Goldberg–type manufacturing process in his basement. He broke through a wall to get the equipment to 3M; an expense report was later submitted. Fry had the equipment up and running when the process engineers came to work in the morning. The manufacturing process for Post-it® Notes initially conceived in Fry's basement was so sophisticated that competition doesn't even try to emulate it—the best of all possible worlds for an innovation.[19]

Senior executives Geoff Nicholson and Joe Ramey knew that Post-it® Notes had an addictive quality simply by watching 3M employees use them. They flew down to Richmond, Virginia, and invaded the business district, handing out pads of Post-it® Notes at banks, office buildings, and conference centers. The response was overwhelmingly enthusiastic and became a harbinger for the marketplace response that would later replicate across the business offices and homes of America.[20]

The company's approach—"here, try this"—was a technique pioneered years earlier by William McKnight, 3M's newly appointed national sales manager, who gave out sandpaper samples to furniture makers in Rockford, Illinois, in 1914, returning later to gather reactions. Nicholson and Ramey intuitively knew Post-it® Notes had natural contagion once consumers saw it. It would leapfrog through networks of people, creating a buzz.

3M validated its "here, try this" approach in the "Boise Blitz," when an armada of 3M-ers descended on the town to sample Post-it® Notes. Conventional advertising methods could not work, because Post-it® Notes, a new-to-the-world product, was very difficult to ex - plain in a thirty-second television commercial. Perhaps an infomercial might have worked. Once consumers had the opportunity to use them it was goodbye staples and paper clips, and thousands of other new uses for the product also surfaced.[21]

In the wake of its success, Art Fry became the poster boy for Post-it® Notes. The corporate spinmeisters wrote a speech for him that he awkwardly delivered on the banquet circuit. The less heralded Spencer Silver retreated to his basement office, perfectly content to be away from the limelight; it was more fun mixing up chemicals with his array of beakers and test tubes.

There were many heroes in the intrapreneurial saga of Post-it® Notes, but nothing would have happened without Spencer Silver pursuing his determined, lonely quest for five years. Spencer Silver and patience: perfect together. Post-it® Notes became the most successful new product in 3M's history primarily because Spencer Silver refused to shut up. And no doubt about it, Post-it® Notes never would have been invented in large bureaucratic corporations like General Motors or Campbell's Soup.

Listerine PocketPaks®

Keith Lerner became the equivalent of Spencer Silver in the development of Listerine PocketPaks®. One way to find new product technology is to attend trade shows. Lerner was at a trade show in Germany when he spotted what would be the technological cornerstone for Listerine PocketPaks®. It was an edible film technology from Japanese company Hayashibara—a coated strip that instantly dissolved in the mouth sold to smokers to freshen smelly cigarette breath.

Lerner returned to the United States totally psyched about the technology, thinking it might have applicability to Warner Lambert's confections group. He set up a round of meetings only to encounter objections like "What would we do with it?" or "It simply won't work." These killer phrases are easy to use and occur regularly in conference rooms, but they stifle creativity and innovation.[22] Every idea has a modicum of merit if given a bit of fresh air to breath, but the oxygen was drained from the room in every meeting Lerner set up.

Lerner remained undaunted; he was inflicted with Spencer Silver's same philosophical musing when the 3M chemist reflected on his funny adhesive—"Surely it must be good for something." Lerner had the same problem Post-it® Notes encountered in its embryonic days. Every product exists to solve a problem. The film technology was a solution to something, but what was the problem it solved?

Lerner began a lonely vigil. For three years, he brought up the idea at every possible opportunity—business meetings, golf and tennis outings, conversations in the company cafeteria, and even the company Christmas party. His was a voice in the wilderness; nobody could generate comparable enthusiasm for the film technology.

Then Lerner had the "eureka moment." In a casual conversation with a market researcher from the Listerine® group, the researcher noted that a need for a portable Listerine® had surfaced in several group sessions with the brand's users. This triggered an internal point of view that a major business opportunity existed for "oral care on the go." Consumers can't walk down the street with a bulky bottle of

Listerine®, swig it down, and spit it out. How do you make Listerine® portable?

The lightbulb went on: Lerner had found the problem that the film technology solved. Listerine® would fight the heartbreak of halitosis on all fronts—in the bathroom and away from home. The concept of "oral care on the go" delivered via the film technology tested well with Listerine® users, and Lerner's passion finally found a home, only because he kept the technology in play with his never-say-die enthusiasm for it.

It would take another five years of development before Listerine PocketPaks® hit the market; product optimization was a major challenge. The director of research and development's first reaction to it was one word: "Yuck." It had to be refined for the American palate to dissolve rapidly while delivering a pleasurable taste.

The research and development group "played around with the basic carbohydrate film, changing flavors and adding surfactants to break up faster on the tongue." For five years, sensory experts, market researchers, dentists, microbiologists, physical chemists, physical chemical engineers, and manufacturing experts embarked on a journey to work out the bugs and kinks.[23]

The manufacturing process was another major challenge. The product was very sensitive to heat and humidity; the conditions had to be perfect, otherwise the film gummed up and was not malleable for manufacturing. The film had to be cut into little postage stamp–size pieces, moved to packaging machinery, and inserted into small plastic containers, which had to be airtight to prevent the product from breaking down. The containers then had to be put into airtight blister packs to protect the product from the humidity.

As Listerine PocketPaks® moved through development, it became clear that the initial volume estimate had to be ramped up, because consumer research indicated an incredibly strong interest in the product. New manufacturing lines had to be ordered and installed. Each line had its own long, tedious process to optimize product quality and get sufficient line speeds. The installation of new lines impacted the production on other lines due to changes in airflow, temperature, and humidity. The process took about a year to complete.

The test market for Listerine PocketPaks® was Canada because limited manufacturing capacity prevented a US launch. The marketing plan's original target segment was older Listerine® users with a need for oral care on the go.

But the marketplace danced to its own rhythm, reconfiguring the target segment definition. Generation X discovered it as a cool, essential lifestyle accessory, deeming it uncool to be seen in public without PocketPaks. It became a social ritual to have the cutesy little dispensers with you at all times. The fifteen- to twenty-four-year-old segment became early adopters of the fashionable breath strip with its intense, high-octane flavors. The original positioning of portability—mouthwash without the bottle—took a back seat to the hedonistic needs of Generation X, who repositioned PocketPaks as the cool, hip breath strip with the toylike package. Very few of PocketPaks's sales volume came from the desire for "mouthwash on the go." The brand had morphed into a better version of the British power brand, Altoids®, not portable Listerine®.

The breath film had natural contagion, just like Post-it® Notes. The buzz briskly swept through the fifteen- to twenty-four-year-old segment. The cash register rung in almost $200 million in the brand's introductory year after being launched in 2001. This was an extraordinary achievement; only 2 percent of new consumer products hit the $100 million level in their initial year.

Post-it® Notes and Listerine PocketPaks® have many similarities, including patience and a culture of collaboration from many different sources. However, a major difference is that Pfizer does not have an intrapreneurial culture like 3M. Lerner defied the existing culture, but not in a disagreeable way. He simply refused—like Spencer Silver—to shut up.

Lerner was a courageous soul from the underground who routinely networked the film technology to those around him. He tolerated their indifference, never became frustrated, and just hung in there until the "eureka moment" struck like a bolt of lightning. Would Listerine PocketPaks® be where it is today without Keith Lerner endlessly talking about the film technology he first saw in Germany?

Pepsi-Lipton Partnership

The two conversations took place about four weeks apart. At PepsiCo headquarters, Craig Weatherup, CEO of Pepsi North America, beckoned the company's marketing lieutenants into his spacious office complete with Picasso paintings. There, he made the following proclamation: "We are going to be a total beverage company. Our product portfolio needs to be reconfigured." It was a pivotal moment in Pepsi's history. Weatherup saw the future, and it was not necessarily a brown, fizzy beverage.

A few weeks later Lipton's vice president, Richard Kundrat, had a meeting with Blaine Hess, CEO of the Thomas J. Lipton Company. He had noticed in *Beverage Digest* that Coke was in negotiations with Nestlé. There was no intrapreneurial philosophy at Lipton, but Kundrat fit the mold. He was a savvy marketer who marched to a different drummer. The textbooks would label him a "change agent"— sometimes called a "turnaround entrepreneur" in academia—with a passion for revitalizing a Lipton business frayed at the edges. Only Hess could give him the green light to move ahead on his mission.

Lipton had existing contracts with 158 Coca-Cola bottlers to distribute and sell Lipton® Iced Tea in cans. Lipton provided the syrup to make the product; the bottlers made it and got it into the stores.

In his meeting with Hess, Kundrat laid out the situation. The relationship was undervalued from Lipton's perspective, because Coca-Cola USA controlled what was put on the bottlers' trucks through its allocation of promotion dollars. The promotion effort focused on Coke's major brands, not Lipton® Iced Tea. In those days, Coca-Cola USA was only interested in selling three brands—Coke®, Diet Coke®, and Sprite®. This was a problem for Lipton. If it wasn't on the trucks or in the vending machines, it meant no sales for Lipton® Tea.

Kundrat proposed that the contracts be shuttled in favor of a partnership between Coca-Cola USA and Lipton. Hess gave his blessing for a meeting between the two companies. In the interim, Pepsi had a meeting with Kundrat expressing a strong interest in finding an arrangement to integrate Lipton Tea into the Pepsi bottling system. Kundrat had this development in his back pocket before setting up a meeting with Coke.

Kundrat flew to Atlanta on a sunny day after Christmas to see Coca-Cola CEO Doug Ivester. Coke's headquarters was deserted as employees enjoyed a holiday respite. The meeting lasted about an hour. Ivester came across as a stuffy, certified bean counter with a tin ear for marketing—a major disadvantage in a marketing-driven company. Ivester saw no merit in a partnership and forcefully reminded Kundrat that Coke would sue if the contracts were broken.

Kundrat left the meeting unruffled. One thing was very clear to him. Pepsi's CEO, Weatherup, saw the future, and Ivester's vision was blurred—a fatal flaw destined to remove him from the CEO's suite in a palace coup led by board members Warren Buffett and Herb Allen about eighteen months later.

Coke's flirtation with Nestlé troubled Lipton. It speculated Coke wanted a global tea and coffee association with Nestlé. On the other hand, Lipton wanted to modernize its tea business beyond little old ladies buying tea bags on their way home. The company was not oblivious to the marketplace success of Snapple's line of iced tea products. It was time for Lipton to join the big parade.

Pepsi was still eager to cut a deal, probably because it had tried a tea product in the Pepsi system and failed. An agreement was reached between Pepsi and Lipton. The two companies would share the revenue, expenses, and profits for seventy-five years; it was a value-added scenario for Lipton's absence in its current relationship with Coke. Lipton pulled the trigger; 158 certified letters were sent to Coke bottlers terminating the franchise contracts.

Coke hit Lipton with an injunction prohibiting the company from selling any product to the soft drink industry. The Lipton lawyers managed to get a summary court judgment in the company's favor. Despite a cozy relationship with Pepsi, Kundrat had a mess on his hands. Pepsi told Lipton that the partnership would move forward only if two-thirds of the country could be freed up in four months. It was a challenge, but not for a determined change agent.

Kundrat swung into action, approaching the two biggest bottlers in the Coke's system—Coca-Cola Enterprises and Coke New York; both agreed to terminate their contracts. Another large bottler, Coca-Cola Consolidated, soon followed. He had the geography Pepsi demanded, but it took him another eighteen months to cut the umbilical cord with the other Coke bottlers. Two things were astonishing about Kundrat's odyssey through the Coke bottling system. Lipton paid a pittance to terminate the contracts. How could Ivester and the Coke bottlers so easily walk away from a crown jewel without a whimper?

In retrospect, Kundrat observed, "Pepsi had the hard assets—250 bottling plants, 30,000 trucks on the streets every day delivering product to stores, and over a million vending machines. We brought only one thing to the party—a powerful brand with incredibly strong equity." His simple, direct statement spoke volumes about the value of a brand's DNA—it's called brand equity.

Pepsi was smarter than Coke in the early '90s, forming strong partnership alliances with Lipton and Starbucks. Ask anyone what comes to mind when the word "tea" is mentioned. The most likely response will be Lipton, not Coke's partner, Nestea. Alas! It could have been different. Coke was offered the partnership opportunity with Lipton. The company could have sold millions of cases every year, but settled instead for table scraps in a weak partnership with Nestlé.

In the early days of the Pepsi-Lipton Partnership, Kundrat pushed for a "double whammy" that marginalized Coke's tea business. The partnership marketed tea in cans and bottles. The later Lipton® Brew was produced on a sophisticated hot fill manufacturing line that produced a high-quality, healthy tea, which helped the image of Lipton's canned tea products in general. Consumers attributed goodness and health to both products, which was perceptual, but perception is reality in marketing.

About five years after the partnership was established, Kundrat met a senior Coke executive on a flight to Florida. The executive confessed to Kundrat after a couple of cocktails in first class, "You really killed Coke's tea business when you put your product in bottles and cans. I wish we had been smart enough to do that." Coke wasn't smart enough, because it passed on the opportunity to partner with someone who understood the tea business like Kundrat did.

The success of the partnership with Lipton encouraged Pepsi to seek out other partnerships, like that with Starbucks and more recently with Izzi in Colorado. None of these partnerships ran the risk of being "Pepsified." Each product kept its core equity, because Pepsi did not want to dominate the relationship, possibly bastardizing the brands. Companies like Coke and Pepsi sometimes fall into the trap of thinking they're the smartest guys in the room. None of Pepsi's strategic alliances with partners have turned out to be "too Pepsi." They are true partnerships, with each side actively participating in innovation decisions.

Kundrat was a classic change agent. He saw the opportunity to revitalize a sleepy, undervalued contractual arrangement with Coke bottlers. He charged into the fracas and fundamentally changed how Lipton integrated tea into the soft drink industry.

Kundrat retired from Lipton after twenty years in the marketing trenches, but his style is typically entrepreneurial. He is still in the beverage business as CEO of NuVim, Inc., makers of a beverage sold in refrigerated juice sections of supermarkets. Old intrapreneurs never die; they just keep surfacing on the chessboard of opportunity.

Lessons Learned

Don't be content with the status quo. Corporations should create an environment where dreamers can wander off the reservation to pursue an innovation initiative at the end of the rainbow. And indeed some companies—think General Electric, Procter & Gamble, and Johnson & Johnson—have moved in this direction with the establishment of chief technology officers who seek out ideas and technology beyond the company's research and development labs.

It is the responsibility of CEOs to create a culture receptive to dreaming. Andrew Grove, former chairman of Intel Corporation, was great at doing this. He "had an exceptional ability to create a work environment that married entrepreneurialism with extreme discipline. He gave his colleagues a wide berth to be innovative and anticipate the future."[24] Intrapreneuring works with the right leader. It should not have to be a shadowy process.

NOTES

1. Kevin Maney, "$3000 Gadget Might Be Globe-Trotter's Best Friend," *USA Today*, September 17, 1998, p. 29.

2. Leslie Cayley, "Losses in Space-Iridium's Downfall: The Marketing Took a Back Seat to Science—Motorola and Partners Split," *Wall Street Journal*, August 18, 1999, p. A1.

3. Merle Crawford and Anthony C. DiBenedetto, *New Products Management*, 7th ed. (New York: Harper & Row, 1990), p. 407.

4. Ibid.

5. Ibid.

6. Jim Mateja, "After 14 years, Ex-GM Boss Still Holds Firm Dear," *Chicago Tribune*, October 12, 2006, http://www.chicagotribune.com.

7. Ibid.

8. Drew Winter, "Engineering/Design; Virtual Turnaround, General Motors Fast Vehicle Development Program," *Ward's Auto World*, June 2000, p. 121.

9. Ibid.

10. Jonathan Welsman, "Bogged Automaker Needs Big Change," *Washington Post*, June 11, 2005, http://www.washingtonpost.com.

11. Ibid.

12. David Kiley, "Pontiac Aztek Goes the Way of the DoDo," July 19, 2005, http://www.businessweek.com/the_thread/brandnewday/archives/2005/07.htm (accessed October 2, 2006).

13. Ibid.

14. Jonathan Weisman, "Biggest Automaker Needs Big Charge," *Wash-*

ington Post, June 11, 2005, http://www.washingtonpost.com/wp-day/content/article/2005/06/10.htm (accessed October 6, 2006).

15. Paul Lukas, "3M a Mining Company Built on a Mistake Stuck It Out Until a Young Man Came Along with Ideas about How to Tape Those Blunders Together as Innovations—Leading to Decades of Growth," CNN.com, April 11, 2003, http://www.money.cnn.com.

16. Gifford Pinchot III, *Intrapreneuring* (New York: Harper & Row, 1985), p. 9.

17. P. Ranganath Nayak and John M. Ketteringham, *Breakthroughs* (Oxfordshire, UK: Mercury Business Books, 1993), pp. 25–37.

18. Pinchot, *Intrapreneuring*, p. 137.

19. Ibid., p. 139.

20. Nayak and Ketteringham, *Breakthroughs*, p. 43.

21. Pinchot, *Intrapreneuring,* p. 141.

22. Crawford and DiBenedetto, *New Products Management*, p. 81.

23. Alex Kuczynski, "Breath Mints. A Hot War for America's Cool Mouths," *New York Times*, February 24, 2002, p. ST6.

24. Jeffrey E. Garten, "Andy Grove Made the Elephant Dance," *Businessweek*, April 11, 2005, p. 26.

⑧

[DEFECTIVE MARKETING INTELLIGENCE]

Marketing research is the function that links the customer with the marketer through information. We are a research nation. On a daily basis, interviewers staff banks of telephones to interview us about everything from soup to nuts. Shoppers are grabbed at malls to participate in fast five- to ten-minute intercept interviews. The Internet has been harnessed as an interviewing environment. For an honorarium, eight consumers are herded into a room in a focus group discussion. As clients sit behind a one-way mirror observing and commenting, a professional moderator guides the groups through a two-hour discussion.

Americans love to talk. In marketing research, they'll discuss anything and everything—decadent dark chocolate as a substitute for spousal affection, bowel movements, hemorrhoid problems, yeast infections, and even their sex lives.

One of the earliest research projects in America was conducted by Charles Parlin, who established the first commercial research department for Curtis Publishing, which owned the *Saturday Evening Post*. Parlin wanted Campbell's Soup as an advertiser, but members of Campbell's senior management believed their condensed soup was too highbrow for the magazine's readers. There wasn't a perceived fit between the *Saturday Evening Post* readers and the Campbell's customer base. Parlin, however, believed soup was a working-man's product.

Parlin rented a warehouse and hired an armada of workers to bring the garbage from Philadelphia neighborhoods to this central location. The workers systematically sifted through the debris, separating Campbell's® soupcans by neighborhoods to disprove the perception of Campbell's management. Parlin's gut instincts proved correct; the garbage from the wealthier neighborhoods contained very few empty cans of soup. However, lots of empty soup cans were discovered in the garbage from the less-affluent areas. This research finding became the cornerstone of a long relationship between the *Saturday Evening Post* and the Campbell Soup Company once it realized blue blood neighborhoods were not its customers.

Marketing research has come a long way since Parlin's early efforts. The expanding corporate need for information to spearhead innovation initiatives and other marketing issues has led to the development of a multibillion-dollar marketing research industry. In *Winning the Marketing War*, Gerry Michaelson describes Procter & Gamble's intense involvement with marketing research:

> P&G will phone or visit over one million people each year to collect information for some one-thousand research projects. Generating this mountain of information is only half the process. It's what P&G does with it that sets the company apart from the corporate pack. The data is funneled to every major segment of the company, where it is sifted and resifted for its impact on P&G's marketing, advertising, manufacturing, and research and development operations.[1]

The romance with marketing research even extends to the field of politics. Currently, members of government in Washington seldom make a move without doing polling research or conducting focus groups designed to measure America's pulse on issues of interest. Strategy gurus sift and resift the information, seeking out the nuggets that resonate with the voting public.

In the innovation game, there exists a rare breed that survives without the need for marketing research. Charles Revlon and Ernest Gallo were superb at interpreting the human condition and the marketplace implications for the product lines at their respective self-titled companies. Their instincts, without the benefits of marketing research, turbocharged the growth of their companies, and new products flourished. Mary Wells Lawrence had an intuitive feel for how to position a new product or service. She became the best positioning strategist on Madison Avenue.

Robert Lutz, General Motors's styling czar, is a car guy to the core with an impressive résumé of achievements—the PT Cruiser® was his baby. Lutz had a strong disdain for how marketing research was used in Detroit, and one of the first dictums out of his mouth in arriving at General Motors was: "Designers shouldn't be slaves to focus groups. What focus groups say they want in their next car is not reliable. The gut instincts of designers have to take over at some point."[2] These marketing immortals discovered innovative ideas without sophisticated marketing research techniques.

However, for the rest of us, marketing research is the conduit to the marketplace, providing the veins of information that guide decision making. The innovation game is a marketing research–intensive process. It starts with a blank piece of paper, and marketing research is the process that must fill these blank pages with sentences and punctuation. It is a discovery process that, hopefully, leads to viable new products and services as a result of doing the required homework with consumers.

In the American Marketing Association's publication *Marketing Management*, it was pointed out that "75 percent more person days and more than double the money were devoted to the early pre-development activities" for successful new products in contrast with those that failed.[3] These early predevelopment activities are very marketing research–oriented—listening to America's consumers talk, searching out big ideas, and making the fuzzy front end of innovative efforts considerably less fuzzy.

ROLE OF MARKETING RESEARCH IN INNOVATION

Packaged goods companies are noted for their marketing research sophistication. The public statements below illustrate the use of marketing research in the new product development process:

> It all started with normal market research. We asked the kids what would make them want to eat more french fries. We started with 50-odd ideas and pared them, through research and testing, down to five.[4]

> We talked to thousands of teens about creating a cola fusion, and they told us two things: Make it berry and make it blue. Teens understand fusion better than any other age group. They live it every day—in their music, fashion, and culture.[5]

What's wrong with this picture? The research spoken of was for blue french fries and Pepsi Blue®. Both became casualties of the great game of innovation roulette. Is the unfounded euphoria simply a case of corporate spin, bad marketing research, or a little bit of both? The marketplace voted; both products were rejected. There is a big difference between purchase decisions and eight teens talking about blue french fries or blue colas in group sessions.

Despite the marketing research sophistication of companies like Kraft and General Mills, nine out of ten of their new packaged-goods products fail. Two marketing research errors surface in the innovation process—omission and commission.

Case #1 Defective Marketing Intelligence: Errors of Omission

In the innovation game, errors of omission emanate from failure to execute critical steps when important predevelopment activity is short-changed or even ignored. Often, this occurs because the timetable is sacrosanct. So the innovation team members, working backward from the date, often find that time is not on their side. Their conclusion: speed is essential if the date is to be met, and some corners may have to be cut.

Skipping critical research steps may be inspired by the desire to save money—a fatally flawed cheapskate strategy that inevitably implodes.

Remember: The evidence is indisputable. Innovation initiatives based on solid homework, especially in the early stages of development, are more likely to be winners. Regardless of the reasons, a rush to judgment creates a situation where essential refinements may slip through the cracks, jeopardizing the new product venture.

In discussing the propensity to move quickly through the hoops and hurdles of the development process, a group session moderator who has personally worked on many different clients and their new product projects observed:

> The biggest change in the past fifteen or twenty years is that there is no time to do it right. For most new products and services, the early up-front exploratory work is shoddy. There is no time for reflection where all the options are explored. It tends to be three focus groups and on to the next step. They end up not understanding the basics of the business.

When marketers manipulate the steps in the development process, to avoid natural detours or refinements that could possibly slow down the project, they start acting as if the consumer is the enemy rather than a friend. The consumer should provide innovation inspiration, not disdain. A marketing research director at a leading over-the-counter drug company remarked, "A strong desire exists to not see the problems and keep the rose colored glasses on. Obstacles are ignored, and the brand team keeps charging [forward]."

As corporate clients sit behind the mirror, observing consumers in group sessions dump on their new product or service, there is a tendency for the new product team to lose its emotional balance. " How can they not like that positioning? It's a winner." In the spirit of Pandering 101, the ad agency often agrees with the client—the consumer is stupid. It is a lot easier to go along than to try to understand the significance of what the consumers are saying and the potential impact it could have on the new product's fortunes. Clients want team players, not obstructionists. Why rock the boat? A plush media budget lies ahead!

If consumers keep making "stupid comments" about the new product or service, it is not unheard of for the client to start beating up on the person leading the discussion, because he or she is considered incompetent. A typical client comment is: "If the moderator properly presented the idea, consumer reactions would be more favorable." What the client wants is a Shakespearean actor from the Old Vic, not a moderator.

As the new product moves closer to the impending launch date, the packaging or advertising copy may be negatively impacted in that both enter at the latter stages of the development process. Sometimes new products slide into test markets or regional rollouts with serious advertising problems. There's always the blithe assumption the copy will get fixed in the test markets or rollout. This happens only on rare occasions.

Because advertising is an essential component in creating awareness and interest for a new product, mediocre or bad copy represents a severe impediment to success. This scenario may exist because the ad agency wasn't given enough time to do the job properly.

We know what's wrong with this picture—the voice of the consumer has been deleted from the equation. Robert Waterman and Tom Peters long ago made the following observation: "The excellent companies are really close to their customers. Other companies talk about it; the excellent companies do it."[6] The error of omission truncates consumer dialogue and eliminates the opportunity for marketing research to help the new products team understand and effectively respond to the voice of the consumer.

Case #2 Defective Marketing Intelligence: Errors of Commission

Errors of commission are committed in plenty of marketing research, but the problem is that the teacher hands out the wrong homework assignment. There is a flurry of misguided marketing research activity. The new product or service is destined for flameout as the misdirected activity takes the innovation venture down the wrong elevator shaft.

New Coke® Follies

It was a major news story. ABC's anchor, at the time the late Peter Jennings, interrupted afternoon soap opera *General Hospital* to bring good news to America. The Coca-Cola Company announced it was bringing back old Coke®. In a moment of insanity, the company had previously decided to scrap its flagship brand in favor of New Coke®, but now the company was hoisting the white flag on that venture. While New Coke® represented a major marketing blunder, it was also a good example of the error of commission in action. I can offer fresh insight into the New Coke® saga, because I was there on a consulting assignment for a major Coca-Cola bottler.

The Market

In the early 1980s, Coke was losing market share to archrival Pepsi. The sales surge was confined to supermarkets: Coke continued to dominate the captive market of fast food, vending machines, and restaurants. But then the unthinkable happened. Pepsi sailed past Coke in supermarket sales by two share points, which represented close to $960 million in cola sales.

There were many sweaty palms in Atlanta—blind taste tests indicated many Coke® drinkers actually preferred Pepsi®. This taste preference had become the cornerstone for the "Pepsi Challenge" advertising campaign. It was a simple commercial in format. Two cola drinkers were asked to sip two unidentified sodas. They were asked for their preference; the identified winning cola was always Pepsi®. There was nothing Coca-Cola could do about this effective ad, because it was true—cola drinkers preferred Pepsi® in this "testing environment."

Pepsi used the challenge campaign regionally in markets where it wanted to build market share at Coke's expense. It was never a full-scale national advertising campaign. It supplemented Pepsi's national advertising.

Coke's senior management attributed Pepsi's supermarket success to the "Pepsi Challenge." The head of market research at Coca-Cola USA assessed the situation as follows: "If we have twice as many vending machines, dominate fountain, have more shelf space, spend more on advertising, and are competitively priced, why are we losing share? You look at the 'Pepsi Challenge,' and you have to begin asking about taste."

Coke's executive brigade began thinking the unthinkable—reformulate the flagship brand to make it sweeter, like Pepsi®. But what the Coke team did not realize was that sip testing—the cornerstone of the "Pepsi Challenge"—favored sweeter formulations, and Pepsi®'s flavor was the sweeter of the two. Pepsi knew this, but Coke did not. Pepsi laid a trap that the Coke executive suite walked right into.

Since ignorance is bliss, the flawed strategic instincts of Coke's management were reinforced with news from research and development that a formula had been developed that beat Pepsi® by six to eight points in blind sip taste tests. Coke did the unthinkable; the untouchable secret recipe was touched. New Coke® replaced old Coke® in the marketplace, and sip-tasting research was a major contributor to the decision.

Coke's Real Marketing Problem

Coke had an advertising problem, not a product problem. Advertising is a major weapon in shaping the images of soft drink brands, especially among young people, the coveted guzzlers of carbonated soft drinks. During the 1980s, Coke bored America with a litany of Norman Rockwell travelogue-type commercials. It became a problem that was destined to plague Coke for the next twenty-five years. The creative style for Coke copy was a throwback to the '70s. The client and its ad agency lived in the happy valley of past advertising achievements like television ads featuring young people on a hill singing Coca-Cola's national anthem. But the world of young soft drink consumers had drastically changed.

Coca-Cola was losing generations of young people with its bland advertising style. The company was eventually forced to bring in "new thinking" about ten years later in an attempt to solve Coke's ever-widening gap with the youth culture. This was a serious targeting issue for Coke.

During this period of Coke's advertising decline, Pepsi® was one of the first brands to recognize that America had become a nation of television babies. The brand tapped into the MTV format using celebrities like Michael Jackson and Lionel Richie to promote its products, especially its flagship brand, Pepsi®. The Pepsi advertising had visual hooks and surprises in contrast to Coke's stodgy look and feel.

Which commercial would appeal to an impressionable twelve-year-old on the cusp of deciding his or her cola preference? A Pepsi commercial featuring Michael Jackson doing the moon walk, or a Coke ad showing happy faces chugging Coke® at the Fourth of July picnic with the American flag waving in the background? Pepsi told young people they were drinking "the taste of a new generation," and an entire generation believed it.

Coke had no relevant statement for the youth culture in the '80s. Pepsi ads repositioned Coke® as the drink for fuddy-duddies. The frat boys drank Pepsi®, while the beverage of choice for senior citizens was

Coke®. Pepsi preempted the youth culture in the '80s and beyond. I evaluated Coke and Pepsi advertising for over a decade and can confidently say that a review of advertising for the two cola brands over the past twenty-five years shows Pepsi® had a decisive edge.

While Coke actually spent more on advertising, Pepsi got more bang for its advertising buck with superior copy as Coke struggled to break through its boredom barrier. This difference, not the sip test in the "Pepsi Challenge," was a major factor in Pepsi's sales spurt. The challenge had a dual impact—it made the cash register ring and paved the way for a flawed research design that set in motion Coca-Cola's historic blunder.

Coke was told its advertising was ineffective from outside sources such as consultants and bottlers, but management refused to listen. It wasn't said once. It was stated many times from many different mouths, but the comments always fell on tin ears in Coke's executive suite. They continued to focus on the *product* as Coke's primary marketing problem.

Lessons Learned

If you pay consultants good money to express their viewpoints about advertising, then listen carefully. They are likely to see the problem more clearly than those close to the advertising, who may have trouble seeing the forest for the trees.

Bad marketing research leads to bad management decisions.

An image-driven business like soft drinks should continuously monitor the impact of its advertising on heavy user segments like teens and tweens. Coke should have known its advertising was no longer relevant to the youth culture.

Problem Definition

Before there can be research objectives, the problem must be properly defined. This may be easier said than done, since most companies struggle with problem definition. William Altier pointed out that "a problem correctly stated is half solved."[7] Because the true problem was not correctly stated, Coca-Cola continued to chase the wrong issue while remaining totally oblivious to its real disadvantage. Altier offers two examples of flawed problem definition:

- Tenants in a large office building complained about the slow elevators. As the volume of complaints reached a fever pitch, building management decided new elevators should be installed. Since there were ten banks of elevators, this would involve millions of dollars and throw the building into chaos for months. Was this the only way to deal with the problem? "In a triumph of lateral thinking, it was suggested that mirrors be placed on the walls around the elevators."[8] This produced a miracle; building tenants no longer complained about the slow elevators. They were too busy using the newly installed mirrors to admire themselves or do some personal primping. There was no change in the product, only a change in the environment.

- British housewives refused to buy frozen fish because of the flat taste. Somehow, there was a taste backlash when the fish were taken out of their natural environment. How could the natural environment be reconfigured? Many solutions were tried, including converting the holds of the fishing fleet into pools where the fish were kept alive, but the flat taste persisted. Nothing worked, and the problem remained unresolved. One day a visitor, upon learning of the problem quite by accident, suggested throwing a combative, predatory fish in the pool to create a more natural environment like the one that existed at sea before the fish were caught.[9] The flat taste problem was overcome at the minor cost of a few fish consumed by the predator.

Note that in both examples true problem definition came from an individual outside the sphere of the problem. The outsider had an appreciative audience listen, unlike the consultants and bottlers who had told an unappreciative audience—the Coca-Cola executive suite—that Pepsi now had the advertising advantage in the cola wars.

These two situations illustrate the complexity of problem definition. Both problems were solved by changing the environment, not the product. Coke needed to alter the environment in which its product operated, not the product itself. Better advertising that connected with the youth culture was the solution to Coke's sales erosion.

Lessons Learned

If the problem is improperly defined, everything else that follows is destined to be a New Coke®–type disaster. Problem definition is always more difficult when subjective emotions drive the definition process.

The Seduction of Numbers

The quest for a New Coke® formulation ended up being the largest research project in the history of Coca-Cola. It took more than two years to complete and cost the company over $4 million.

On the week that New Coke® was launched, the head of marketing research at Coca-Cola USA attended a marketing workshop in Florida. At a cocktail party, he remarked with a martini clutched in his hand, "If you saw the numbers from our New Coke® research, you'd understand why we made the decision." Coke had technically correct data, but it was misleading in that it allowed the company to chase the wrong business problem. The unaware Coke executive suite had been seduced by funky numbers. Numbers are fragile; they represent a surface façade of a complex process. Beneath lies a chain of issues that impact the quality of these numbers—problem definition, research design, how questions are asked, and even the analytic skills of those who interpret what the numbers mean.

Never forget Hodock's Law of Marketing Research: Ask a question. Get an answer. Consumers will answer marketers' questions, even the bad ones, but sometimes consumers are oblivious to their problems. Gillette research, for example, indicated men were satisfied with their blue blades. In reality, customers were walking around with nicks, cuts, and scratches on their faces. It was only when they saw an alternative—Wilkinson Sword® stainless steel blades—that complaints about blue blades surfaced. Gillette users started to think about their product differently.

Gillette asked a lot of questions about its blue blades in surveys. Nowhere in the research files could indications of product dissatisfaction be found. Ask a question. Get an answer. The principle instrument of quantitative marketing research—a questionnaire with questions complicated by the undercurrents of a complex research process—remains a delicate thing. As New Coke® proved, a rating scale does not necessarily mirror real life.

Somehow, often rather naïvely, we feel that if a substantial number of consumers tell us what is important in buying our products, their responses are like money in the bank. After all, they come from consumers, who vote in the marketplace with their dollars. Coke had research with lots of consumers—about two-hundred-thousand cola users—voting for the sweeter formula, but the numbers were a siren song seducing smart executives to meander down the wrong strategic path.

Marketing research is as much an art form as a science. The data produced in numerical form comes from defining the problem, research design, and how the questions are asked; and proper analysis of the responses is critical. Coke struck out on all these dimensions.

Numbers are our God. Since this is how we measure things, we place them on a pedestal. But remember Hodock's Law—questions in marketing research can produce good or bad numbers. Which is which? How do we know?

Unfortunately, we are trained to run with the numbers, irrespective of their quality. All the new products that fail have bad numbers in the initial sales forecast; these are typically rooted in optimistic assumptions that make innovation initiatives look promising. Numbers are blithely accepted, whether it's New Coke® research or the sales forecast for a bad new product.

The architects of New Coke® can possibly find solace in this observation. Others also have succumbed to the seduction of numbers. Our nation experienced a national trauma fueled by misleading numbers. In the Vietnam quagmire, secretary of defense Robert McNamara, a Harvard-trained MBA cultivated at the Ford Motor Company, was dedicated to the use of analytic techniques and kept demanding numbers to help measure and evaluate our progress in the Vietnam War. Servicemen were asked to collect all manner of numbers—body counts, villages where the headmen slept at home, and so on—to satisfy McNamara's penchant for data. McNamara believed the numbers; he used them to tell officials in the Johnson administration that progress had been made and victory was just around the corner.

McNamara's system of measurement—in effect his research design—was flawed just like New Coke®'s marketing research was, but they both produced tons of numbers. Coke's executive suite and Robert McNamara are perfect together.

Lessons Learned

Since innovation is a discovery process, it is heavily dependent on marketing research. To take a bare canvas and paint a landscape, a company needs consumer insight and strategic nourishment. The numbers that surface from marketing research are not infallible if proper interpretation, among other things, is not present.

Marketing research is like a siren song. You feel you control it, because you sired it. Like all offspring, however, it has a life of its own. Both good and bad numbers will appear, but how can you tell them apart? The moment of truth comes early in the discovery process:

- Work through all the options to seek the true definition of the problem.

- Avoid the internal spin that can lead to New Coke®–type strategies that are emotional rather than substantive.

If these two objectives are achieved, the probability of delivering good numbers increases dramatically in the innovation game.

An Issue of Validity

There are two important criteria in marketing research—reliability and validity. Reliability means the survey can be replicated many times producing essentially the same findings. New Coke® research had reliability.

Validity means the research measures what can be found in the real world. The survey findings from a sample can be comfortably projected to a larger population. New Coke® marketing research lacked validity on two fronts:

- Coke never told consumers its flagship brand would be withdrawn from the market and replaced with a new sweeter-tasting formula.

- Coke research was too one dimensional. Sip testing occurred at central locations and was influenced by the format used in the "Pepsi Challenge" commercials that had traumatized Coca-Cola's senior management.

Since sip testing favors sweeter formulations, the numbers from that research process can be deceptive. Sip testing is only one piece of the puzzle. It can be used as a first step in refining flavor formulations, but the next logical step should have been to give consumers a couple of six packs of New Coke® to drink at home under normal usage conditions. This approach would have provided better numbers to guide decision making.

On a hot August afternoon after cutting the lawn or playing tennis, cola users don't take a few sips of their Coke® or Pepsi® and walk away. They chug it. This is another aspect of the real world the Coke marketing research failed to measure.

In defending the New Coke® marketing research program, President Donald Keough claimed the deeply rooted feelings associated with Coca-Cola could not be measured. This assertion is pure hogwash. Any competent research director could have given Keough several research designs to measure the psychological commitment to a one-hundred-year-old brand that is considered holy water among its hard-core users.

It takes time, patience, and an open mind to root out Coke's important congenital associations. What Coke failed to bring to its cola party was an open mind.

Brand equity is the stored value of a brand built up over years of promotional effort. What perhaps is most astonishing is how Keough and his cohorts so easily walked away from one hundred years of Coca-Cola®'s brand equity. They either didn't understand its value or deliberately chose to ignore it. Either way, it is a case of unenlightened management charging into an embarrassing quagmire.

Lessons Learned

Insightful marketing research requires that reliability and validity be demonstrated. One without the other doesn't work. Coke's research had reliability—it could be replicated—but not validity—it was unsubstantiated in the marketplace.

If an established brand is an important part of the innovation initiative, the equity value must be understood and respected or a New Coke® shadow will loom on the horizon.

Fortuitous Marketing

Coke benefited from a fortuitous scenario. The retail trade credited Coke with brilliant marketing. The perception was that the company deliberately took old Coke® off the market to build the demand for it.

On top of that, consumers were equally generous in their assessment of the situation. Consumers had a positive built-in equity for the company; they thought of Coke as a caring corporation. Their perception was reinforced when the company listened to the wave of protest letters and phone calls pouring into Coke's headquarters in Atlanta. Indeed, the company did deliver on that built-in equity consumers harbored for Coca-Cola® by bringing back old Coke® and restrategizing its portfolio of cola products.

While the company fully intended to scrap its flagship brand, there was a contingency plan to assess the New Coke® launch. The company conducted tracking interviews on a daily basis with consumers across the fruited plains of America. There were also store audits in key markets.

In the tracking interviews, Coke got an earful. The negative buzz had swept across America. In a mere five weeks, the company knew New Coke® was dead meat. The toothpaste was out of the tube and no amount of marketing effort could get it back in.

A senior Coke executive picked up the phone and called New York. The Schecter Group, a New York–based package design consultancy, flew to Atlanta to initiate work on a package for the rebirth of Coca-Cola Classic®.

Lessons Learned

Coke lucked out. Don't bet on fortuitous marketing coming to the rescue very often in innovation debacles. At least one smart move was in play on Coke's behalf—it had a contingency plan in place. Every marketing plan for a new venture should have a contingency plan. The company needs to ask itself what potential potholes and barriers might impair innovation success.

Conflicting Information

The heart of the research plan for New Coke® was quantitative, hardcore numbers, but the marketing research department also conducted focus group sessions, which are softer in tone and texture than survey numbers. Many researchers believe that quantitative research—hard data—is science, truth, and justice. On the other hand, qualitative research—the group sessions that New Coke® executed—is best suited for generating ideas and hypotheses. Making important marketing decisions on focus groups alone is very risky. In reality, there are violations of this rule of thumb every day in marketing circles.

While Coca-Cola didn't make this mistake, maybe it should have been less rigid in its attitude about group sessions. Coke's limited quantitative research on this issue "estimated that somewhere between 10 to 15 percent of Coke® drinkers would be alienated with the move to a sweeter formula, with about half of them accepting the inevitability of the switch."[10]

The group sessions indicated a different pattern. There were always one or two hard-core Coke® drinkers in each group who became visibly and vocally agitated about the notion of the brand being taken away from them. Their intensity was so pervasive that by the end of the group sessions, most of the participants also became dissatisfied that America's icon brand was being dumped. The agitation and frustration was basically what surfaced in the real world. It became unfashionable to say anything nice about New Coke®. The cow was out of the barn, and Coke couldn't do anything about it—time to call in the Schecter Group.

Lessons Learned

Qualitative and quantitative data should be viewed as complimentary, not adversarial. In the New Coke® scenario, the qualitative data did the best job of predicting ultimate real-world behavior, whereas the quantitative research lost true consumer sentiment in the numbers.

When there is conflicting information or data, rational people should try to understand the difference. Such an exercise was not possible, because Coke had lost its objective balance. The head of marketing research was an agricultural economist by training; he favored numbers over the "unreliability" of qualitative research.

Life beyond New Coke®

Coca-Cola came out of its innovation debacle smelling like a rose due primarily to the company's swiftness in responding to the negative feedback about New Coke®. Coke stock soared to an all-time high; Wall Street and investors were delirious. Several prominent members of the New Coke® fiasco received huge bonuses. Life was good for them, while a couple of midlevel marketing researchers were terminated. Life was not so good for them.

In the '80s and '90s, Coca-Cola moved through a period of unparalleled prosperity. The company was like an iceberg—calm and comfortably serene on the surface, but underneath there was considerable manipulating and maneuvering. Coca-Cola's best salesperson was not on its sales force; it was the company's legendary CEO, Roberto Goizueta, who had convinced Wall Street that the global consumption of Coke® was unlimited. His "sell job" gave Coca-Cola stock a nice lift. The company inflicted debilitating price increases on its bottlers to make its numbers look good. The bean counters also participated in the internal charade by shifting debt and assets to the company's bottling organization, Coca-Cola Enterprises.

In the interim, Coca-Cola still had an advertising problem; impactful image-driven advertising directed at the youth culture is essential for survival in the soft drink category. Coke lost several generations of the youth market because of an acute case of advertising mediocrity that spanned almost three decades.

Take this test—walk into any college or high school classroom and ask the students which soda is cool, Coke® or Pepsi®. The thunderous response will undoubtedly be "Pepsi®." Ask the same question about the advertising for these two brands, and expect the same response—Pepsi® has better ads. Coke® is not a trendsetter with youth culture.

Coke had a brief period of advertising prosperity in the early '90s with the "Always Coca-Cola® campaign." The "Always" theme hit the right chords—leadership, competitive superiority, and product quality—with a bundle of commercials that were zap-proof. And then Coke drifted back into its haze of advertising mediocrity.

One could argue that New Coke® was more than an embarrassing innovation debacle. Here was a marketing-driven company that could not identify its true marketing problem, even after spending over $4 million in marketing research. New Coke® was the tipping point that swung the pendulum in Pepsi's direction. Today, "Archrival Pepsico has eclipsed it [Coca-Cola] in many important ways, including stock performance, earnings growth, talent development, and buzz."[11]

NOTES

1. Gerald A. Michaelson, *Winning the Marketing War* (Knoxville, TN: Pressmark International, 1987), p. 34.

2. David Kiley, "New Blood Infuses Big Change at GM," *USA Today*, October 9, 2001, http://www.usatoday.com/money/auto2001-10-09-9M-lutz .htm (accessed December 27, 2006).

3. Barton G. Tretheway, "Everything New Is Old Again," *Marketing Management* (Spring 1998): 5.

4. Associated Press, "Get Ready for Chocolate French Fries," December 25, 2003, http://www.usatoday.com/money/retail2002-02-11-funky-fries .htm (accessed January 20, 2004).

5. Pepsi-Cola North America Press Release, May 7, 2002.

6. Thomas J. Peters and Robert H. Waterman Jr., *In Search of Excellence* (New York: Harper & Row, 1982), p. 156.

7. William J. Altier, "From Experience a Perspective on Creativity," *Journal of Product Innovation Management* (Spring 1988): 157.

8. Ibid., p. 158.

9. Ibid., p. 157.

10. Robert M. Schinder, "The Real Lesson of New Coke: The Value of Focus Groups for Predicting the Effectors of Social Influence," *Marketing Research* (December 1992): 26–28.

11. Dean Foust, "The Queen of Pop," *Business Week*, August 7, 2006, p. 45.

⑨

[MARKETING DISHONESTY]

nnovation initiatives are a high-risk game; most new products fail to achieve marketplace success. Our previous chapters have pointed out the major factors that underscore flawed innovation. However, there remains one other miscue that must be addressed to complete the journey down the yellow brick road of innovation.

Each failure had a sales forecast that met, or even exceeded, the company's financial criteria for new ventures. The finance department approved the numbers. Members of senior management nodded their heads in approval. The board was equally compliant. Everybody jumped into the boat; the numbers supported the new venture, and it sailed through the system untouched, only to experience a "thumbs down" from consumers in the marketplace.

The serene façade of approval is often underscored by a symptom that is very hard to eradicate—marketing dishonesty.

While enthusiasm, conviction, spirit, and creativity should flourish within the hearts and minds of those on the innovation team, judgments must remain totally, even brutally, objective. This is easier said than done. The lack of objectivity operates on two levels: unconscious and conscious.

UNCONSCIOUS MARKETING DISHONESTY

People fall in love with what they create—movies, television pilots, novels, art, and, yes, even new products. And all too often that love is blind. Objectivity eludes the creator; normally rational people become evangelical salesmen for their dreams rather than practical, objective business executives.

President Harry Truman once remarked, "The buck stops here." But in flawed innovation initiatives, the brakes are never applied. The new product, with its many warts and blemishes, lunges forward, sweeping across the marketing landscape like an uncontrollable brush fire.

Campbell Soup's CEO, David Johnson, believed in the potential of Intelligent Quisine®. The Coke executive suite was convinced New Coke® was the right thing to do. The Procter & Gamble scientists believed Citrus Hill™ was a better-tasting orange juice than Tropicana® and Minute Maid®. Motorola's engineers were misguided in their faith and devotion to the Iridium™ project, but they believed in their fantasy of a worldwide telecommunications system. Ford's MBA crowd believed in the cheap Jag strategy.

These were well-meaning people who wandered off course because they became passionately enamored with what they created. But let's face it—optimism has limits. The marketplace disagreed, and that's the only vote that counts in the innovation game.

CONSCIOUS MARKETING DISHONESTY

On the conscious level, marketing dishonesty is more insidious. In this scenario, blind passion may still be part of the equation, but the innovation team consciously pushes the envelope across the line of propriety. There are disquieting signs or signals that all is not well with the new product, but the enthusiasm for plunging forward to marketplace failure is uncontested.

Unfavorable data or information might be ignored, perhaps even suppressed, under this circumstance. There might be the blithe assumption that some miracle will surface and make it all right. Successful innovation initiatives are not products of miracles, but simply taking a good idea and executing all the basic steps that are part of the discovery process. The reward goes to those who excel in executing the thousands of details associated with the dirt of doing.

Either way, conscious or unconscious, marketing dishonesty means resources are wasted, valuable time is lost forever, and shareholder value may be diminished depending on the magnitude of the mistake. Oftentimes, nobody takes the blame, and many get promoted. Some even get rewarded—think about the juicy bonuses received by the Coke executive suite after the New Coke® fiasco.

Remember Robert Lutz's observation about the Pontiac Aztek®? "We'd fire the guy who greenlighted the Aztek® if we could find anyone willing to admit it." There's often no accountability, even though many participants help implement a new product blueprint. It is understandable why innovation teams are willing to "run bad ideas up the flag pole" in lassiez-faire–type innovation environments.

Case #1 Marketing Dishonesty: Campbell's Souper Combo™

The Concept

We often walk into a restaurant and see it on the menu—a cup of soup and a sandwich, the blue plate special for the day. This was the base concept behind Campbell's® Souper Combo™, a combination frozen soup and sandwich ranging from grilled cheese to a hamburger. The idea was tested in a concept test and performed very well—two-thirds of the consumers in the test said they "definitely or probably will buy" the product. The intended target audiences were latchkey children, adults who wanted an easy lunch for the workplace, and those who wanted a fast meal at home after laboring all day in the vineyards. Two things drove the favorable response:

- The convenience in terms of saving time; Americans live in the fast lane, and reducing food preparation by a few minutes represents the equivalent of saving them a decade as they rush through their fast-paced lifestyles.

- Souper Combo™ was additionally a hearty meal, consisting of two of America's favorite food items—soup and a sandwich—reinforced by a very clever brand name.

There was nothing to suggest the idea should not move into product development.

Which Forecast Is Right?

Research and development delivered the product, and Souper Combo™ was tested in a controlled store test in Marion, Indiana, where the distribution was forced as opposed to a natural sell-in by the Campbell's sales force. The Souper Combo™ innovation team also had diary data tracking household purchases and focus groups with buyers of the brand. It was a good portfolio of marketing research for evaluation purposes.

A funny thing happened on the way to the forum before Souper Combo™ was moved into national introduction. Two sales forecasts surfaced from different parts of the company. The marketing group estimated Souper Combo™ would be a $68 million business after four months in test. Senior management was delighted with the news, because Campbell's policy said a new product must promise $70 million to merit national introduction. Souper Combo™ was almost there. Senior management licked their chops in anticipation.

But the marketing research department started to revise the forecast as more data became available. New products have an awareness-trial-repeat flow; it takes a long time for repeat purchase patterns to firm up for new product ventures. The marketing research department did not see a strong repeat pattern occurring in the later reviews of Souper Combo™'s household panel data. The department's final estimate was that Souper Combo™ probably would be a $40 to $45 million business.

The innovation team didn't want to hear talk about a revised forecast. It was too far off the mark from the $70 million threshold level. The team that created the product remained giddy about the original $68 million forecast, perfectly content to gloss over the fact that the forecast was based on trial sales. The innovation team didn't acknowledge that the jury was still out, and no one knew whether Souper Combo™ could get repeat purchases, a critical dynamic in a forecasting scenario. Trial is nice, but adoption is even better.

Marketing presented the more optimistic forecast for sales, which prompted management to greenlight Souper Combo™ for national introduction. The general attitude was that with a little fine-tuning the brand might easily exceed the $70 million threshold. The sky is always bluer in the conference room.

It is astonishing that senior management did not ask any questions about the trial and repeat curves for Souper Combo™ or challenge the basic assumptions used to build the $68 million forecast. Even the company's numbers-oriented financial department greenlighted the optimistic forecast without asking any hard questions about its internal components. This shows, once again, the seduction of numbers. Numbers are blithely accepted because we put them on a pedestal, failing to realize they might have feet of clay.

An innovation team can manipulate the numbers in various ways to get any forecast they want. It's easy to do—use optimistic assumptions, and management sitting further up the food chain may blindly accept the numbers. Upper echelon management often trust what marketers tell them, even though it could be a bouillabaisse of marketing dishonesty.

Dead-on-Arrival Product

Souper Combo™ was a classic example of a flawed product that never should have been launched. One former Campbell's executive said the innovation team believed research and development could make product adjustments as the company raced toward the national launch. Here are some product adjustments that never materialized:

- A convenient approach to food preparation was made very inconvenient with excessive packaging; one version of Souper Combo™ had eleven separate packaging components. This made it very difficult for children to use, and consumers had to throw out a pile of garbage after making their meals. The now defunct *Garbage Magazine* selected Souper Combo™ for its "environmental disaster of the month award." The magazine's notoriety gave the brand an unhealthy dose of negative buzz.

- The product was a nightmare to work with. The soup was a block of ice; it took twice as long to microwave than was initially anticipated. The directions were confusing, and the preparation process was awkward—put soup in, take soup out, put sandwich in, take sandwich out and put soup back in, and so on. The preparation logistics were complex and cumbersome. In addition, the sandwich was never cooked thoroughly and was often cold on the inside. It was easier to prepare a bowl of soup and a sandwich from scratch rather than fight with Souper Combo™'s nightmare instructions.

- The price point at the time was high, about three dollars for soup and a nuked sandwich. This was important, because the price was never mentioned in the Souper Combo™ concept test. This is not unusual. Reviews of client concept tests often show that price is ignored. But the price of the product is a critical piece of information that should be an integral part of the research.

- The packaging graphics were tepid, bland, and unappetizing for a food product; the brand name was barely legible, inhibiting the package's stopping power at the point of purchase. All this added up to a lack of in-store visual impact.

Mismatched Positioning

The basic idea behind Souper Combo™—a fast, convenient soup and sandwich—had strong consumer appeal as reflected in the favorable concept test and trial sales in the marketplace, but the product could not deliver on Souper Combo™'s positioning promise. This was a classic case of a mismatched positioning—consumers didn't receive the benefit from the product that they expected.

Postmortem

The product should never have made it through the development process, and the only reason it had to endure the embarrassment of a national introduction was the inflated sales estimate served up to management by the innovation team.

The market share of Campbell's® condensed soup had been in steady decline for two decades, and it was not surprising that management was receptive to good news for a change. We make no judgments about whether the innovation team's rosy view of the product's future was conscious or unconscious, but this was a serious marketing error.

Lessons Learned

Concept testing is only one small piece of the innovation jigsaw puzzle. A favorable concept test doesn't mean much if the product can't deliver the promised benefits. This scenario inevitably leads to a mismatched positioning.

The price should always be mentioned in the stimulus material used in concept testing. It is surprising how many concept tests conducted by consumer packaged-goods companies never mention the price in the concepts shown to consumers. It strongly suggests that innovation teams are trying to hide something in their exuberance to move their ideas forward.

Numbers are not infallible, nor are the people who serve them up for management consumption. Senior management has to be more involved in understanding the guts of the profit and loss estimates for innovation initiatives. How were the numbers put together? What are the assumptions that drive these numbers? Otherwise, management runs the risk of being snowed with a fairy tale forecast.

The initial sales for new consumer packaged-goods products come from trial and repeat purchases. Souper Combo™ never should have gone national, based on a mere four months of in-market data; there was not enough time to get an understanding of the brand's long-term repeat rate, a critical dynamic in forecasting.

Case #2 Marketing Dishonesty: Crystal Pepsi®

The Market

As beverage companies like Coke and Pepsi moved into the '90s, consumer preferences started to shift with new drinks from Snapple, Arizona Iced Tea, and other companies. The term assigned to the newest interlopers in the category sandbox was "New Age beverages." This became a catch-phrase that encompassed a wide range of noncarbonated drinks competing with Coke® and Pepsi®.

Three childhood friends from Brooklyn began selling pure fruit drinks to healthfood stores in the Greenwich Village section of New York City. Distribution expanded with increasing demand for the drinks, and soon the three friends found themselves running a $525 million company called Snapple.

Don Vultaggio and John Ferolito were beer distributors by trade, but they could not help but notice the success of Snapple and the marketplace's thirst for ready-to-drink iced teas. They jumped into the competitive fray with Arizona® Iced Tea, featuring a unique packaging strategy focused on bright, colorful Southwestern graphics. Two Brown University graduates started Nantucket Nectars. A classic serial entrepreneur, John Bello, started SoBe, which he later sold to Pepsi. The beverage landscape was burgeoning with successful entrepreneurial ventures built around New Age beverages.

Coke didn't get it. One senior Coke executive remarked to Richard Kundrat, the architect of the Pepsi-Lipton partnership, "New Age isn't our bread and butter." And when Coke did try to get it, the result was Fruitopia®, a new product flop. Pepsi, however, understood the new biorhythms of the marketplace. That's why it executed the partnership with Lipton, but Pepsi was about to stub its toe.

Two things caught Pepsi's eye. One was real—the trend to noncarbonated beverages—while the other was a superficial fad—the romance with clear products that implied purity. The latter spawned a litany of clear products, even a clear beer from Miller and a clear whiskey from Brown Foreman. So, why not create a clear Pepsi®?

On a Clear Day You Can See Crystal Pepsi®

Crystal Pepsi® was a clear cola-flavored beverage 100 percent naturally flavored, with no preservatives or caffeine. Its objectives were murky. One of Pepsi's major marketing gurus believed the 1990s would be the era of clear products; the company's other high priest of marketing viewed Crystal Pepsi® as an entry into the New Age beverage segment.

The clearness of the product provoked consumer interest, because it connoted purity to some consumers. So maybe it was Pepsi® without the "ingredient bad guys"—nasty things like artificial colors and chemicals with long, unpronounceable names. This perception should have alarmed Pepsi, because it denigrated its flagship brand by implying that regular Pepsi® had impurities. Other consumers simply viewed Crystal Pepsi® as a New Age beverage that would taste like Clearly Canadian® or Mystic™. Crystal Pepsi® would fail to live up to either expectation.

One of our clients, Coca-Cola Consolidated, was a major Coke® bottler located in the south; it was concerned about the impact of Crystal Pepsi® when it rolled into its markets. We conducted a simple exercise in group sessions in which consumers viewed an ad for Crystal Pepsi® and then discussed their feelings and attitudes about the product as it was depicted in the ad. We then gave each consumer a large cup of Crystal Pepsi® to enjoy. Crystal Pepsi® was introduced with the positioning statement "You've never seen a taste like this." Here's how consumers reacted to the slogan:

- Two or three consumers immediately spit the drink back into their cups. The pained look on their faces said volumes about the taste of Crystal Pepsi®.

- The other group session participants were a bit more polite, but they were equally unimpressed with the product's taste and told us so.

The bottler's fears were negated after we saw this scenario repeated in other group sessions. We became convinced that the "never seen taste" was destined to be brief and quickly forgotten. It clearly wasn't going to work.

A Pepsi technical specialist told Rick Kundrat, the founder of the Pepsi-Lipton partnership, that the Crystal Pepsi® formulation contained nutmeg, which contributed to the taste issue. A sales promotion executive with access to Crystal Pepsi® marketing research said the data indicated a taste problem that was never corrected.

Despite the red flags, the clear cola was forced through the Pepsi bottling system. Since the taste problem surfaced early in the development process, why was the beverage introduced in the first place? Pepsi's senior marketing gurus ignored the research data and input from outside consultants because they whimsically believed they were right about Crystal Pepsi®'s merits.

Brand Equity Issues

Crystal Pepsi® was a major violation of Pepsi®'s brand equity that had been built up over decades of promotional effort. There was an inevitable taste expectation when the Pepsi name was used on the product. Pepsi® addicts expected it to taste like Pepsi®, of course. Consumer taste reactions were graphically described in such unflattering terms as foul, sewer water, lacking character, and simply lousy. These were not desirable Pepsi® attributes.

Another brand equity issue was Crystal Pepsi®'s not-so-subtle insinuation that the flagship cola had bad stuff in it. The denigration represented a serious case of brand malpractice. Why risk putting the flagship brand Pepsi® in a "no-win situation" by implying that Crystal is perhaps a better alternative?

Once a new product gathers critical mass, it is almost impossible to stop. Only the CEO or the board could apply the brakes that would have kept Crystal Pepsi® from driving out of the garage. Both, unfortunately, had faith in the success equation they heard from the company's senior marketers.

Was this conscious or unconscious marketing dishonesty? We cannot make that judgment; we only know that Pepsi's flirtation with clear was withdrawn from the marketplace a year after Crystal Pepsi®'s national introduction.

The Son of Crystal Pepsi® Returns

Somebody up there in the executive suite still liked the idea; the clear cola went back to the drawing board. It surfaced again as simply Crystal. There was not much the troops in the marketing trenches could do about the resurrection except obediently march forward to another fiasco.

There was one smart move in this reiteration; the new name wasn't linked with the Pepsi® brand name. The company did learn something from the prior debacle, but the learning curve was still incomplete. The marketplace response to Crystal was even worse than the first time around, and Pepsi finally shelved its romantic fling with clear colas.

Lessons Learned

Don't mess with the company's cash cow. The equity of a brand name like Pepsi® takes a long time to evolve. It should be treated like a crown jewel, and any misuse of the name should be carefully avoided.

It's been said before, but it is worth repeating. Brand equity is like a savings account. Marketers should make deposits, building up the stored value of the brand. Crystal Pepsi® was a serious withdrawal from the savings account. It was Pepsi's version of New Coke®.

There is nothing wrong with recycling a failed new product if there is merit in doing so. There was not a shred of evidence that the clear cola warranted a resurrection. Pepsi confused uniqueness with preference. Crystal Pepsi® was a unique beverage, but with no sound reason to exist. It failed to deliver a consumer benefit other than curiosity.

Case #3 Marketing Dishonesty: Apple Newton

The Boardroom Brawl

John Scully had a remarkable marketing reputation during his tenure at Pepsi. He was responsible for the very successful "Pepsi Challenge" advertising campaign, which drove Coke crazy and pushed the company into the disastrous New Coke® strategy. Madison Avenue viewed him as an advertising genius.

Scully's marketing credentials intrigued Apple cofounder Steve Jobs. He viewed Scully's marketing prowess and his technical expertise as a powerful combination. The story has been told many times. Scully was lured to Apple by Jobs, who reportedly asked him, "Do you want to spend the rest of your life selling sugar water, or do you want a chance to save the world?" Jobs became relentless in his pursuit of the seasoned marketing veteran.

Scully joined Apple in 1983 as president and CEO. In the beginning, the two personalities had a comfortable business relationship, and the honeymoon period lasted for two years. Apple was no different than any other company; it lived by the numbers—sales and profits.

The sales figures became bleak. Jobs was responsible for steward-ing the Macintosh®/Lisa division. In 1985 sales of the Macintosh® "had fallen way short of Jobs's projections of 500,000" units.[1] Apple's 1985 first-quarter sales results were ominous. "Macintosh® revenues were only 10 percent of the [Jobs] projection, meaning that Apple would have to write off unsold inventory."[2] Moreover, Apple's new product pipeline was barren, and product design was presumably Jobs's expertise.

The sour sales set the stage for the disintegration of the relation-ship between the two senior executives; they started to bicker. Scully blamed Jobs for the sales erosion in Macintosh®. In an office con-frontation, Scully complained that Jobs's ineffective management style was hampering Macintosh®'s marketplace performance. "Scully wanted Jobs to find another cause to champion and leave running the Macintosh®/Lisa division to grownups."[3] The latter was a reference to the rather strong perception among senior executives that Jobs lacked maturity, although his design genius was still widely heralded on the Apple campus.

In turn, Jobs viewed Apple's precarious situation as a function of Scully's inability to cut costs in problem-plagued divisions like Apple II. The Apple board was placed in a difficult position. Each side was given an opportunity to present its case to the board.

The board was confronted with a dilemma. Who presented the better case? Which one was more qualified to lead Apple? The board liked Scully's calm, experienced management style. His brief presen-tation to the board was impressive. It restored their confidence in Apple's future. Conversely, the board was less charitable to Jobs, telling him "he was a punk kid who should shut up and let John run the company."[4]

It was the end of an era, as Apple's two cofounders, Wozniak and Jobs, were no longer part of the management team. Wozniak had left earlier in a falling out with the mercurial Jobs. It was not the first time an entrepreneur had lost control of his love child. It also happened to Rod Canion at Compaq, who founded the company. Company growth can be a curse for entrepreneurs if they fail to fine-tune and hone their management skills as the organization expands. This became Jobs's curse. The Apple board didn't see the growth, making Scully the more palatable alternative.

Apple returned to financial respectability under Scully's management team composed of older, more experienced executives. There was still a major challenge for Team Scully. The new product pipeline remained barren.

Apple loyalists, right or wrong, despised Scully, whom they considered incompetent. Scully knew the scuttlebutt in Apple's corridors said he was technically inferior to Jobs. Scully wanted to establish a technical legacy that would endure long after he left the Apple campus. He named himself Apple's chief technology officer in an effort to polish up his own technical apple.

Apple engineers had been working on a skunk works project to create an Apple handheld computer called Newton. For several years, they toiled in relative obscurity. A presentation was made to Scully and the board in 1990 to keep the project alive. "Scully became enamored with what he saw."[5] He viewed Newton as the signature product that could enshrine his technical reputation.

Calendar Innovation

Scully set a Newton ship date for April 2, 1992. That ended Newton's status as a pure skunk works research project. It was time for the rubber to meet the road. The innovation team was under great pressure to deliver a finished product. Three Newton models emerged, and Scully selected the smallest version for development. But there was still a massive amount of development work to do in order to meet Scully's launch date. Apple's engineers worked fifteen- to twenty-hour days; the pressure was so intense that one software engineer committed suicide.[6]

Scully did a strange thing as his innovation team burned the midnight oil. He was noted for making visionary proclamations for the consumption of the press, and he became the poster child and spokesperson not only for Apple, but also for the cyberspace industry as a whole. Scully was a charismatic public speaker, whereas in private "he was painfully shy, and preferred to eat lunch alone since he found it difficult to engage in small talk."[7] The transformation in his public persona was amazing.

Scully made one of his visionary proclamations as the keynote speaker at the Consumer Electronics Show in Las Vegas on January 7, 1992, just a few months before the Newton's launch. He decided to stir up the audience, making the case "that personal digital assistants (PDAs) would be commonplace in the next decade. Scully never mentioned the Newton by name" in his keynote address, and his vision about PDAs turned out to be impeccably correct.[8]

His statement did tip off competition that something big was taking place at Apple. It was a foolish gesture possibly influenced by his low-tech image with the Apple purists who found it difficult to accept that "a Pepsi guy" could run the company. Several competitors did a good job of speculating what Apple was up to. Competitors eventually caught up and surpassed Apple's pioneering PDA effort.

After Jobs was ousted, it was Scully's intention to stay at Apple for five years. During Newton's development, Scully lost interest in the company's day-to-day activities, and he delegated most of the company business to his management team. However, two passions were in play. One was the Newton project, which he wanted his signature on. The other passion was government issues related to technology and political candidates like Bill Clinton.

A Development Process Awash in Pressure

The development pace remained fast and furious as Apple poured $500 million into the Newton effort. Apple's engineers were burned out; "psychologists were brought in to monitor their mental health."[9] The innovation team was confronted with two challenges. They needed to have workable models available for important industry trade shows, and Scully's ominous launch date was hovering on the horizon.

Every public presentation of the Newton technology miraculously worked, and the demos generated an avalanche of press coverage about the Newton. However, huge technical issues in the research and development labs jeopardized Scully's mandated launch date every day.

Nobody wanted to tell Scully the truth about the technical problems, because they were afraid to rain on his parade. Moreover, they were correct in their assessment; Scully had no interest in hearing about problems. He had adopted the Nike® slogan at this point for Newton—just do it.

There were three delays in Newton's launch date, much to Scully's displeasure. The Newton was finally "pushed and shoved" into the marketplace with major technical glitches; the innovation team was fully aware of the product issues. The first Newtons were shipped with "over a thousand documented bugs."[10] The politics overrode the inevitable customer dissatisfaction that came with a technically flawed PDA, but Scully's vision was fulfilled—the Newton was one of the first handheld computers of its type. It also became another victim of "timetable tyranny."

In a twist of irony, Scully suffered the same fate as Steve Jobs— the numbers had gone sour. Although Scully had taken Apple from annual sales of $600 million to $8 billion, Apple lost $183.5 million in the third quarter of 1993. The board asked for his resignation. Scully was back in Connecticut at the time the Newton was launched, oblivious to the flaws, because his most trusted lieutenants were afraid to let him know the truth about the product.

An Issue of Ethics

This was a serious ethics issue. The company was not doing that well, as reflected in Scully's departure, yet senior management poured over a billion dollars into a product that would inevitably fail. This was a bad deal for the company's shareholders, and Apple's board had a fiduciary responsibility to ask some probing questions about the Newton's progress, or lack of it, but it never acted in the best interest of the shareholders. Everyone was too busy pursuing personal agendas and sweeping Newton's problems under the rug.

Would it have not been refreshing, after the Newton debacle, for someone in senior management—preferably the CEO—to have said, "We messed up by rushing Newton to market, and the product wasn't very good. We will never sacrifice product quality again in our future innovation efforts. We have a fiduciary responsibility to use our shareholders' money more wisely"?

Product Issues

In many ways, Newton was viewed as a brilliant design by high-tech pundits—"a pen-based digitized note pad designed to capture data and ideas."[11] But the handwriting recognition feature had an erratic performance; it often came up with bizarre and sometimes humorous interpretations of what was really intended as input. Others viewed the clunky Newton as not much better than traditional methods of "capturing information like electronic address books, pen and pencil, calendars, etc."[12]

The price tag on the Newton—$800—was considered steep, even for a fancy executive toy. The Newton was lampooned in the *Doonesbury* comic strip and the popular satirical television show *The Simpsons*. Both focused on the comical results associated with Newton's not very efficient handwriting recognition feature. These visible displays of Newton's ineptness rapidly turned the buzz from positive to negative.

About four years after the Newton flop, the smaller Palm™ Pilot hit the marketplace with stunning acceptance. Scully was right; there was a consumer need for PDAs. The Palm™ Pilot succeeded where Newton did not, because it met the needs of business professionals. It functioned flawlessly, was easy to use, and snuggly fit into a pocket or purse—something the clunky Newton could never do. And the price was right.

Later Newton models were greatly improved over the "bug-infested" initial entry, but Palm™ captured two-thirds of the PDA market. Only two hundred thousand Newtons were in use at the peak of its popularity. Although Apple didn't realize it at the time, it had laid the groundwork of consumer research for the next generation of PDAs to enter the market.

Steve Jobs Returns

In the irrational world of Apple, a more mature, experienced Steve Jobs returned to steward the company fortunes once again after eleven years in exile. Not surprisingly, he expressed open disdain for Scully's pet project, the Newton. He referred to it as the "funny looking scribble machine with no keypad."[13] It was payback time—Jobs trumped Scully. The Newton innovation team knew that Jobs would jettison the product. Many of them immediately flocked to Palm™ Pilot, helping to make it a marketplace success.[14]

Apple officially killed off the Newton, but the product had developed a cult following. Ardent Newton fans demonstrated in the company parking lot on the day it died; company officials served cookies and coffee to the demonstrators, but the decision to kill Newton was final. Some of these same devotees take their Newtons to Apple events and wave them silently in protest. It doesn't deter Steve Jobs from making a great keynote speech, which is his specialty at such events. And Apple has prospered with the return of a more mature, experienced Steve Jobs—think iMac®, iPod®, iTunes®, and iPhone®. The man is a design genius.

Lessons Learned

If you start with the technology, the technology will drive the product. Products are solutions to problems. It is better to start with consumers and discover what product solutions they want. Newton trumped Palm™ Pilot in creating the technology, but Palm™ Pilot succeeded because it was designed to meet the needs of business professionals. The Newton innovation team didn't spend enough time talking with the customer; the group was too busy designing hot, proprietary technology.

Companies can pay dearly for being first to market if they shortcut the development process, establish irrational launch dates, and prioritize speed to market over product quality. The following successful software franchises came late to the party:

Adobe Photoshop®
Intuit's Quicken®
Microsoft Word®

Each of the above franchises dominates its respective market segment. It isn't always true that "the early bird gets the worm."

Case #4 Marketing Dishonesty: Arthritis Foundation Pain Relievers

The Market

Tylenol® dominated the over-the-counter pain-reliever market, but nothing is forever. A new competitor, Advil®, cut into Tylenol®'s sales; the active ingredient in Advil® is ibuprofen, previously only available in the prescription drug Motrin®. This was a classic prescription to over-the-counter switch, and Advil® benefited from the positive prescription heritage of ibuprofen. It also had a strong competitive advantage—longer-lasting pain relief when compared to Tylenol®.

Johnson & Johnson did not have an ibuprofen brand. It needed to protect Tylenol® in some way and stop the infiltration of Advil®.

A Bad Idea Resurfaces

In 1960 the American Dental Association granted its seal of approval to Crest® for the brand's cavity-fighting protection. Procter & Gamble poured heavy advertising dollars into the endorsement, and Crest® became the dominant brand in the toothpaste market for three decades.

About thirty years later McNeil, a Johnson & Johnson company, rediscovered the Crest® playbook. Its objective was to find an endorsement for a line of parity pain relievers. Perhaps, if the right one was found, some of that Crest® endorsement magic could rub off on the new venture. The Arthritis Foundation eagerly offered the use of its name for a flat fee and a royalty based on sales. The magic had been found.[15]

Thus, Arthritis Foundation Pain Relievers was born. McNeil launched a line of nonprescription analgesics—aspirin, acetaminophen, ibuprofen, and acetaminophen with diphenhydramin—sold under the foundation's name. The brand was positioned as a full line of pain relievers with ingredients effective for minor arthritic pain. Every purchase helped fund a donation to the Arthritis Foundation to be used for research in seeking a cure for this debilitating disease. That was the party line.

Millions of Americans suffer from the pain and limitations of arthritis; it is a huge market. And to tap into it, America's favorite nanny, Julie Andrews, became the spokesperson featured in the introductory advertising for Arthritis Foundation Pain Relievers.

This was basically a licensing agreement. McNeil agreed to pay the Atlanta-based foundation $1 million annually in exchange for the trademark, and each consumer purchase would not necessarily increase the amount of money given to the Arthritis Foundation.[16]

Although the chemical compounds and patented packaging sounded impressive, there was nothing unique about the line. The products were already available under other brand names such as Bayer®,

Tylenol®, and Advil®. While the targeted segment was arthritics, it was anticipated that nonarthritics also were likely to try the pain relievers, because a pain reliever effective against the "mother of all pain"— arthritis—was expected to be effective for less severe pain. Was this marketing hustle or marketing dishonesty? It's your call.

This was a line concept, and the history of line concepts was not promising. They seldom work, and this concept had been tried unsuccessfully before in the analgesic category. Remember Bayer® Select? Bad ideas never fade away; they simply resurface in another part of the marketing pasture.

The Bad Result

This venture died an early, merciful death. Consumers were smart enough to detect a charade when they saw it; they weren't going to pay a premium price for a line of private-label pain relievers masquerading as a major advancement in pain management. There was more to this scenario than a weak product idea falling down the elevator shaft; this was an unholy alliance with unforeseen consequences for the parties involved.

McNeil and the Foundation were accused of deceptive marketing by nineteen states.[17] Ask yourself again: was this marketing dishonesty or marketing hustle? Both may apply in this case. State attorney generals had become a very potent force in marketing in the late '90s; they were responsible for bringing the tobacco industry to its knees with the Grand Master Settlement in 1998.

In a news release from the state of Florida, that state's attorney general, Bob Butterworth, commented:

> These drugs contain analgesics common to other pain reliever products and were developed with no assistance from the Arthritis Foundation. The Foundation was paid over one million dollars for the use of their name.[18]

In essence, the attorney generals from nineteen states said that the proposition was deceptive and misleading. This established an important precedence in marketing—frivolous positioning may get you in trouble. Marketers must be acutely aware of the damaging consequences that misleading positioning statements can bring. Duplicitous cause-related marketing serves nobody very well. Partnerships between corporations and nonprofit organizations must be carefully examined for propriety.

Episodes like Arthritis Foundation Pain Relievers established a potential precedence for corporate legal departments to get further involved in the marketing and innovation process. Now they have a rationale to review concept statements, strategies, partnerships, and who knows what else. This gives corporate lawyers newfound power should they choose to exercise it. The depth of their involvement probably will vary from company to company.

Concern about the law is another headache for corporate marketers to deal with, exacerbated by the fact that lawyers can often qualify as the most uncreative people around the corporate corridors. Their specialty is covering posteriors, but don't expect creative suggestions from them about strategies and positioning statements. Life got a little more hellish for marketers whose legal department demanded deeper involvement in the innovation process.

It is astonishing that the Arthritis Foundation and McNeil got involved in this embarrassing quagmire. The foundation was greedy, and McNeil acted irresponsibly. How could senior management ap - prove this positioning charade? Although McNeil admitted no wrong-doing, the case was settled for close to $2 million. The settlement split $1.7 million among nineteen states and forced McNeil to pay the National Institute of Arthritis and Musculoskeletal and Skin Disease $250,000 for scientific research related to arthritis prevention.[19]

Lessons Learned

The Arthritis Foundation Pain Relievers product line was an embarrassment. Smart companies may do dumb things in traveling through the treacherous terrain of innovation. Questionable positioning gimmicks like this one may provoke an encounter with law and order, and not the television program on NBC.

Positioning is about substance, not marketing tricks. Consumers can see through the smoke and mirrors. A superficial positioning like Arthritis Foundation Pain Relievers never works.

There was no historical perspective in the creation of the product, either. The answers are not in the stars; they can be found in the filing cabinets of history. If McNeil had opened the first drawer, Arthritis Foundation Pain Relievers never would have taken its first baby steps. An analgesic line concept had been tried before by Bayer® and failed. McNeil should have known this.

Case #5 Marketing Dishonesty: Pontiac Aztek®

As previously noted, there are eight viruses associated with innovation initiatives that have gone awry. Moreover, several of these viruses are usually associated with innovation debacles.

The Pontiac Aztek® was not an exception to this phenomenon. Because General Motors rushed the vehicle into the marketplace anticipating annual sales of seventy thousand units, it was a victim of "timetable tyranny." The Aztek® had serious design flaws that doomed its marketplace acceptance, but the timeline was met. "Get it out" became more important than "get it right."

The General Motors bean counters insisted that an existing minivan platform be used because it was cheaper, further compromising the Aztek®'s aesthetics. This mistake is our old friend, "fatality in frugality." A third mistake that surfaced, however, was marketing dishonesty. The Aztek® was an embarrassing faux pas.

Sanitized Marketing Research

The development of a new car involves an enormous amount of money. The major tools for consumer input are focus groups and clinics. The latter involves taking the car around the country, showing it off to a cross section of consumers geographically and demographically. The Big Three's fondness for this approach is "old school." The Asian connection prefers to rely more on dealer networks for important input about design and styling issues.

General Motors should have dropped the hammer on the Aztek® when it did so poorly in the clinics, but senior management never heard anything negative about it. Kay Polit, a senior consultant at A. T. Kearney, a major consulting company, noted the prime source of Aztek®'s problems was "the lack of honest information flowing from focus groups up to the executive level."[20] The Aztek®'s styling was poorly received in focus groups, and the unfavorable consumer responses should have been a cause for major concern among the Aztek® project team, which was made up of a bunch of young designers out to make a name for themselves.

George Peterson, president of Auto Pacific, Inc., confirmed Polit's observation: "What we hear is that they kept taking the Aztek® to focus groups, and it kept getting rejected, but they just didn't listen to their own research." Peterson speculated that the Aztek® team kept going back to groups to find a viable target segment, but they never found it. Instead they plunged forward, knowing the vehicle was destined to flameout once it hit the market.

The research accurately predicted that the Aztek® was a hopeless cause, but the reports sent to the executive level were spruced up to make things appear better than they were. Senior management made decisions about the Aztek® based on information that was heavily edited and modified.[21]

This was blatant marketing dishonesty cultivated by a culture senior management had created. By the time a General Motors car got through the group sessions and clinics, so much money had been spent on it that it would be "a career killer for the team leader to inform senior management that the vehicle missed the mark."[22]

John Scully never heard the bad news about the Newton, and the General Motors executive suite didn't want to hear any bad news about its drab, dowdy cars. It's a helluva way to run one of America's largest corporations. It was also a bad deal for General Motors shareholders.

General Motors®'s Corporate Culture

The corporate culture at General Motors became one of fear, where it was politically incorrect to tell the truth about a flawed vehicle. Three years before it hit the market an outside consultant who was working on a project for General Motors was told by the project team that the car would bomb. And yet, the project team trudged forward because senior management endorsed the project. The prediction came true; the car died in the marketplace. Aztek®-type scenarios became regrettably common in the General Motors culture.

It is difficult to compete with the Asian connection when General Motors executives have become obedient wimps. Where were the Marlboro men? They weren't working at General Motors.

The Marlboro Man Cometh

A Marlboro man finally did show up at General Motors in the form of Robert Lutz. One of the good moves made by Richard Wagoner, the new CEO at General Motors, was to hire this industry maverick. Lutz was a cigar-smoking, martini-drinking, jet-attack aviator in the United States Marine Corps with a distinguished career at Chrysler, where he reached the position of vice chairman. Lutz was viewed in Detroit as instrumental in transitioning Chrysler into the world's hottest car company before its current problems. Lutz was a no-nonsense car guy to the core with an intuitive feel for styling and design.

The grapevine chitchat in Detroit's auto circle was that one of Lutz's first meetings at General Motors involved bringing the design team into a large conference room. He looked them square in the eyes and said, "I don't care to know how the Aztek® got from A to Z, but just tell me how it got from Point A to Point B." Rumor had it there was no response; the room was eerily quiet. As pointed out earlier,

Lutz led the charge to do a quick-fix on the Aztek®, but it was beyond salvation. It was a vehicle that never should have rolled off the assembly line. But it did, because of dishonest manipulation of marketing research.

There can be a silver lining in every storm cloud. Lutz used the Aztek® episode to revitalize styling and design at General Motors. He stressed to design teams that exterior styling was paramount and much more important than interior features. He repeatedly pointed out that the Aztek® was a vehicle with a lot of nifty interior features, but car buyers never saw or experienced them, because they immediately shunned the ugly car's exterior. Lutz has since made it a personal rule to never look at any consumer research until the exterior styling and design have been put to bed.

Lessons Learned

The long-term effect is always bad news compounded when management only wants to hear good news. Poor management of focus group data prevented the Aztek® from succeeding. Focus group research is very delicate. One can hear whatever one wants to hear to fit a preconceived bias. Focus groups, when properly prepared and effectively conducted, can make valuable contributions to the innovation process. In the Aztek® scenario, the maligned focus groups didn't fail General Motors. The design team associated with them failed General Motors, fueled by a culture of intimidation. Senior management should always see the original report from the marketing research supplier, not a sanitized summary from those with vested interests.

NOTES

1. Tom Horby, "Good-bye Woz and Jobs: How the First Apple Era Ended in 1985," October 2, 2006, pp. 3–6. http://www.lowenmac.com/orchard/06/1002/html (accessed October 16, 2006).

2. Ibid.

3. Ibid.

4. Ibid.

5. Tom Hormby, "Scully's Dream: The Story behind the Newton," p. 5, http://www.lowendmac.com/orchard/06/0207.htm (accessed October 16, 2006).

6. Ibid., pp. 9, 10.

7. Ibid. p. 8.

8. Ibid.

9. Ibid., p. 10.

10. Ibid., p. 12.

11. Merle Crawford and Anthony C. DiBenedetto, *New Products Management*, 7th ed. (New York: Harper & Row, 1990), p. 84.

12. Ibid.

13. Rod Cambridge, "Whatever Happened to Newton," October 7, 2006, http://www.toppocket.pwp.blueyonder.co.uk/Newton.html (accessed November 15, 2006).

14. Ibid.

15. Milt Freudenheim, "Marriage of Necessity: Non-profit Groups and Drug Makers," *New York Times*, August 20, 1996, p. D2.

16. Ibid.

17. Jay Novak, attorney general of Missouri press release, October 16, 1996.

18. Attorney general of Florida press release, October 16, 1996.

19. Ibid.

20. Gary Kobe, "How Focus Groups Failed Aztek, PT Cruiser," *Automotive Industries* 181 (February 2001): 9.

21. Ibid.

22. Ibid.

(10)

[WHAT'S IT ALL ABOUT?]

We have moved through the eight basic mistakes associated with flawed product innovation. These are not mutually exclusive. Several of these innovation viruses surface in almost every setback.

In the innovation game, mistakes are inevitable. Though they have the power to illuminate and make us smarter when we stub our toe, they nevertheless keep getting swept under the rug. We should take umbrage to this for many reasons, not the least of which is the fact that misguided innovation costs corporations and their shareholders millions, if not billions, of dollars.

Most corporations could double their bottom lines with improvements in launching new products. There is no more juice left in the orange as corporations have downsized, cut costs, and extended their flagship brands to the point of no return. Corporations have looked everywhere for profit improvements, except at their dismal new product track records. It is one of the few remaining silos left with the tantalizing potential to improve the bottom line big time.

Corporate marketing activities are under attack for accountability and return on investment (ROI), despite the Garden of Eden with low-hanging money fruit waiting to be plucked in the backyard. A modest improvement in the innovation batting average would be worth a great deal to the bottom line.

What is surprising is the inferiority complex corporations have about their ability to play the innovation game. An article in *Advertising Age* noted the following:

> The problem is marketers don't feel their companies are equipped to deliver [successful new products]. Rating their companies out of 100 in terms of their competence at selecting the most viable new product concepts, marketers awarded an average score of 32%. They gave themselves 34% for their ability to design new products and went only slightly higher, 38%, in rating their launch marketing (advertising, PR, etc.) skills.[1]

As we move down the yellow brick road of innovation toward a final destination, it is of value to keep the following very much in mind:

- The problem of flawed innovation represents an important issue for everybody—investors, corporations, employees, and America.

- Critics have called it corporate America's legalized fraud. It is not as sinister as the Enron or WorldCom scandals in most cases, but it can come closer than one would wish.

WHY PRODUCT INNOVATION
IS EVERYBODY'S BUSINESS

Big Buck Mistakes Equal Investor Pain

Innovation is a high-stakes game; every major debacle carries a hefty price tag, as the examples below illustrate:

Classic New Product Failures

Failure	Company	Loss
Edsel	Ford Motor Company	$1 Billion
Video Disc	RCA	$600M
Iridium™	Motorola	$6 Billion
Olestra	Procter & Gamble	$1 Billion*
New Coke®	Coca-Cola	$250M*
Premier	RJ Reynolds	$300M
Home PCs	Texas Instruments	$600M

*Estimated by industry sources

The large financial losses are misleading, because opportunity costs are never factored into the write-off equations. In other words, what would companies have earned by investing their time and dollars elsewhere?

Stock ownership has moved from Wall Street to Main Street, reinforced by 401(k)s and other employer pension plans. About 52 percent of Americans own stock, and shareholders are big losers in the game of innovation roulette. It is their money that is tossed around to chase bad ideas like colored french fries, clear colas, and ugly cars nobody wants to buy. Flawed innovation robs shareholders of higher dividends or capital gains should they decide to sell and move to greener investment pastures. Some other examples of investor pain:

- Kraft's Ooey Gooey chocolate chip cookies promised a warm, moist homemade-tasting cookie similar to the kind your grandma used to make. Unfortunately, consumers didn't agree. They complained about the cookie's unorthodox texture. As it turns out, Ooey Gooey cookies were neither moist nor chewy.[2] Retailers returned carloads of Ooey Gooey to Kraft, and the company paid $17 million to pull unsold cookies off of store shelves.

- Pfizer lost a cool $100 million in market capitalization over a period of just a few days when the FDA told the company to stop advertising Celebrex®. The new pain reliever was initially developed for older people with chronic pain, but it was marketed to a much broader audience of baby boomers. The shift to a broader base was made because the initial segment—people over the age of sixty-five—was too small. By overprescribing Celebrex® to a broader target audience, Pfizer created a blockbuster drug that encountered safety concerns several years after its initial launch, but the drug helped inflate the price of Pfizer's stock in the short term. However, when the concerns about safety surfaced, Pfizer's stock immediately dropped by 11 percent in one day with more declines to follow as the news about Celebrex®'s woes continued to intensify. Overall Pfizer stock lost a quarter of its value—money that came out of shareholders' pockets.[3]

- The Polaroid pension plan required employees to put 8 percent of their salary into company stock. The inability of Polaroid to innovate and harness the digital imaging revolution destroyed the company's value. It also destroyed the retirement dreams of Polaroid employees. When the company filed for Chapter 11 bankruptcy protection, its stock sold for twenty-eight cents a share. Not exactly a pension windfall.

Shareholders need to look at the innovation practices of the companies in their investment portfolios in a more critical way. This may be easier said than done due to time constraints, and it does, after all, require effort in the form of homework. But the perspiration and energy expended can be invaluable. The choice is ours.

Less Room for the Little Guy in the Innovation Game

Supermarket retailers became exasperated with the continuing cycle of clearing out failed new products from warehouses and store shelves. Their solution was to make manufacturers pay new product slotting fees, which put a price on every new product SKU (stock keeping unit) coming into supermarket chains. These fees could be as high as $30,000 per SKU, depending on the product's location in the store. Slotting fees add millions to the cost of introducing new products. While the supermarket trade has found a new revenue source in slotting fees, marketers absorb the money as a cost of doing business. This does not, of course, deter them from continuing inefficient innovation practices. Reflecting upon the predictable death of Wahoos™, a new "me too," salty snack from General Mills, an East Coast supermarket executive observed in *Advertising Age*: "No amount of marketing could help Wahoos™, since there is nothing unique, different or interesting about it."[4]

Supermarkets get slotting fees, but consumers lose. Before slotting fees, product innovation often surfaced from smaller companies that had to try harder to make an impact on consumers. In the world of slotting, the little companies find the "innovation fees" a financial burden. They don't have the leverage to negotiate with supermarket chains the way Campbell's® Soup or Kraft can. The price of entry becomes prohibitively high.

Here are some examples of smaller companies permanently altering the marketing landscape with innovative products:

- Stokely Van Camp, an obscure processor and marketer of fruits and vegetables, launched Gatorade® down the innovation path. The brand was sold to Quaker Oats, and Gatorade® became a power brand, to the dismay of Coke and Pepsi.

- Irresistibly decadent Häagen-Dazs® ice cream came from the fertile mind of Reuben Mattus. He hypothesized correctly that Americans thought the rest of the world ate better than they did and would pay more for ice cream with a foreign mystique. He innovated a great-tasting ice cream with a tongue-twisting name and printed a map of Sweden on the carton for concept authenticity. The rest is marketing history. Mattus sold his goldmine business to Pillsbury in the 1980s for $70 million.

- Small companies such as Snapple, SoBe, Mystic, and Arizona fueled the move away from carbonated soft drinks to fun and funky noncarbonated drinks while Coke and Pepsi watched the action.

- A small Minnesotan company, Minnetonka, Inc., started the trend toward liquid soap and body washes. Colgate bought its primary brand, Softsoap®, in 1988.

- The first diet cola, Diet-Rite®, did not come from Coke or Pepsi. It came from Royal Crown Cola International, maker of RC Cola.

- The Peter Hand Brewing Company marketed one of the first lite beers—Meister Brau Lite. The company knew how to make it but wasn't very good at marketing it. Miller came along and bought the Lite® recipe and, very importantly, the Lite® trademark.

- Wilkinson Sword®, an obscure sword company from the United Kingdom, introduced American males to stainless steel blades while the Gillette Company stood on the sidelines watching.

- A small Texas shoe company invented Heelys®, the sneaker with a wheel in the heel. It quickly became a hot item among the target audience of six- to fourteen-year-old kids. Heelys® addicts can glide on the wheel or pop it out, converting it to a sneaker perfect for walking or running. Nike, Adidas, Reebok, and others let this one pass by. They were too busy making money selling regular sneakers.

And some product innovations surface from the garage, a favorite innovation environment for inventors. That's where Steve Wozniak and Steve Jobs invented the personal computer. They tried to peddle it to Atari and Hewlett Packard but were turned down. They went back to the garage to start their own small company, Apple.

The Cornucopia of Real Choice Narrows

Marketers believe that choice is good, an essential ingredient in delivering customer satisfaction. They worship at the altar of line extensions and customizations in an effort to provide choice, but the world of slotting has produced an environment of monotonous repetition, dominated by look-alike extensions such as Wahoos™, not genuinely differentiated products like Gatorade®. Today, one of General Motors's major business problems is the illusion of choice in its attempt to market too many look-alike models. General Motors has trapped itself in a sea of sameness with its cars. Emergence from this quagmire will prove to be exceptionally challenging.

Honda and Toyota outsmarted the Big Three with their choice strategies. In the early invasion of the US market, allocation of their research and development resources focused on three brands—Civic®, Accord®, and Camry®—rather than attempting to spread the effort across unwieldy product lines. When these brands were well established with American consumers, Honda and Toyota expanded their choice offerings by attacking other segments dominated by the clueless Big Three, most notably trucks and SUVs.

THE LONG REACH OF FLAWED INNOVATION

The death of Soft Batch® cookies or Pepsi Twist® is not a national tragedy; America woke up the next day and went to work. But flawed innovation can have long tentacles, and America can sometimes wake up with a hangover as a result of flawed innovation. Some of us may even find ourselves standing in line at the unemployment office— think General Motors or Merck.

Case History #1: The Impending Death of the Big Three

The Good Times Are Over

In the Eisenhower administration, Secretary of Defense Charles Wilson, former CEO of General Motors, remarked, "What is good for General Motors is good for the country." While the statement was viewed as arrogant in some quarters, Wilson wasn't far off the mark. We would gladly trade today's Detroit for Wilson's glory days at General Motors, when Honda and Toyota weren't around.

Today, amid intensified competition from foreign brands, Detroit's Big Three carmakers struggle to eke out profits or reverse losses. They sell their cars with a combination of patriotism and financing gimmicks. The domestic car market looks like our political map. The blue states love foreign brands. Patriotism still sells Detroit brands in the red Rust Belt states, but even the diehards are fast souring on the Big Three. They have lost their innovation edge. The only true escape from the open faucet of rebates and incentives is to regain that edge by making and selling better cars.

The buyers of foreign brands are the cream of the car market— younger, better educated, and wealthier. Detroit has lost them, perhaps forever, and reversing share losses will be profoundly expensive, difficult, and perhaps impossible. The Big Three will be fortunate to retain what they have.

GM, Ford, and Daimler-Chrysler failed to understand that they are in the business of seduction and entertainment. A car is more than a chassis and four wheels. Car buyers want to be entertained with razzle-dazzle features, designs, and models, not "pedestrian retreads." While Detroit slept, foreign brands enticed and entertained car buyers with emotionally electrifying features, options, and designs, creating "gotta have" cars.

The Social and Economic Impact

Ford's chairman, Bill Ford, has pointed out the widespread impact of the industry in terms of generating income for America in terms of manufacturing power, employment, and retail. The industry accounts for an important chunk of America's gross domestic product (GDP)—anywhere from 3 to 4 percent of the total, depending on whose calculations are used.[5] Over five million Americans are employed in the automobile industry, with a compensation contribution of $250 billion. In other words, the ups and downs of business in Detroit directly impact America at the grass roots.

Membership in the United Auto Workers Union (UAW) has declined by half from two decades ago. The average car has fifteen thousand parts supplied by three thousand firms, two-thirds of which employ twenty or fewer people.[6] These suppliers are an important part of the nation's manufacturing foundation. With a shrunken business base, thousands of jobs have been eliminated in the UAW and automotive vendors.

The cradle of our domestic automobile industry is the Midwest, and economic ripples have spread across the region. Michigan especially is a microcosm of the Big Three's innovation hangover. Un - employment remains stubbornly high. State tax receipts are down. The state budget has been slashed, dropping many programs at the community level. The Canadian province of Ontario has replaced Michigan as the largest producer of cars in North America. The cars made in Ontario are cheaper, because the Canadian government subsidizes healthcare.

Roads don't get fixed. Tuition programs for higher education get scrapped. Vocational training programs for the unemployed disappear. The list is endless. The Big Three's innovation funk has devastated the social and economic fabric of the state.[7]

Domestic auto suppliers are at risk. Delphi, Lear, and Visteon employ more workers in Michigan than Chrysler. These three companies have red ink on the books and junk bond ratings. All three outsource jobs to China in an attempt to stay afloat with a reduced business base.[8]

The state of Michigan is struggling to deal with the mess spawned by the Big Three. State officials are openly courting Japanese auto manufacturers to relocate to Michigan.[9] The UAW doesn't object. Any job is better than no job. Union halls are no longer towing foreign cars from their parking lots. Even the trade unions have faced the inevitability of Detroit's demise.[10]

In the aftermath of the Big Three's innovation misery, all of America feels the pain—weak stock prices, earnings short of expectations, lousy American-made cars with quality problems and embarrassing recalls, closed factories, unemployment, lower wages for those left behind, outsourcing of jobs, the potential demise of Buick and Pontiac, and a serious erosion of the tax base in communities dependent on car sales.

A New Competitor on the Horizon

China is moving from a bicycle to a car economy. The Chinese are moving into car manufacturing just like their Korean and Japanese counterparts. They bring many cost advantages to the table, including cheap sources of labor. Their cars will reach our domestic shores in eight to ten years. The Asian connection continues, reinforced with a new competitive face. This is a major potential problem, not only for the beleaguered Big Three, but also for all of America. Much of the solution to the problem ultimately lies with innovation. Perhaps one of the Big Three American car companies should consider a partnership with a Chinese car maker. It is better to be a partner than a victim.

Case History #2: The Polaroid Debacle

A Can't-Miss Investment Misses

Polaroid was a member of the Nifty 50, hyped by Wall Street as one of the fifty best stocks for investors to buy in the 1970s because of the company's innovative products and management practices. This "can't-miss investment" was selling at ninety times earnings. Stockbrokers told their clients of Polaroid stock: "Sit on it. It's a great retirement nest egg."

On October 12, 2001, the $2 billion Polaroid Corporation filed for voluntary Chapter 11 bankruptcy protection in Delaware. The company was buried under a mountain of debt. It had run out of cash and time. The "can't-miss investment" went kaput. Polaroid stock was selling for twenty-eight cents a share.

Catch a Falling Star

The catalyst for Polaroid's birth was a vacation in New Mexico. A Harvard dropout, Edwin Land, took pictures of his daughter. She innocently asked, "Why can't I see the pictures now?" It seemed like a logical question that deserved an answer. In an hour, Land had conceived a product concept that provided the answer.

In 1947 Land stunned an American Optical Society meeting in New York with his demonstration of a single-step photographic process that developed pictures in sixty seconds. Land was on the cusp of inventing an entirely new industry—instant photography. The process was later reduced to ten seconds. The company sold its first Polaroid camera a few months later at Jordon Marsh, a Boston department store.

Under Land's stewardship, Polaroid® became one of the ten most recognizable brands in the world. Polaroid used the legendary ad agency Doyle Dane Bernbach to create an iconic brand. Polaroid ads charmed America. The only commercial ever made by legendary actor and director Sir Laurence Olivier was for Polaroid. The company was destined to enjoy forty profitable years, based on one great idea. Nevertheless, there were dark days ahead at the end of that rainbow.

Polaroid's Innovation Machine Goes Haywire

In a twist of irony, the genius of Edwin Land led the company down the path to a major innovation disaster. Land was obsessed with achievement and had a strong desire to top his instant photography innovation. Why not pursue instant movies?

Land insisted on moving forward with Polavision™, which was destined to be short-lived and not very well remembered. This instant movie system consisted of a bulky camera and a special device to instantly view the film. It recorded a two-and-a-half-minute movie with no sound, hardly an inspiring technical achievement when video cameras with superior technical flexibility were surfacing. Land's unassailable innovation track record had been tarnished.

Polavision™ became a $300 million innovation blunder. An infuriated board forced Land to resign as CEO. He left the company in 1982. Polaroid's successor CEOs were engineers with no instincts for the biorhythms of the marketplace. Polaroid's product research pipeline lost its direction. The critical blend of Polaroid's savvy engineers and marketing magicians disintegrated. Most of the best market - ers, like Peter Wensberg, senior vice president of marketing during Polaroid's glory years, left the company.

Now let us fast-forward to 1991. That year, Polaroid was awarded $935 million from Kodak in a patent infringement suit.[11] Polaroid could have used the money to pay off debt in fighting a hostile takeover from Shamrock Holdings, or the money could have been used to fuel innovation efforts, which had the potential to generate cash flow for debt repayment. Polaroid chose the latter option; there would have been nothing wrong with this, had the company's execution been better.

Polaroid pursued a dry film technology for the medical community that would replace conventional x-rays. A new $300 million plant was built in New Bedford, Massachusetts, to produce the dry film. Another $300 million was spent on the company's research and development program. The product was never launched after over $600 million was invested in it.[12]

Another big chunk of the Kodak settlement—$300 million—was used to build the new Captiva™ camera with a smaller format film than the original goldmine product, the SX-70, but two problems doomed Captiva™.

Marketing research indicated the camera would not sell if priced above $60. Polaroid decided to slap a $120 price tag on it. The Captiva™ revenue forecast assumed there would be a high level of repeat purchase for the camera after the introductory year. But selling cameras was not like selling potato chips or shampoo, products that need to be replaced all the time. Cameras like Captiva™ are sold once. That's it! There are no repeat purchases. The high price for the camera and a profoundly short-sighted repeat purchase forecast emasculated Captiva™'s potential from the start. A stock analyst said, "Essentially, the $925 million was pissed away," a stunning indictment of Polaroid's innovation virus in the post-Land era.[13]

In 1995 new executive blood was ushered into Polaroid's headquarters in the form of Gary DiCamillo from Black & Decker. The new CEO proclaimed that Polaroid would introduce twenty-five new products a year, reflecting the company's rich technical assets. It was quite a proclamation. Not even Procter & Gamble, with its vast resources, could introduce twenty-five new products in a year.

Polaroid continued to spend large amounts of money on projects that went nowhere. Even innovations that initially looked successful had problems below the surface, the most notable example being I-Zone®, the best-selling camera in America in 1999.

The I-Zone® was designed to create consumer loyalty in teenage girls. It took thumbnail-size photos that could be printed as stickers "affixed to binders and assignment books."[14] Unfortunately, there was no loyalty in the teen girl segment, and Polaroid should have realized this fact. Teen girls float from one fad to the next, and I-Zone® became a fad, not a trend. It also had product problems: imaging quality was inconsistent, the stickers were too small, and the film price was too high for cash-starved teenagers.

At one point in its life, Polaroid seemed indestructible. Its innovation machine fell victim to a disease that the late Harvard professor Ted Levitt called "marketing myopia." Just as railroad companies thought they were in the railroad business, when they were really in the transportation business, Polaroid thought it was in the instant picture business, when it was really in the business of visually capturing and sharing memories. Company hubris kept Polaroid from recognizing that its best innovation scheme would have been to move to digital imaging.

Conversation about digital imaging had floated around the corridors of Polaroid for years. If the company had jumped on it with its engineering savvy, Polaroid could have brought digital and instant together seamlessly. Instead, the company was anchored to the belief that Polaroid's monopoly in instant photography would sustain the company forever.

Loyal Polaroid Employees Get Shafted

Edwin Land created a paternalistic work environment. It was not unusual for Land to have lunch in the company cafeteria, chatting with the workers while munching on a fried bologna sandwich. In *Boston Magazine*, Glenn Rifkin described Land's caring attitude:

> Land believed that a company could be far more than a collection of employees, products, and earnings statements. Under his paternalistic hand, Polaroid became a corporate family, routinely named one of the best places in the world to work. Land rejected conventional wisdom regarding compensation and benefits. Even in the parking lot, spaces were allocated not by rank but by seniority.[15]

Polaroid employees were lifers. They came to the company fresh out of high school and college with the intention of staying forever. They had good jobs, benefits, and a caring leader.

As Polaroid slipped into its downward spiral, the good times were rolling in the executive suite. Three months before the bankruptcy filing, DiCamillo was given a $1.4 million bonus by the board and an additional $25,000 for legal expenses that might incur from a bankruptcy filing. Ten months earlier the board gave CEO DiCamillo a two-year employment contract extension and a $795,000 bonus, which was more than his annual salary. It was a very generous gesture from the board, considering Polaroid's underperformance relative to the S&P 500.[16]

Six weeks before the bankruptcy filing, five board members received special payments ranging from $63,000 to $275,000 for services rendered. Retention bonuses and incentives totaling millions of dollars were set up for 155 key employees to stay with the reorganized company. Eight key employees became owners.[17]

One Polaroid executive who fled before the final meltdown was the CFO, Judith Boynton. For less than three years as the CFO, she received the following package: a lump sum pension payment of $638,000, stock worth $510,000, and severance checks of $17,308 every two weeks until Polaroid filed bankruptcy. Not a bad payday for less than three years of service. It reflected generous rewards for senior executives who made decisions that pushed Polaroid down the elevator shaft.[18]

What did the loyal Polaroid employees get?

- Polaroid cut off health benefits and life insurance payments to thousands of its retired workers. Dental, health, and life insurance coverage had to be obtained in the private market for those who could afford it. Polaroid didn't even tell its retirees that the coverage was eliminated. Many found out as they attempted to fill prescriptions or showed up at hospitals for surgery.

- Promised severance payments were terminated.

- Polaroid employees were required to allocate 8 percent of their salary to company stock ownership, with a stipulation that the stock could not be sold until they left the company. Others bought Polaroid stock through brokers outside the company. The stock became worthless. Retirement savings went up in smoke.

- The depleted Polaroid pension fund is now managed by a federal government agency.[19]

While the executive suite feathered its nest, loyal Polaroid workers were left holding an empty bag.

THE ILLUSION OF COMPARATIVE ADVANTAGE

We are afflicted with a heroic assumption that America has a perpetual monopoly on product innovation and design. It is our comparative advantage; a nineteenth-century theory from English economist David Ricardo explained "why cloudy and cool England exported woolens to Spain, which in turn exported wine to England."[20]

We naively assume that emerging economic markets, such as India, are content to perform menial backroom tasks for us using their comparative advantage—lower-paid, highly skilled labor. Is that all there is for these workers—examining patient x-rays, muddling through tax returns, and telling a credit card user in Hoboken that the late fee can't be taken off the Visa card?

In *Business Week*, Roger L. Martin makes an astute observation: "Capabilities are not static. Advantages are not permanent."[21] We laughed at the initial offering of cars from Toyota and Honda—cheap looking and tacky. We are not laughing anymore. Americans are intoxicated with their styling and design.

The Asian companies that trumped American cars acquired their comparative advantage the old-fashioned way—hard work. Japanese engineers and designers would stand around supermarket parking lots on hot Saturday afternoons in August watching homemakers load groceries into the trunks of their cars. They wanted to build better, more consumer friendly car trunks. Where were the General Motors and Ford executives on weekends—playing golf or tennis at the country club?

The Asian connection worked twenty-four/seven to understand our culture. We take coin trays in cars for granted, but the idea came from Honda's CEO. On business trips to the United States, he found himself fumbling for change at tollgates. He immediately realized cars needed coin trays. Everyday happenings are often triggers for product design creativity. Nevertheless, hundreds of Ford and General Motors executives went through tollgates without a spark of inspiration. The companies who enter the market at a disadvantage work harder to find their comparative advantage.

That's the point. It is a mistake to assume our global competitors "won't attempt to develop a capability because it seemingly conflicts with an existing one—in this case low cost versus innovation expertise."[22] In personal computers, Taiwanese manufacturers, such as BenQ and HTC, were dismissed as low-cost players forever destined to scrounge for table scraps. However, it was an erroneous assumption, as Roger L. Martin points out:

> Taiwanese companies actually had more engineers, held more patents, and performed more research and development. And in recent years they've dominated ever-more-sophisticated segments in the industry.[23]

We can no longer count on the brain drain—the flight of intellectual talent to the United States—for our engineering and scientific base. In Silicon Valley, about one-third of the scientific and engineering communities is foreign born.[24] One of the cofounders of Sun Microsystems came from Germany; another emigrated from India. Gururaj Deshpande, from India, founded Juniper Networks. The state of California estimated that within its borders over three thousand companies are owned by Indian entrepreneurs.[25] Immigrants with sophisticated technical backgrounds flocked to our shores to pursue dreams and ambitions that would not be possible back home. Our product innovation benefited from the exodus over the past three decades.

This pipeline may cease; emerging economies now offer incentives—stock options and equity—to keep their talent from fleeing. In a global world of outsourcing, good jobs are now available in China or India for scientific talent—a phenomenon unheard of a decade ago, when the United States was the only job market alternative. Now they return home to do what they did best in America—create technology, jobs, and wealth.[26]

Unfortunately, in American society, our best and brightest want to be investment bankers rather than engineers or scientists. Our base of scientific talent is dwindling—a major deficiency for innovation initiatives in the current global high-tech sector. We are losing an advantage as America sleeps through this problem.

In industrialized nations, the highest concentration of entrepreneurial activity can be found in North America. We take for granted that America will continue to be the cradle of entrepreneurial activity fueling our innovation engine—people like Reuben Mattus and Steve Jobs, tinkering around with little acorns that grow into big oak trees.

Our faith is bolstered by the belief that failure—an inevitable outcome associated with risk-taking entrepreneurial activities—is viewed as a disgrace in other cultures, especially Asian societies. Milton Hershey declared bankruptcy several times before stumbling upon the Hershey® bar. Will the entrepreneur in Malaysia or the Philippines accept cultural scorn and bounce back like Hershey did?

While China and India produce brilliant students, their rote approach to education does not necessarily crank out graduates who are very good at thinking out of the box. And indeed American companies have complained that it is difficult, though not impossible, to find professional managers with good critical-thinking skills in Asia. They are either bureaucratic or very rigid in thinking about business problems.

The entrepreneurial success equation is not necessarily a function of college degrees. Michael Dell, Bill Gates, Ted Turner, Thomas Edison, the Wright brothers, and Colonel Sanders never graduated from college, but they were entrepreneurs who changed the landscape of our lives. So what will the global map of entrepreneurial activity look like in 2030? Will North America still be the citadel for entrepreneurs? Does our presumed comparative advantage—entrepreneurial endowment—carry us through an innovation war with global parameters?

It didn't happen in the automobile industry. The only constant in innovation roulette is change. These days Ford and General Motors are experts on the fortunes and misfortunes of change. While many factors fueled the Detroit decline, one of them is lackluster styling and design:

- The Pontiac Aztek® looked like the hunchback of Notre Dame.

- The Buick LaCrosse® is a car designed for grandmothers.

- The Honda Fit®, a subcompact, sits on dealer lots for a mere two weeks or less. Ford's comparable product, Focus®, languishes on dealer lots, victimized by boring design and more than twelve recalls since its 2000 introduction. It will take Ford three years to fix the Focus® problem because of long lead times.[27] Honda is not about to throw in the towel. It'll be shaking and baking in design studios, too, over the next three years.

- The MBA crowd at Ford destroyed the styling and design legacy of Jaguar® by attempting to market a cheap Jag that looked like a Taurus®. Both Mercedes-Benz and BMW stretched downward, but they did it right, retaining the elegant styling and design of the parent.

And the beat goes on. The young, restless, and affluent prefer the styling and design of foreign brands. That's their comparative advantage.

In the innovation war, product design can be a potent weapon, as the rapidly shrinking Big Three have discovered to their dismay. For years, General Electric appliances were viewed as durable and reliable, but not very exciting. The appliance unit was available for the right price. Then GE strategic planners noticed a demographic trend—empty-nesting baby boomers were refurbishing their homes, using their disposable income for expensive personal indulgence with the kids out of the house. The first place usually refurbished was the kitchen. That meant new cabinets, floors, countertops, and, of course, appliances.

GE's bland appliances became opulent and pricier, targeted to this affluent, high-rolling segment. Sales surged as baby boomers dipped into their discretionary income for ovens, dishwashers, and freezers with maximum sizzle. In the vernacular of the Boston Consulting Group's portfolio analysis, GE appliances moved from dog to star. No major new technology was involved in the revival—it was simply a case of smart styling and design that made the cash register ring.[28]

These are the extremes of product innovation and design. General Electric used it skillfully to revitalize its appliances, and sales soared. The dysfunctional Big Three struggled with it. We know the rest of that story. Therefore, American companies—many of which have pretty tired designs—are blissfully naive if they assume global competitors will not focus on this weakness. An English professor returned from her trip to Europe and asked me, "Why are the products in Europe better designed than ours?" If an English professor noticed the weakness, so will the design-conscious Germans, Scandinavians, and Asians.

Here's the compelling question: are there other American industries with product creativity issues that are set to experience a Detroit-type meltdown? Our comparative advantage—product innovation and design—remains an asset only if we play the game of innovation roulette with an intensity never displayed in Detroit. Nothing is forever, including comparative advantages.

WHY DOES FLAWED INNOVATION FLOURISH?

Flawed innovation flourishes with relative ease in corporate America for seven major reasons.

Reason #1: The Curse of "Me, Too"

In a landmark study reported in the *Harvard Business Review* in 1976, J. Hugh Davidson evaluated one hundred new products equally divided between successes and failures. One of his principle conclusions: failures were "undistinctive me-toos with a very low chance of success."[29] Conversely, the new product successes had important points of difference. Not much has changed since Davidson's observation: witness the mad rush of food and beverage companies to emulate warmed-over versions of competitive products. There was no meaningful point of difference to justify their existence. America doesn't need two hundred brands of salsa, and yet many sit gathering dust on grocery shelves. This is choice morphed into madness. While there is validity to Davidson's findings, an important question remains: how do these "me, too" products, whether its General Motors or Kraft, slip through the corporate checkpoints?

Reason #2: The Marketing Kindergarten

In corporate America, the innovation game is often a training ground for inexperienced marketers. Many of these yearlings are MBA graduates who have never managed anything in their lives. They lack the sophisticated set of skills essential for managing the product innovation process in pressure situations.

Business schools have morphed into trade unions. In many corporations, one of the Ten Commandments appears to read: Thou shall not enter our marketing ranks without an MBA. A capricious corporate culture convinced that business schools are producing—with assembly line efficiency—an elite corps of decision makers throws marketing neophytes into the complicated innovation fray.

Internal studies at major consulting companies, such as McKinsey and the Boston Consulting Group, have found that liberal arts graduates perform as well, and sometimes better, in the management consulting field than their counterparts from MBA programs.[30] While this suggests that corporations should get over their bias that favors MBA graduates over students with liberal arts backgrounds, recruiters trudging across college campuses see major differences between the two.

In interviewing MBA students for jobs, "arrogance is the MBA graduate's biggest sin by far in the eyes of recruiters."[31] One recruiter observed, "They need to check their egos at the door when they start work."[32] A recruiter once made this statement to me: "Students with liberal arts backgrounds are a more rewarding interview. They are more focused. They have done their homework about the company. They are not shopping around for the best salary, playing one company off against the other. They write better than many MBA students."

In fact, liberal arts graduates may bring a better aptitude to the innovation process than MBA graduates. The latter are trained for quantitative analysis—spreadsheets and crunching numbers are their aphrodisiac. The early stages of the innovation process are an unstructured journey through the forest of discovery, which requires assembling hundreds of Lego blocks into a meaningful pattern. This discovery process is an art form. Consumers' invisible stripes are made visible using soft skills such as intuition, inferences, feel, creativity, and emotional intelligence—these are qualitative skills business schools choose to write off with their penchant for quantitative techniques and analysis.

These skills are very much a part of the early exploratory, predevelopment activities carried out in new ventures; what happens first counts disproportionately in successful innovation. Several studies reveal that the winners in the innovation game spend proportionately more time, money, and manpower exploring the full range of possibilities in the earliest stages of innovation initiatives.

This brings us back to the MBA tenderfoots wading around in the pool of product innovation, weighed down by inexperience and, occasionally, attitude. In their energetic drive to achieve, they may ignore counsel or advice that suggests trouble lies ahead for the new venture, sacrificing—consciously or unconsciously—sound business judgment.

While MBAs are impatient for results, there is no patience for reflection, rethinking, and regrouping when barriers surface that represent impediments in the development timeline. Delays are viewed as the enemy, and red flags or distress signals from consumers are rationalized away, fueled by a results-oriented drive that has gone awry.

When moving a flawed new product forward, it is very likely that this misguided youthful exuberance never has to be explained, because, as pointed out later, marketers are moved around with great frequency, and accountability gets lost in a game of musical chairs. When the books are closed on another product failure, the stewards of innovation malfeasance are either working on another project or pursuing achievement in another company.

The tragedy for shareholders is that these flawed, capricious decisions never take into account the shareholder money that is being thrown around. You can bet that the architects of failure would make better decisions if it were *their* own money being flushed down the drain.

Reason #3: Marketing Waltz of Musical Chairs

There is an accountability problem in the innovation game. New products are moved through something akin to a NASCAR® pit stop. The brand manager working on a new product for six months moves to mouthwash. The mouthwash brand manager moves to shampoo. The players are constantly rotated around the chessboard. Since some MBA graduates have the unrealistic expectation that their careers are in a constant skyrocket mode, the MBA ego must be stroked with upward mobility. Corporations acquiesce, because they are afraid of losing their MBA talent pool to the lure of a better-paying opportunity.

In discussing General Motors' ugly duckling, the Pontiac Aztek®, Robert Lutz, GM's styling and design czar, observed the company was having trouble pinpointing who was responsible for the car. Accountability in corporate America becomes illusive in the innovation game —unless, of course, the innovation succeeds, in which case many claim ownership.

Reason #4: The No-Bad-News Syndrome

Marketing research departments are responsible for interpreting the voice of the consumer—the good, bad, and ugly. Since innovation is a discovery process, it is the job of marketing research to take a bare canvas and paint the marketing landscape for the innovation team.

Most of the case histories cited in this book involved heavy marketing research investments. The problem is that innovation teams only want to hear the good news; negative news gets rationalized away, even though it can save the company and its shareholders bundles of money.

What often happens is warning signs in the development process —especially the fuzzy front end, where there is need to illuminate the darkness with learning—are rejected, because the innovation team is racing toward a launch date that was promised to management. When marketing research becomes a voice in the wilderness, the required homework does not get done.

In another scenario, marketing research loses its objective balance, becoming a cheerleader for flawed innovation, as was the case with New Coke®. The spigot of objectivity is turned off, because reality might get in the way.

Reason #5: Comatose Board of Directors

Boards of directors come in various tones and textures. When the topic of conversation is product innovation, many boards become comatose. They either act as a "rubber stamp" for what management wants to do, or they are asleep at the switch. Complacent board members neither hear nor see any evil, and they ask no questions.

Imagine sitting on the Heinz board listening to a business plan for chocolate and blue french fries. Once the sands of time had flowed through the hourglass, Heinz's profits and earnings were adversely affected in this attempt to reinvent an American food icon, the french fry. Where were the probing questions from the Heinz board about this silly venture? A few questions would have been a small price to pay for stronger corporate governance from the Heinz board, protecting its shareholders from an innovation disaster.

Reason #6: Marketing's Freudian Id

In studying research and development expenditures at a thousand companies, Booz, Allen, and Hamilton consultants Barry Jaruzelski, Kevin Dehoff, and Rakesh Bordia reported the following finding:

> When it comes to getting a substantial return on an R&D investment, a key is how the innovation process is handled. The tighter the links among R&D, marketing, sales, service, and manufacturing, the greater the chances for success.[33]

The concept of "tighter links" leads one to reflect upon marketing's Freudian id. Freud believed that the human personality is comprised of three interrelated forces forming a synergistic process that governs behavior—the id, the superego, and the ego. In Freud's theory, the id is viewed as a silo of primal and impetuous drives requiring immediate satisfaction regardless of how despicable the behavior might be. The role of the superego and ego is to constrain the impulsive drives of the id; they become the "brakes" to keep the id in check.

In innovation initiatives, the marketing id tends to go wild, because there are no brakes. While there is supposed to be security checkpoints in the development process, the marketing id finds ways to maneuver around them. When important research findings are ignored or rationalized away, this does not optimize marketing research's contributions in a total team effort; it does diminish the chances for successful innovation.

In *Guns of August*, author Barbara Tuchman describes how Great Britain, France, and Germany historically spent a decade preparing for war. Each side had to match or top the other in terms of weaponry. War became inevitable once the momentum was set in leading up to August 1914—a catalytic event initially referred to as the Great War.

Product innovation has its own "guns of August." Innovation initiatives also can build momentum to the point where nothing will stop the product from being launched—not even dire news. As the momentum carries the blemished idea forward through the development process, attempting to stop it is analogous to trying to derail a runaway train.

Don Schultz, a faculty member at Northwestern's Kellogg Graduate School of Management, noted that a study conducted by Cranfield University among nonmarketing senior executives in major United Kingdom corporations found that "marketing people were described as slippery."[34] Their behavior in the innovation process reinforces the perception.

Product innovation is too important to be left in the hands of the marketing department. Everybody in the process—manufacturing, research and development, marketing research, and finance—should be involved, adding value in their own way to achieve tighter linkage. The stewards of new products are prone to mute the voices of dissension; their marketing superiors choose to ignore—either consciously or unconsciously—the behavior.

We take our cars to the mechanic when the brakes don't work. Well, the brakes need to be relined in the innovation process—critical quality control checkpoints must be taken seriously to offset the impulsive drive of the marketing id to protect bad ideas.

In some cases, the passion to pursue a bad idea comes directly from the CEO—think, as an example, of John Scully's obsession with the Apple Newton. There was a need for PDAs, but not the overpriced, poorly designed Newton. Nobody would dare tell him the truth about it, because the golden rule was in play—those with the gold rule. The "guns of August" fired away in Apple's research and development labs with marketing waiting in the wings to spend even more money on a bad idea. But when CEOs veer off on innovation tangents destined for an ugly implosion, where are the brakes?

The relining of the brakes must come from a board of directors. They represent the superego and ego in the innovation process. While the board hires professional management to steward the fortunes of the company, it also has a fiduciary responsibility to spend the shareholders' money wisely. Apple sank more than $500 million in development costs chasing Scully's folly;[35] the development cost coupled with money spent attempting to market Newton made it approximately a $1 billion mistake. When the prize cattle companies hire—CEOs like John Scully and Raymond Gilmartin—who chew up bushel baskets full of money with nothing to show for it, boards must find the courage to apply the brakes.

How do boards sort out truth from fiction? How do they stand up to charismatic CEOs with a persuasive spin that shades the truth? As will be discussed further, boards need innovation committees comprised of objective and experienced outsiders who are not board members. Their role is to assist the board in assessing innovation initiatives. The innovation committee should audit the product innovation in a systematic, objective process that allows the board to raise the hard questions that often go unasked. Their observations might come as a surprise—perhaps even a jolt—to the board's tranquility. The board can then decide what action should be taken. These cultural changes must come from the board, because right now there are no brakes to check the impetuous nature of the marketing id. They must become the superego and ego in innovation initiatives. An innovation committee helps the board fulfill this critical role.

Reason #7: CEOs Need Short-Term Results

CEOs must create shareholder value, or they will find themselves unemployed. No CEO saves his or her job by pointing out how happy the employees were at the annual Christmas party, or citing good news from the latest round of customer satisfaction surveys.

To create shareholder value (improve the company's stock price), CEOs can cut costs, but there is only so much fat to cut. The other path to success is via innovation, which creates lasting shareholder value. Most companies attempt to move down both paths. The problem is that many companies are superb at cutting costs, but their innovation efforts are what lawyers might designate as "innovation malpractice."

The average CEO spends less than 2 percent of his or her business life on new products. These corporate types don't understand why it takes so long for new products to move through the pipeline. They are under pressure from Wall Street for quarterly results. The best money manager in America, investor Warren Buffett, remarked, "Making the numbers for Wall Street while running a business can be, and usually is, stupid."

CEOs frequently dance the Wall Street tango, and a big part of it involves pushing the innovation button. They hope the new products in the pipeline will have merit. They may well not have been told the unvarnished truth about them. The reality is that many roll the dice on the new products game table anyway, knowing full well that nine out of ten are destined to fail.

Duke University and the University of Washington conducted a survey of CFOs (chief financial officers). The study, "Economic Implications of Corporate Financial Reporting," found publicly traded companies make business decisions that hurt their long-term vitality because of profit pressures.

While aggressive accounting gimmicks are less prevalent recently due to the dawn of a new era of investor scrutiny, many CFOs surveyed said "they would be willing to sell assets, give their customers incentives to buy more products than they need, or cut spending on maintenance or research and development."[36] In other words, these companies are willing to sacrifice long-term shareholder value to hit unrealistic earnings targets. This is the Wall Street tango alive, well, and thriving.

Missing earnings targets is viewed by the market as a reflection of an underlying weakness in the company—"like seeing one cockroach, you know that there are a one hundred behind the wall."[37] Uncomfortable decisions are foisted on CFOs by the market's myopic focus on earnings. CEOs want the numbers, and nothing else matters; it is their report card.

In *Marketing Management*, Tim Ambler discussed the role of brand equity in "understanding and nurturing the sources of cash flow."[38] We have paraphrased a couple of his observations to illustrate the mania of CEOs for numbers. In the typical scenario, CEOs force an endless litany of "forecasts and re-forecasts" with relatively little concern about the source of the money. At companies like Apple, the money comes from real innovation. The pile of money doesn't get any bigger no matter how many times CEOs have the bean counters tally it up. The pile does get bigger with products like Prius® and iPhone®.[38]

Merck needed the numbers. It is alleged that it continued to sell Vioxx® even after an early clinical study suggested potential health risks. Polaroid needed the numbers. It moved forward with an inflated sales forecast for Captiva™. Bernie Ebbers needed the numbers at WorldCom, only he did his manipulating on a larger, grander scale. They all danced the Wall Street tango. The music entices desperate CEOs to resort to desperate behavior, scrambling to achieve unrealistic financial targets in an effort to please the Wall Street mercenaries.

NOTES

1. Beth Snyder Bulik, "The New Product Paradox," *Advertising Age* (October 4, 2004): 1.

2. Sarah Ellison, "Kraft's Stale Strategy," *Wall Street Journal,* December 18, 2003, p. B1.

3. Jeffery Brown, "Risk Assessment," PBS.org, December 17, 2004, http://www.pbs.org/newshour//bb/heaalth/july-deco4/Celebrex.html (accessed August 19, 2007).

4. Stephanie Thompson, "Sales Decline; Retailers Yank Wahoos from Shelves," *Advertising Age* (July 7, 2002): 45.

5. "Economic Contribution of the Auto Industry," Ford Motor Company, May 2005, http://www.ford.com/su345inability/report.htm (accessed December 12, 2006).

6. Danny Hakin, "With Delphi Filing, Tougher Times for Auto Industry," *New York Times*, October 10, 2005, p. C2.

7. Louis Uchitelle, "The End of the Line as They Know It," *New York Times,* April 7, 2007, p. B8.

8. Ibid.

9. "Governor Pitches Michigan to Japanese Automakers at 2005 World Expo in Japan," Office of the Governor of Michigan press release, July 25, 2005.

10. Hakin, "With Delphi Filing, Tougher Times for Auto Industry."

11. Glenn Rifkin, "Losing Focus," *Boston Magazine* (January 2002), http://www.bostonmagazine.com/articledisplay.htm (accessed January 28, 2005).

12. Ibid.

13. Ibid.

14. Ibid.

15. Ibid.

16. T. Paradisco, "Polaroid's Final Days Come Into Focus," August 26, 2003, http://www.fool.com/community/pod/2003/030826.htm (accessed January 14, 2005).

17. Ibid.

18. Jeffery Krasner, "Compensation to Former Executive at Polaroid Demonstrates System of Rewards," *Boston Globe*, March 17, 2002, http//www.accessmylibrary.com (accessed August 18, 2007).

19. Stephanie Armour, "Polaroid Retirees Lose Benefits," *USA Today*, January 14, 2002, p. B1.

20. Roger L. Martin, "What Innovation Advantage," *Business Week*, January 16, 2006, p. 102.

21. Ibid.

22. Ibid.

23. Ibid.

24. Daniel T. Griswold, "Let High Teen Workers In," Cato Institute, March 30, 1998, http://www.cato.org/dailys/3-36-98.html (accessed August 18, 2007).

25. Kevin Maney, "Indian Entrepreneurs Increasingly Go Home to Join Tech-Industry Explosion," *USA Today*, August 23, 2006, p. 3B.

26. Ibid.

27. David Kiley, "Blurred Focus," *Business Week*, June 19, 2006, p. 69.

28. Claudia Deutsch, "GE's Bland Appliances Grow Sexier and Pricier," *New York Times*, September 17, 2006, p. C1.

29. J. Hugh Davidson, "Why Most New Consumer Brands Fail," *Harvard Business Review* (March/April 1976): 120.

30. Jeffrey Pfeffer and Christina T. Fong, "The End of Business

Schools? Less Success Than Meets the Eye," *Academy of Management Learning and Education* 1, no. 1 (September 2002), http://www.20monline .org/publications/articles/bschools.asp (accessed July 10, 2007).

31. Ronald Alsop, "How to Get Hired," *Wall Street Journal*, September 22, 2004, p. R7.

32. Ibid.

33. Paul S. Brown, "R&D Under the microscope," *New York Times*, December 24, 2005, p. C5.

34. Don E. Schultz, "Marketing Gets No Respect in the Boardroom," *Marketing News*, November 24, 2003, p. 9.

35. Tom Hormby, "Scully's Dream: The Story behind the Newton," p. 5, http://www.lowendmac.com/orchard/06/0207.htm (accessed October 16, 2006).

36. John Graham, Campbell R. Harvey, and Chivd Ragjool, "Survey Finds Financial Executives Will Sacrifice Shareholder Value to Meet Earning Expectations," February 9, 2004. http://www.dukenews.duke.edu./2004/ survey.htm. (accessed November 10, 2005).

37. Ibid.

38. Tim Ambler, "What Does Marketing Success Look Like?" *Marketing Management* (Spring 2001): 13.

⑪

[RULES OF ENGAGEMENT]
Shareholders

There are three important players in the innovation game: investors, corporations, and business schools. Because the fate of investors and corporations are intertwined, both prosper with innovations like the all-in-one iPhone® or Mach 3®. But all product innovations are not created equal; failures widely outnumber successes, and both parties pay a hefty price because of this.

Business schools also have a stake in these failures on two significant fronts. First, until they better comprehend the marketplace realities of the innovation process, they will not be in a position to teach others about it. Second, they have to figure out how to successfully transfer this knowledge to their students, in a manner that properly prepares students for these realities.

There is a set of principles that can help each player deal with the innovation challenge. This chapter focuses on insights that can help shareholders make better choices.

Corporations can't be separated from their shareholders. It is not about them and us. When corporate boards and professional management tolerate innovation chicanery, they are letting their shareholders down at the end of the day.

First and foremost, shareholders have to act like the business owners that they are, and this certainly involves being sensitized to the wasteful innovation shell game played with their money. Frivolous innovation emasculates the value of their stock. The following suggestions and tips are food for thought.

FOUR TIPS FOR SHAREHOLDERS

Tip #1: Shareholder Silence Is Not Golden

The typical annual report delivered to the mailboxes of America's shareholders trumpets the company's new products launched during the past year, thereby generating positive vibrations with shareholders and Wall Street. It is a rite of passage, intended to show the stakeholders that the company is aggressively playing the innovation game.

What they don't trumpet is the new products that failed—those that disappeared into the bowels of the balance sheet, many of which were prominently featured in annual reports from prior years. Some speculate that the emphasis on product innovation in annual reports is the ultimate spin, since so many of the trumpeted innovations are here today and gone tomorrow.

Since shareholders are the big losers in the grand game of innovation roulette, they need to speak up, in tangible ways, about slovenly innovation practices of the blue-chip corporations in their investment portfolios.

Fifty thousand letters protesting New Coke® got the company's attention. A couple hundred phone calls from irate mothers forced JC Penney to take a risqué jeans commercial that glorified the teenage midriff off television. Three hundred phone calls from angry A&P customers compelled the supermarket chain to put a new product—

NuVim®—back in their stores after delisting it. Home Depot's imperial CEO Robert Nardelli was sacked, the direct result of an investor revolt, although he departed with a $210 million exit package, an outrageous gift from Home Depot's board.[1] Nardelli surprisingly resurfaced as CEO in the Chrysler takeover, presumably hired for his cost-cutting expertise honed at General Electric.

Two tenacious shareholder dissidents, Robert A. G. Monks and Nell Minow, were instrumental in forcing Sears to sell off its most precious, profitable assets—Coldwell Banker, Dean Witter, and Allstate —businesses that had propped up a faltering retail operation. Shareholders could now see the abominable performance of Sears's core retail business, because finally there was no place to hide the unremitting litany of management blunders.[2]

Two decades ago, shareholders had relatively few options. They either went along with management or sold their stock. But that was before the rise of the individual investor, fueled by employer pension plans, institutional investors, and corporate meltdowns like Enron. Today, there is critical mass. Shareholders have tools of empowerment—letters, telephone calls, and especially the populist medium of the Internet. Cyberspace is a rich environment within which to facilitate the voices of disgruntled shareholders.

Tip #2: Look for Bench Strength

In athletics, winning teams have bench strength. Reserves come off the bench in critical moments to ice the victory. Corporations have the same need. The winners have a deep bench of executive talent.

This was part of the legacy Jack Welch left behind at General Electric. He fostered the development of people, creating what many considered to be the most talent-rich company in America. He actively groomed several contenders for his job. While Jeffrey Immelt succeeded Welch, the two losers immediately became CEOs at Home Depot and 3M. Astute investors should always follow "the exitors" from talent-blessed companies to their new homes.

In the GE scenario, this was a win-lose strategy. The vanquished James McNerney became CEO at 3M, "where he raised both productivity and its stock prize."[3] He later did the same thing at Boeing. The other vanquished candidate, Robert Nardelli, was less successful in his CEO stint at Home Depot.

Dirk Jager had a seventeen-month reign as CEO at Procter & Gamble—the shortest in the company's history. After Procter & Gamble stock lost one-third of its market capitalization during Jager's rein, it was time to go to the bench. Enter A. G. Lafley, waiting in the wings. He faced an immediate problem: Procter & Gamble's new product cupboard was bare. The last big hit was Pampers® disposable diapers. For almost three decades, the company enriched its product portfolio through acquiring companies—such as Richardson Vick and Noxell—with power brands—like Nyquil®, Olay®, and Cover Girl®. Lafley knew the innovation stagnation had to be reversed.

He quickly refocused the company's core product competencies, with a product-innovation strategy designed to unify development around core products like Crest®, Tide®, and Pampers®. This enabled Procter & Gamble to regain dominance in oral hygiene and disposable diapers, which Colgate and Kimberly Clark had taken away with new products such as Total® and PULL-UPS® training pants. Lafley's core strategy was great for earnings.

He also opened up the innovation process beyond Procter & Gamble's internal research and development group. For decades, Procter & Gamble's scientists had advocated a policy that product development was their domain. Outside innovation was not welcomed. But Lafley was willing to outsource innovation, moving beyond the narrow-mindedness of the company's scientific community. His approach to open innovation did bear fruit—Swiffer® and the battery-powered SpinBrush® are shining examples. Today, about one-half of the ideas, products, and technologies that Procter & Gamble works with come from outside sources.

So, as Lafley's impact illustrated, bench strength is a blessing in the innovation game. In discussing the demise of former CEO Carly

Fiorina at Hewlett Packard, an executive recruiter observed, "She did not develop enough effective lieutenants."[4] What she ended up with was a weak management team with no bench strength.

Tip # 3: Look for Board Strength

Basketball coaches win games with strong rebounding on the offensive and defensive boards. Do the companies in your stock portfolio have board strength? Boards of directors come in various shades and degrees of commitment and competency. Some boards are floating in the twilight zone. When Coca-Cola's former CEO, Douglas Daft, came to the Coca-Cola board with a proposal to steal Gatorade® away from Pepsi at the eleventh hour, the board turned him down. Daft wanted Coca-Cola to be a total beverage company, capitalizing on the trend to noncarbonated beverages. The Coca-Cola board still believed, regrettably for its shareholders, that "Coke is it." It micromanaged the business to the point of determining which Coke commercials should be aired. A board that treats the acquisition of Gatorade® and advertising copy as equally important is truly adrift.

Today, Coca-Cola's shareholders would be better off with Gatorade® than tired production innovations like Coke® with lime or Vault®, the company's second attempt to derail Mountain Dew®. These are perfect examples of "innovation lite"—an attempt at innovation with a noticeable lack of calories. Perhaps the board itself should be viewed as a tired product badly in need of innovation.

Then there was the Hewlett Packard board. They brought in Carly Fiorina, a CEO change agent. Not only was it her first CEO position, but she also knew nothing about Hewlett Packard's computer and printer businesses. Yet the board approved her strategy to acquire Compaq® as a "backdoor" way to bring innovation to the company. This board-approved strategy failed, and the Hewlett Packard stock lost over half its value. While Fiorina was forced to vacate the premises with a $21 million severance package, the Hewlett Packard board was still in place.[5] Where was the shareholder rage for this board's accountability failure? The theoretical role of any board is to keep a watchful eye on management, representing the interests of shareholders, but the stark reality in many cases is that shareholders must monitor the board if they want to protect their investments.

Business Week, in a special corporate governance issue, developed prescriptives for optimizing board performance in 2002. They can easily be modified to fit the innovation challenge, because board members need to be better connected with the innovation process taking place on their watch:[6]

- Boards have finance, audit, nominating, and compensation committees. They do not, however, audit marketing. While we know marketing does not want to be audited, the financial records of companies are audited constantly, whether they like it or not, because somebody has to be looking out for the investors. So why not do the same for marketing's performance via an innovation committee composed of outsiders who are not board members to ensure objectivity?

- Corporate boards have a dilemma. While a few may look like Stillman's Gym, a famous New York City boxing emporium where the blood flows freely, most boards have a gentlemanly demeanor. There is a tendency to be nice and avoid asking the hard questions. Such love fests do not get the job done for shareholders. Direct challenges in the boardroom can be layered with decorum and etiquette, but boards have to find ways to be active and independent.

- One way to achieve this is to have boards put together a process for reviewing and evaluating board policies and decisions on a continuing basis. This process of self-evaluation should include an annual retreat—without the CEO. Since board members may lack group dynamics skills, an outside facilitator should be used to achieve maximum productivity. The annual retreat should be a training ground for new board members. They should understand the role of product innovation in the corporation. They should be coached in the art of asking probing questions about new ventures—including, of course, challenging the assumptions in the profits and losses for these ventures. The innovation committee can help board members refine their skills in these areas.

- Financial literacy of board members should be up to speed. In the WorldCom fiasco, billions of expenses were counted as revenue to keep Wall Street happy. A passive board had no inkling about the creative accounting practices going on in board meetings. CFO Scott Sullivan counted on their passivity and ignorance to make the sham work.[7]

- In his prime, Sam Walton visited every one of his Wal-Mart stores at least once a year. He also visited the competitors' stores. Sam learned a lot wandering up and down store aisles. Lafley, Procter & Gamble's current CEO, also makes frequent store visits. These visits provide valuable insights about customers and brands. Boards should be involved on this level as well. They should look, listen, and talk with customers in stores where the company's products are sold. It is one of marketing's moments of truth and an eye-opening learning experience. Home Depot's directors are required to visit twelve company stores a year. It should be a function of the innovation committee to help board members understand what to look for in relevant retail environments. These trips should occur quarterly. They will contribute better-equipped board members ready to judge the merits of sanitized presentations about "can't-miss" new products.

- Good former CEOs are ideal board members because of their depth of understanding about how the innovation game is played. That's good for shareholders. The problem is that they often sit on too many boards. *Business Week* recommends that such "board sitters" should be involved with three companies at a maximum. Two is even better. Professional board members earn a lucrative living, but they have difficulty maintaining shareholder interest as a high priority if they are spread too thin among too many boards.

• In the TV show *Survivor*, show participants vote lesser competitors off the island. The same principle should apply to board members with a confidential appraisal of their individual performances. It should be the responsibility of a board chairperson to steward the review process. Those with unfavorable appraisals should be asked to resign.

• The annual report should have a running section on the cost of product innovation over the past ten years, providing a historical context for innovation initiatives in the company. No more sweeping expensive new product mistakes under the rug. Shareholders have the right to see the cost of good and bad product innovation.

While the line is delicately thin between good board governance and the undermining of CEOs, boards can no longer complacently watch flawed innovation chew up shareholder value. Shareholder rage is the best way to institute an activist board culture.

Tip #4: Who's behind the Steering Wheel

Investors lick their chops when a new CEO takes over an underperforming company. The stock usually does gain value in these moves, but all that glitters is not gold. In real estate, it is "location, location, location" that counts. In assessing a new CEO, shareholders should be concerned with "background, background, background." Shareholders have to do their homework and move beyond the hype that can flow from the corporate PR machine. New products succeed because the innovation team does its homework. Shareholders have to do their homework, too.

The CEO's Background

The first basic question to ask of a new CEO is: what's your background? When Louis Gerstner first went to IBM, the company was in dire straits. Wall Street wondered how a "cookie man" (Gerstner had been Nabisco's CEO) could solve the company's deeply rooted problems. But analysts were too focused on chocolate chip cookies. The fact is Gerstner had already experienced success at American Express as well as Nabisco, but IBM didn't make cookies or peddle credit cards. Wall Street's consternation was perhaps understandable.

But the Wall Street crowd also overlooked another important period in Gerstner's business career—the years he spent as a key executive at McKinsey & Company, a management-consulting firm. In hundreds of consulting assignments, Gerstner learned how to sort out critical issues from irrelevant ones. His consulting experience trained him in the understanding of what customers wanted. Indeed, Gerstner's focus on customers and services at IBM was a major contribution to the revival of the company's stock.

Shifting to the background of another high-tech CEO, the already mentioned Carly Fiorina, paints a different picture. She came to Hewlett Packard as a high-powered sales and marketing executive from AT&T and its equipment making spin-off, Lucent Technologies. Both companies flamed out in the high-tech implosion of the late 1990s; her managerial spurs were won in business environments that were hardly symbols of success. AT&T was very much like the airline industry. The company did not survive after losing the protection of government regulation.

Marketing guru Al Ries commented on Fiorina in *Brandweek*: "She was a great front person. If she just had someone whispering Marketing 101 principles in her ear, she'd have done a lot better."[8] Half of the wealth of Hewlett Packard shareholders disappeared under her reign. Where would Hewlett Packard be today—or AT&T for that matter—if Louis Gerstner had occupied the chief executive suite?

John Scully found the Apple challenge more daunting than the

"Pepsi Challenge." After he failed to remake Apple, Steve Jobs returned from exile to tidy up the Apple landscape. The hand-held Newton, Scully's teacher's pet, never sold. Jobs marshaled a string of innovation successes—iMac®, iPod®, iTunes®, and iPhone®—that reversed Apple's fortunes. Scully's Pepsi background was an impediment to success in the swift currents of Silicon Valley. Jobs was there from the beginning when the valley was a mere infant.

Nevertheless, a guy who started out selling brownie mix made the grade in Silicon Valley. It helped Microsoft's CEO Steve Ballmer's transition that his career was initiated at the "academy of marketing," Procter & Gamble, where his basic marketing and business skills were honed. Moreover, unlike Scully, he did not start out at the apex of the pyramid in his indoctrination to the dynamic and challenging world of high-tech. He gradually earned his stripes under fire, but for Scully it was immediately sink or swim. Scully's background was a riptide that carried him out to sea without a safety jacket. When Jim Kilts left Nabisco and Kraft and ended up at Gillette, former Kraft colleagues promptly bought the stock. Kilts instantly understood the business problems of the underperforming company, based on his experiences in the food companies. In contrast, Gary DiCamillo took over the reins at Polaroid with an improbable background in power tools, far removed from selling cameras and film. He plowed Polaroid into bankruptcy. Background does matter.

Initial Impressions of the CEO

Initial impressions are very important; shareholders need to watch the initial moves of a new CEO very closely. Gary DiCamillo, as mentioned previously, came to Polaroid as the first outsider CEO in the company's sixty-year history. One of his earliest statements was that Polaroid would introduce twenty-five new products in the next year. This was a spin statement, made with Wall Street in mind. Polaroid shareholders should have sold their stock the minute that statement surfaced. They were being led down a primrose path.

On the other hand, when Jim Kilts had his first meeting with Wall Street's financial analysts, he refused to make rosy predictions about Gillette's future earnings, despite repeated attempts by analysts to back him into a corner with unrealistic forecasts. Good first impression. Kilts was not going to dance the Wall Street tango.

Jim Kilts went on sales calls, roamed Gillette warehouses, and talked with customers in stores. Gerstner spent weeks roaming IBM's research labs learning the business and culture before making his first moves. Both were very skillful in massaging the informal network that exists in all organizations.

Kilts and Gerstner were taking a page from the management stylebooks of Edwin Land, Sam Walton, Bill Packard, and Walter Hewlett. It is management by wandering the halls, listening, and learning. The troops in the trenches can tell you a lot. Edwin Land ate in the company cafeteria several times a week. Carly Fiorina ate lunch at her desk alone. Which one was in a better position to know what was going on?

The CEO's Team

Who's on the team? Shareholders should watch this development closely. Astute CEOs surround themselves with people who tell them the unvarnished truth. In Gillette's transformation, Jim Kilts replaced two-thirds of the company's senior management. Twelve people reported to him directly, and ten were imported from outside Gillette. Most of the team, like Senior Vice President Peter Klein, had worked with him before. The people who worked under Kilts knew what they were getting into. This raised the truth quotient and also narrowed the hiring risk.

This contrasts with DiCamillo's Polaroid team. He surrounded himself with the very Polaroid executives who had driven a stake through the company's heart. There was no possibility of fresh thinking. Most of DiCamillo's outside hires stayed at the company for three years or less. This should have scared shareholders into selling.

The CEO's Style

Another issue indeed: What is the CEO's style? Carly Fiorina became the poster girl for *Business Week, Fortune,* and other business publications. She refused to hire a chief operating officer.[9] She either dumped or scared away HP's best managerial talent.[10] After her demise, the same *Business Week* that lionized her noted, "Many who spent time around her came away with the impression that she was mostly interested in burnishing her own image."[11] Fiorina seemed enamored by her fame—a character flaw that did her in and cost HP shareholders a lot of money.

CEO styles come in various hues. One style is quiet leadership devoid of a "me" orientation. Another style is the high-profile CEO with a fondness for the limelight like Carly Fiorina. Which style is best for shareholders? A *USA Today* editorial makes the following recommendation:

> Try taking this test: Can you name the CEO of Starbucks, one of the few US companies that has mastered the art of growing without losing quality? Can you name the CEO of Southwest Airlines, the only major airline to achieve profitability in the face of an industry wide economic disaster? Can you name the CEO of Harrah's, the world's largest gaming company, which has figured out how to combine high-quality service with the ingenious use of information technology? Very simply, most people can't, which speaks volumes about the quality of these CEOs. If you are really looking for CEO advice, here's the best advice. The best-known CEOs are the ones you least want to listen to. Don't believe in legends and superstars; follow a leader who's not interested in seeing his or her picture on the cover of a magazine.[12]

In contrast to high-profile CEOs, Louis Gerstner was a man of mystery during his IBM tenure. It was impossible to gain access to him for interviews or public appearances. He insisted that his senior executives adhere to the same principles. On the eve of his retirement,

Gerstner was an enigma. Gerstner never made public speeches about his greatness. Instead, he let his accomplishment at IBM be his public persona.

Jim Kilts operated the same way. He seldom made public appearances. His demeanor, though very competitive, was conservative and reserved. "A country club gentleman" would be an appropriate description. He was highly respected by those who worked with him, a group that included CEOs at Campbell's Soup, Hershey, and Mattel.

New CEOs must always confront two basic issues—cost control and innovation. Pomp and glitz doesn't get the job done on either end. What is required is putting on the overalls and becoming involved with the dirt of doing. That's what Gerstner and Kilts did best.

NOTES

1. Eric Dash, "Nardelli Receives $210 Million to Go," *New York Times*, January 4, 2007, p. C4.

2. Sandra Guy, "Shareholder Revolt Bearing Fruit," *Chicago Sun Times*, March 24, 2005, http://www.suntimes.com/output/business/cst-fin-sears.htm (accessed March 24, 2005).

3. Claudia H. Deutsch, "GE Magic Can Fade After GE," *New York Times*, January 4, 2007, p. C1.

4. Henry, David, Dean Foust, and Emily Thorton, "Can Anyone Save HP?" *Business Week*, February 22, 2005, p. 28.

5. Gary Strauss, "21 Million Severance Package Eases Exit," *USA Today*, February 9, 2005, p. 2B.

6. John A. Byrne et al., "How to Fix Corporate Governance," *Business Week*, May 6, 2002, p. 74.

7. Floyd Norris, "Market Place; Ebbers and Passive Directors Blamed for WorldCom Woes," *New York Times*, June 10, 2003, p. C1.

8. Diane Anderson, "Tech Marketing," *Brandweek* (February 14, 2005): 17.

9. "Now Who Will Save Hewlett-Packard," *Business Week*, February 21, 2005, p. 96.

10. Ibid.

11. Louis Lavelle, "Three Simple Rules Carly Ignored," *Business Week*, February 28, 2005, p. 46.

12. Alan M. Weber, "Overrated: Business Superstars," *USA Today*, April 26, 2005, p. 13A.

⑫

[RULES OF ENGAGEMENT]
Corporations and MBA Programs

Corporations need to improve their innovation batting averages. Ten prescriptives are offered here for consideration. Implementing even a few would drastically improve innovation initiatives and boost bottom-line performance. The last silo for profit enhancement in corporations is attacking frivolous innovation; bottom lines could easily be doubled at companies struggling with innovation initiatives, like Ford, Kraft, Coca-Cola, and so many others.

Our journey ends with a focus on MBA programs and the opportunity to confront the innovation challenge at its roots. MBA programs, especially those with high status in the eyes of executive recruiters, are body shops for America's corporate elite. Their graduates are bright, eager, and analytical, perhaps to a fault. They are also inexperienced tenderfoots with, oh yes, flaws in their fabric.

It is not unusual for them to bring attitude, illusions of grandeur, and ethical lapses to the innovation process. Remember the two forecasts for Souper Combo™? The company's innovation team leader at the time was the proud bearer of an MBA degree from one of the leading business schools. Recruiters complain that "some of the prestigious [business] schools clearly suffer in their ranking because their elitism rubs off on some of their students."[1]

More recently mass hysteria swept through many of the upper-echelon business schools as a result of a study reported in *Advertising Age*. The principle conclusion of the study was that underperforming companies had more marketing MBAs "per square foot" than high-performance companies.[2] Three prescriptives follow to help MBA programs plug the leaks in their vessels. Corporations and shareholders would benefit greatly from their implementation.

TEN PRESCRIPTIVES FOR CORPORATIONS

Prescriptive #1: Quit Playing the Wall Street Numbers Game

Before Jim Kilt's arrival, the Gillette board announced it would no longer provide quarterly financial estimates. It believed these estimates drove CEOs to make short-term decisions that negatively impaired the company's long-term vitality. A key board member, Warren Buffett, who has long advocated that managing a business to please Wall Street's insatiable appetite for rosy numbers was management stupidity, influenced the decision. All boards are not necessarily comatose; the Gillette board did the right thing.

In his encounter with Wall Street, Kilts refused to let the analysts bulldoze him into a corner with respect to Gillette's future earnings. Shareholders benefited hugely from the stance taken by the Gillette board and Kilts. The new management team, led by Kilts, unlocked the slumbering giant's potential without Wall Street looking over its shoulder. The Gillette stock stabilized, and profits returned in about thirty-six months. More companies should adopt the Gillette position; Wall Street will kick, holler, and shriek, but it'll get accustomed to this new way of doing business profitably.

Prescriptive #2: CEO Involvement

CEOs must create an innovation culture in their companies. Some CEOs are detached, relying on senior managers to hover over the company's innovation process. This is a mistake, because the feedback from the vineyards about innovation initiatives may be distorted. Other CEOs fall in love with pet projects—think, for example, of David Johnson's unfulfilled fantasy for Intelligent Quisine® or John Scully's romantic fling with the Newton at Apple. They each became evangelical salesmen for money-losing, ill-fated ventures, blinded by their misguided passions. This innovation virus is no better than detachment. Both leadership styles are likely to make a major dent in shareholder value.

What is the right balance? In today's global marketplace, CEOs must not be afraid to "shake things up" in sculpting the innovation culture. Here are four CEOs who transformed the innovation culture from what they had inherited from their predecessors:

Chief Executive Officer	Company
Ed Zander	Motorola
Mark Schwab	Crayola
Jeffrey Immelt	General Electric
A. G. Lafley	Procter & Gamble

The Inheritance Problem

In the '90s, Procter & Gamble's sales were stagnant because the company had lost its innovation spark. In a mere eighteen months, the stock had lost half of its value. Shareholders called their brokers with instructions to sell Procter & Gamble. Employees and retirees who depended on Procter & Gamble stock for a secure retirement were disoriented and confused. The industry bible, *Advertising Age*, carried a front-page article with a damning headline, "Does P&G Still Matter?"[3]

As A. G. Lafley, newly anointed CEO, walked into his office on his first day on the job, he knew a blood transfusion was needed. The Procter & Gamble family had fallen apart. In his first two weeks, Procter & Gamble stock plunged almost another eight dollars. Lafley had a mess on his hands.

Mark Schwab didn't inherit a Lafley-type mess when he walked in to become Crayola's CEO (formerly Binney & Smith). What he did inherit was a sleepy company with a boring product line that was blessed with a strong brand name, rich in brand equity. Schwab's challenge was to jump-start the innovation process.

When Ed Zander came to Motorola from Sun Microsystems, he inherited a company wallowing in an innovation funk and self-pity. Remember the audacious Iridium™? The company had lost $6 billion when it placed its bet on this global satellite telecommunication system. Motorola had lost its innovation courage as a result of the experience. The company needed an attitude adjustment.

Jeffrey Immelt replaced the legendary Jack Welch, the apostle of Six Sigma and the maestro of the potentially brutal Session C meetings, where Welch personally reviewed several hundred of General Electric's top managers, including his handpicked successor Immelt. Under Welch's stewardship, "The skills GE prized above all others were cost-cutting, efficiency, and deal-making. What mattered was the continual improvement of operations, and that mindset helped make GE a marvel of earnings consistency."[4] While Immelt had not forgotten the lessons learned from the master, he was determined walking into the CEO's office to sculpt a corporate culture where GE managers were not afraid to take calculated risks in the dicey game of innovation roulette.

Each CEO has a unique style. Brooklyn-born Zander has an infectious pepper-pot personality. Lafley possesses a gentlemanly reserve. Schwab tends to be playful and curious. Immelt is affable and high-energy. Wholesale change in corporate cultures sounds simple, but it is not easy to achieve. Chris Galvin, a descendent of the company's founding family, was too timid to pull it off at Motorola. William Ford was in over his head in attempting to lead the family dynasty out of the wilderness of an acute case of Ford's innovation malaise. In reengineering the innovation culture at each company, our four highlighted CEOs tended to focus on four major areas. They got the job done, despite their disparate styles and personalities:

- Tear down the silos
- Seek outside perspectives
- Know the details of the innovation menu
- Make innovation everybody's business

Tear Down the Silos

The employee populations in large corporations tend to live in silos with no cross-fertilization or communication between them. There are turf battles. Department loyalty takes precedence over everything else. These destructive issues are a natural by-product of the human condition. Zander inherited a severe "silo syndrome" when he walked across Motorola's threshold to replace the ineffective family scion, Chris Galvin.

A 2006 article in *USA Today* described Motorola's silo chaos as follows: "The company units for too long had operated as warring tribes as Motorolans called it. The different business units would fight each other, often, harder than they fought outside competitors. The units had different strategies and clashing products. They even had separate booths at major trade shows."[5]

Zander used his inspirational leadership skills to get Motorola's innovation teams to come out of their silos. The idea was to cross-fertilize skills and expertise—think company-wide, rather than across a strategic business unit. The newfound cohesion led to the technically advanced, wafer-thin RAZR cell phone—a huge hit in the marketplace. But Zander can't rest on his laurels. He must find a replacement for the RAZR, which is losing its cool to competition like iPhone®. The cell phone business is volatile. Customers addictively seek out "gotta have" phones with new cool features. Innovation is a formidable challenge in this fast-paced industry.

Lafley inherited a different kind of silo problem. Procter & Gamble's research and development team had a rigid "not invented here" philosophy; the company's scientists were suspicious, skeptical, and unreceptive to innovation from the outside. They held up Tide®, Crest®, and Pampers® as symbols of their scientific superiority while the company moved through an innovation drought. This attitude was allowed to prevail for decades, until Lafley finally mandated that outside innovation was not only essential but welcomed at Procter & Gamble. Today about half of Procter & Gamble's innovation initiatives come from outside sources.

The same problem existed at Crayola. Research and development had built a moat around the department, sending outsiders a direct message: "We're very busy in our castle, please do not come in." Mark Schwab knew the moat, and all other company-wide barriers, had to go if Crayola wanted to revitalize its fatigued product line. The strategic goal was to move from crafts to toys. It bordered on an impossible mission with a recalcitrant research and development department on Schwab's hands.

"Research and development's super secret laboratory" became more open under Schwab's persuasive guidance. The channel for idea generation was blasted open.[6] "Instead of individual groups that focused on crayons, markers, or toys, the door was opened for any product ideas to come from anywhere in the company. The R&D group, previously isolated, now shares its ideas monthly."[7]

Seek Outside Perspectives

Corporations tend to become insular, singing a stale party line drumbeat. The borders are closed, making it difficult for fresh perspectives to surface. When William Ford finally, and wisely, threw in the towel, Ford's new CEO, Alan Mulally, was criticized by the Detroit establishment because he drove a Lexus. It's actually good to use the competitor's product. This was a fresh perspective Detroit chose to ignore. The insular Ford executives weren't going to learn how to make better cars driving Fords.

Corporations such as Procter & Gamble and General Electric preferred to grow and fertilize with loving care their own flowerbeds. They nurtured the farm system, rotating promotion-worthy executives around the chessboard. Key General Electric executives moved every two or three years. Family nurturing promoted group thinking, but it did not necessarily open up creative ways of thinking about consumers, markets, and competitors. The Procter & Gamble way became the only way. Group thinking is a recipe for troubled times. It's what caused Coca-Cola to miss the wellness trend. The Coke family didn't believe America wanted to drink beverages other than its cola brand.

Immelt broke GE's cherished tradition of promotion-from-within. A 2005 *Business Week* article observed, "In sales and marketing alone, GE has hired more than 1,700 new faces in the past few years, including hundreds of seasoned veterans such as David J. Slump, a former ABB Group executive who is the chief marketing officer of GE Energy."[8]

Immelt even promoted an outsider, Sir William Castell, to the position of GE's vice chairman because he liked his cerebral way of thinking about marketing opportunities. There were no two-hour commutes for Castell. The headquarters of Castell's strategic business unit, GE Healthcare, was located in his hometown in England by Immelt's edict.[9] These types of decisions would have been unheard of in the Jack Welch era.

Mark Schwab knew Crayola's innovation renaissance required fresh eyes from the outside. He brought in Tom Prichard from the animation company Pixar to steward marketing and product development. Prichard immediately identified messless craft toys as a major opportunity for the company. An example of the renaissance was Crayola's Color Wonder Sprayer™ described in *USA Today* as "an airbrush that sprays out a colorless mist, yet works like spray paint on Color Window paper."[10] It came in four different fun and funky, kid-friendly colors. It was a "wow! product" that excited kids and moms alike, reflecting the new face of innovation at Crayola. It wasn't the usual in-the-box marker or crayon thinking.

While Procter & Gamble terminated thousands of employees under Lafley's reign, including senior executives and scientists, it also hired hundreds of designers who had worked at other companies and industries. It was part of Lafley's strategy to bring novel, fresh thinking to Procter & Gamble's innovation initiatives that had become robotic and unimaginative.[11]

Know the Innovation Menu

Some CEOs have only vague notions about what may be coming down their particular yellow brick road of innovation. They may not hear the unvarnished truth about new ventures—think, for example, of the senior management at Campbell's Soup or General Motors as they signed off on Souper Combo™ and the Pontiac Aztek®. Savvy CEOs know what is going on, but they also don't try to micromanage the innovation process. They let their troops do their thing, but there shouldn't be surprises about what's going on.

On major new products close to marketplace introduction, Lafley sits in on fifteen long and grueling research and development meetings a year. His archrival, CEO Ian Cook at Colgate, also does the same thing every month—tracking, monitoring, and reviewing the ten most important innovation initiatives in the company. Lafley also spends three full days with the company's design board comprised of outside designers who provide points of view about the company's forthcoming new products.

Motorola's CEO spark plug, Ed Zander, had adopted Lafley's hands-on approach a long time ago at Sun Microsystems. He spends one or two days a week at Motorola's design center in downtown Chicago hanging out with the techies. The design center visits are motivational, because it is difficult to resist Zander's infectious personality cultivated on the streets of Brooklyn. The visitations also keep Zander abreast of product development issues. He is never clueless about what's on Motorola's innovation menu.

Innovation Is Everybody's Business

Innovation is too important to be left solely in the hands of the marketing department. Innovation-centric CEOs get everyone involved in the process. Mark Schwab's innovation philosophy is that everybody should be engaged in the innovation game. Nobody should be sitting on the sidelines. Crayola has an open-door policy; anyone, regardless of title and rank, can submit new product ideas. Each idea gets its day in court.

The suggestion box technique worked at Toyota. The company received annually an average of twenty suggestions per employee, about ways to build better cars and achieve cost savings, with its employee suggestion policy. Employee ideas resulted in $230 million in annual savings.[12]

General Electric CEO Immelt established and leads the commercial council, composed of about a dozen senior marketing and sales executives. Phone meetings are held every month, along with quarterly strategy sessions. Each council member must submit three innovations that can generate at least a $100 million in incremental growth. The council debates the merits of each submission.[13]

Lafley created an "innovation gym" that trains Procter & Gamble managers in the art of integrating design into product development. The company has seventy worldwide "technology entrepreneurs" searching the globe for technical breakthroughs.[14] It's Lafley's version of intrapreneuring. Although it wasn't mentioned in Procter & Gamble's annual report, Lafley unofficially became the company's chief innovation officer. He has left no stone unturned in his quest for big ideas.

The Bottom Line

In Search of Excellence identified sixty-two companies labeled America's best in the 1980s by informed sources. Many of these "excellent companies" have disappeared or experienced lean times.

Companies move through periods of greatness, prosperity, and despair. Nothing is forever.

Procter & Gamble was an innovation disaster in the '90s. While Gillette may have leaped to greatness in the eyes of some observers, it was alleged that Warren Buffett forced the board to bring in Jim Kilts as CEO in the wake of the company's missing earnings estimates for four-teen consecutive quarters. Kilts brought the company back to a level of respectability. Procter & Gamble had bench strength while Gillette did not. Procter & Gamble turned its misfortunes around with one of its own while Gillette turned to the outside to remedy its headache. In both sce-narios, innovation played a major role in the turnarounds.

The pattern is clear. CEOs must be innovation activists who walk the walk as much as they talk the talk. This represents one of their most important responsibilities. There is no room for detachment or misplaced passion in an innovation war that spans the global market-place. Shareholders benefit immensely from this hands-on, walk the talk approach.

Prescriptive # 3: Challenge Assumptions in Preliminary Sales Forecasts for New Products

Decision making is more art than science, but number crunching is inevitable. Since there are good numbers and bad numbers, it is easy to find numbers that look good to support a bad idea. Numbers are not in-fallible. When placed in the wrong hands, they can seduce and deceive.

In the innovation game, a favorite trick of innovation teams is to use marketing models to justify moving bad new product ideas for-ward. Marketing models require assumptions; crafty managers can feed them to higher-ups, which in turn leads to an inflated sales forecast that senior management finds acceptable.

As pointed out earlier, Souper Combo™ had two internal sales fore-casts from the same marketing research project. The less optimistic one, developed by the marketing research department, never crossed the desk of senior management. The optimistic forecast was presented to senior management and, not surprisingly, was accepted. When Souper Combo™ perished in the marketplace, Campbell Soup's marketing researchers did not find the product's death the least bit surprising.

The Souper Combo™ team's forecast was—take a guess:

a) Optimistic

b) Simplistic

c) Dishonest

d) All of the above

Marketing people can, and do, cook the books with deceptive numbers. Management must focus on the assumptions behind the numbers and challenge them aggressively. Nothing should be taken at face value. A few probing questions can save millions of dollars.

How are the assumptions supported? Are they simplistic? Does the category sandbox have any cash cows or sentimental brands? What scenario planning has been instituted for the inevitable competitive response from these brands? Is it realistic to expect the trade to take on an elaborate line extension? The list of questions can go on, and they have to be asked. Instead of "don't ask, don't tell," the focus must shift to "do ask, tell all."

One safeguard against optimistic assumptions is a sign-off process. Before senior management reviews a new product plan, key players in the innovation game—manufacturing, marketing finance, and marketing research—must review the plan and sign-off that the assumptions are correct, balanced, and not distorted. Differences between marketing and functional areas must be resolved before the plan moves forward. This mitigates the "creative number crunching" that comes with superficial assumptions. The plan senior management ultimately sees is the unvarnished truth—a much-needed tonic in the innovation game.

Specious assumptions must be flagged early. When bad ideas, like Souper Combo™ or the Pontiac Aztek®, maneuver through the review process, the final scenario is inevitable—fail late and, regrettably, fail expensively.

Prescriptive # 4: Have the Courage to Kill the Love Child

Whether it is a sculpture, painting, television script, or a new product, we fall in love with our creations. But our love is blind, because the emotional connections are deeply rooted. Nevertheless, judgments must be brutally honest.

Although perhaps easier said than done, managers must have the courage to kill their carefully nourished children when the evidence warrants it. Innovation teams may try to beat the system. That is why built-in safeguards in the development process are an absolute requirement in making sure flawed new products are not kept in play.

When Carlos Gutierrez, our current secretary of commerce, became Kellogg's CEO, he immediately pulled the plug on two innovation nightmares—Breakfast Mates™ and Ensemble™. Breakfast Mates™ was prepackaged milk, cereal, and a spoon sold in grocery dairy cases. Since cereal at breakfast had become a soggy concept, this was an attempt to make it portable. However, by the time Breakfast Mates™ arrived at work, the milk was warm. Who wants to eat cereal with warm milk? Americans didn't find this acceptable. Gutierrez mercifully put Breakfast Mates™ out to pasture.

Ensemble™, introduced with much fanfare, was a line of psyllium and oat-based products: pastas, cookies, potato snacks, frozen entrees, and cereals. While the problems with it could fill several pages in this book, it was, simply put, a line of healthy foods designed to lower cholesterol levels. Sound familiar? That's right—it was Intelligent Quisine® revisited with the same problem—most Americans with high cholesterol are unaware of that fact.

Since Ensemble™'s sluggish sales lacked Kellogg's famous snap, crackle, and pop, Gutierrez lowered the hammer. National rollout plans were scrapped. Ensemble™ was exiled to romp in the pasture with its buddy, Breakfast Mates™.

Fredrick the Great said, "The mark of a great general is to know when to retreat, and how." The most difficult decision facing a CEO is canceling innovation efforts the company is counting on in its financial forecast. What will Wall Street say? However, taking small losses early prevents bigger losses later. Shareholders benefit when bad ideas clogging the innovation pipeline are flushed out.

Prescriptive # 5: Too Many Cooks Spoil the Stew

Continuity is essential in the innovation game. The marketing waltz of musical chairs—moving people around without a compelling reason to do so—should be discouraged. Too many elephants make for a crowded dance floor. Senior decision makers on innovation teams should remain intact. When the players are moved around the chessboard too frequently, bringing in a new manager for an ongoing innovation effort creates the possibility, even the probability, of second guessing decisions that have already been made. There is no ownership in the accomplishments of the former manager, and a strong tendency to put new fingerprints on everything creeps in. The wheel is irresponsibly reinvented.

A failed new product's champion should follow it out the door at its launch, assuming ongoing management responsibility for a specified period. Continuity has another advantage. It takes care of the accountability problem.

Prescriptive # 6: Bring Something New to the Party

The high priests of marketing need to confront the curse of the "me, too" product. The world does not need another pancake syrup, even when it carries a powerful brand name like Eggo®. Money is saved—and dropped to the bottom line—when companies abandon their penchant for developing warmed-over versions of products already available. Give consumers a real difference or forget it. An innovation like DiGiorno frozen pizza, which brought a new, real taste benefit, is worth more than fifty short-term, avarice-driven line extensions. Before DiGiorno arrived on the scene, frozen pizzas sold in supermarkets tasted like cardboard.

The spoils belong to the first one or two innovative brands that successfully enter the category sandbox. The later entries nibble on the scraps, and they are not worth the shareholder dollars they squander. Pepcid® AC, Advil®, Gatorade®, Prius®, and Smirnoff Ice® are examples of value-added products that have achieved segment dominance by being the first of their kind with carefully crafted introductory strategies. Competitive entries that followed have not been able to dislodge them from their perches of dominance.

Prescriptive # 7: Stamp Out Marketing Amnesia

Our corporate cultures often suffer from marketing memory loss. There is no historical perspective taken into account. The same innovation mistakes continue to be made. We have seen the movie before. We know how it ends.

Since 1890, toilet paper had been a relatively quiet category. The tranquility was disrupted in January 2001 with Cottonelle® Fresh Roll-Wipes, the only dispersible moist toilet paper on a roll with a plastic dispenser that clipped onto a regular toilet paper holder. Kimberly Clark invested over $100 million in the product's research and development, backed by thirty patents, to give us RollWipes. The company predicted first-year sales of $150 million; some company pundits estimated the category potential to be $500 million. The product dropped off the radar screen in eighteen months.

While it would take several paragraphs to list the litany of problems associated with the demise of RollWipes, here's a news bulletin for Kimberly Clark: Procter & Gamble and American Can tried moist toilet paper in the '80s. It failed both times. Kimberly Clark must have known about these prior debacles. The evidence was there. Those who do not remember history—or deliberately choose to ignore it—are bound to repeat past mistakes.

Why not establish a knowledge base of past innovation, on a category basis? Young "marketing puppies" should review the database every time a new product thought creeps into their heads. It might be advisable for chief marketing officers to do the same.

The company's proprietary knowledge base should include all product successes and failures in the category. The data and information should be developed and updated by outside sources. Outsider consultants, with no axe to grind, ensure objectivity in building the knowledge base. This affords management the opportunity to learn from mistakes without playing the "blame game."

Prescriptive #8: Where's the Truth Squad?

As a recipe for survival, CEOs should embrace skeptics, not true believers who tell them what they want to hear. A conference room full of "yes-executives" never illuminates the darkness. This is especially critical in product innovation. How does the CEO differentiate fairy tales from reality? Where is the truth squad?

CEOs can find truth in many places. The marketing research department should be a member of the truth squad, but it often is not granted that function. Pepsi Blue® was researched. It failed. Blue french fries were researched. They failed. Souper Combo™ was researched. It failed. Over $4 million was spent on New Coke® research. It failed. The fact is, most product failures had hefty marketing research budgets associated with their development. How can this be?

The basic elements of the marketing research process are transmitters (researchers), receivers (marketers), and messages. Transmitters and receivers must work together for maximum effectiveness. However, because transmitted messages are often negative, it is predictable that marketers resist accepting them. In order to minimize this inevitability, market researchers must bring added value to their messages, regardless of whether the news is good or bad. Many marketing research departments are lost in a forest of technique and numbers. There is little focus on business issues. In working with a value-added research department, a vice president of marketing said, "This was a good presentation. I don't remember a single number. I do know what our problems are and how to fix them."

What constitutes a value-added research department? One that has management's respect. How does it get respect? The department leader comes out of the silo and interacts with marketing rather than waiting around for marketing to make its latest research request. He or she knows the business issues as well as the marketing counterparts. This allows executives to be more effective in recommending research steps. Think about this. If a division has eight different brands, the manager must understand these businesses as well as, or perhaps even better than, the respective marketing groups. That is why the vice president of marketing liked the presentation. He saw the solution to his problem, not a bunch of numbers.

Value-added research departments are members of the truth squad. They get invited to the important meetings because they walk into conference rooms with solutions, not boring presentations. Management wants and needs business insight. Presentations that draw management's attention are about substantive business solutions, reinforced with a dash of showmanship to keep the audience from falling asleep. Many market researchers regrettably lack this skill set.

Marketing research is like a siren song. It sounds good, like the prospect of an ice cream sundae. You feel you control it, because you sired it. Like all offspring, it will deliver what's demanded of it. If added value is what's desired, then hire researchers capable of delivering it, and spell out the expectations clearly. The alternative is to let the marketers run the asylum with sanitized optimism.

The value-added concept requires a special kind of leadership and training to make it work. Since most researchers aren't trained to think in this context, they are rarely invited to sit down at the table with other disciplines, such as finance, research and development, and manufacturing, at important management meetings. The lack of leverage puts researchers on the sidelines as spectators rather than players.

In a quest for value-added, one company hired a consultant from McKinsey with no formal training in marketing research to head up its marketing research department. Between attending important management meetings with the other key players in the innovation game, it was this person's responsibility to train the marketing research department in how to implement the value-added concept.

This novel approach puts the right person in the function—one who has the respect of senior management. Otherwise, marketing research has no leverage or influential voice in the innovation process, despite its heavy involvement in that process.

Recognize that this illustration is oversimplified. Not all research departments should be run by graduates of Bain, BCG, McKinsey, and other elite consulting environments. This represents a complex problem that has been festering for decades. An entire book could be written about it.

However, the fact remains: if senior management does not respect the leadership of marketing research, the disciple becomes impotent. The current model is broken; it needs to be fixed. The choice for corporations is relatively simple—do something about it by finding the right person or live with the illusion that the marketing research department is clicking on all cylinders. But the illusion may breed a blemished innovation ledger.

Prescriptive # 9: Ethics Boot Camp

When the sales forecast is fudged for a new product, this is an ethics issue. When bad news about a new product is rationalized away or swept under the rug because the mantra is "full steam ahead," this is also an ethics issue. Both happen in the innovation game when marketing's impulsive and unrestrained Freudian id overpowers the logic of the innovation team. Corporations spend millions on employee training, but how much is focused on ethics to help marketers navigate through gray areas?

For every major product innovation, the innovation team should attend an ethics boot camp early in the development process, before marketing and technical issues are addressed. This should include everybody on the team, including ad agencies. It is difficult to imagine that agencies and their clients did not know Vioxx® and Celebrex®

were overprescribed drugs, peddled to consumers with minor pain who could have used less expensive alternatives like Advil® and Aleve®. So what we've got is an ethics issue, because both advertisers and ad agencies formulated the strategy to target pain.

Bayer® Select was a line of aspirin-free analgesics. One item in the line contained acetaminophen (the core ingredient in Tylenol®). There also was an ibuprofen product (the active ingredient in Advil®) in the line. There was nothing unique about Bayer® Select. The products were already available, under the strong familiar brand names of Tylenol® and Advil®. In a postmortem about Bayer® Select's death, an agency account executive working on the project remarked, "We knew it was a lousy idea, but we loved the $40 million ad budget." Unenlightened self-interest wins again. The entire innovation team should have attended an ethics boot camp.

Some might argue that the agency had an obligation to point out the folly of Bayer® Select. However, would any agency walk away from a large budget that would hurt the agency's bottom line? Where does the accountability lie?

Over the years, line concepts seldom work—think of Intelligent Quisine®, Ensemble™, Arthritis Foundation Pain Relievers, and so many other big, expensive failures. Shouldn't Bayer®'s innovation team have recognized this? Marketing amnesia strikes again, but perhaps it wouldn't have if, as pointed out earlier, there was a knowledge base of past innovation blunders to guide the internal innovation process.

The accountability issue here lies with the board, which should have vetoed this silly venture. The board members might have done so if, as previously pointed out, they had an innovation committee composed of outsiders to assist them in making decisions about funding innovation initiatives. Then there is no need for Bayer® Select or an ethics boot camp. Remember: the Board must be the superego and the ego in the innovation process.

Prescriptive # 10: Corporate Endowments

Corporations interact with business schools on many levels. They make sizable donations, fund basic research, and send executives to workshops and seminars. Corporations need to walk the ethics walk—endow ethics chairs at business schools. These chairs should be populated by bright, dedicated academics who are interested in ethics scholarship.

Corporations should not hesitate to open up their information vaults to academics with an interest in ethics scholarship. Let them sit down with the merchants of marketing to better understand the seemingly endless stream of cases involving flawed innovation. Is there a pattern of ethical issues that underscore death on the altar of blemished innovation?

THREE PRESCRIPTIVES FOR MBA PROGRAMS

Our focus now shifts to the relationship between product innovation and MBA programs. New product courses tend to be taught with a focus on the best corporate practices that lead to success. But the problem should be looked at from the opposite angle. The failure rate for new products is high because of the *worst* practices that deplete shareholder value and corporate profits. The discussion of the best corporate practices isn't doing much to reduce the high rate of failure.

There are major ethical issues associated with flawed innovation. These cover a scale of problem areas—from outright lying and fudging profit and loss statements, to overenthusiasm and overoptimism, to a misunderstanding of the cumulative effects of optimistic assumptions, to reliance on simplistic assumptions. These issues are seldom taught in MBA new product courses, and many of the people engaging in this behavior in the real world are MBA graduates. There is more to ethics than the big-name corporate scandals like the downfall of Enron's Jeffrey Skilling.

The MBA is a pedigree—a passport to walk across the threshold of America's corporate elite. Many will be tossed into the innovation game totally unprepared for the complexity of the assignment. Because they have been told in business schools that they are ready to manage, they will attempt to do so, often with dire results. On the other hand, they are just doing what the system has asked them to do. Now it gets complicated because corporations often do not have clear, publicly stated policies—other than "get the product launched"—regarding what is expected of marketing staff as they play the innovation game. So anything goes.

Prescriptive #1: Ethics Renaissance

WorldCom and Enron have stimulated more interest in ethics courses in our MBA factories. A 2004 article in *Business Week* suggested current efforts are malnourished, as reflected in Columbia's business school struggle with the teaching of ethics to their MBA students:

> Some professors found teaching ethics a burden, so it showed in their teaching. The thought of earning an F in a class called ethics spurred rumblings of discontent. It implied to some students that they were unethical. That led Profs to switch from the standard bell shaped curve to a pass/incomplete grading system.[15]

The heavy lifting in business schools is directed at everything but ethics. Ethics is a soft subject marginalized by the emphasis in these schools on analysis and quantitative techniques. There might be a course or two on ethics buried in the catacombs of the curriculum. High-profile professors never teach ethics courses. They want to teach their specialty (competitive strategies, etc.) and make a lot of money on outside consulting projects. Professors under pressure to be published in prestigious academic journals and attend symposiums have no incentive to get involved with the subject of ethics, a topic that does little to build their careers. The teaching of ethics may be left to the B team.

A *USA Today* survey among MBA students suggests that their ethical fabric is frayed at the edges.

ETHICS OF MBA STUDENTS

Percent of MBA Students Who Would

Buy stock on inside information	52%
Reveal corporate secrets to spouse/family	50%
Let a gift sway purchasing decisions	26%
Pay someone off to close a business deal	13%

Would you hire an MBA student with this set of values?

At the universities of Maryland and Pepperdine, MBA students are sent to prisons to talk with white-collar criminals about the ethical lapses that led to their incarceration. An overnight stay might be even more sobering. While this is a small step in the right direction, it is the kind of innovation and fresh thinking MBA programs need in the ethics area.

While there are several ethical issues associated with flawed product innovation, here's one that occurs with great frequency: product failures widely outnumber successes, but each failure had a rosy sales forecast that was spoon-fed to senior management. The underlying assumptions behind the forecasts were either misleading or overly optimistic—perhaps fueled by the innovation team's thirst for personal advancement and résumé building.

This is an ethics issue—manipulating the numbers for new product forecasts—that's rarely covered in the MBA classrooms. Since ethics is barely recognized in the curriculum, this is understandable, but not necessarily comforting to shareholders as marketing plays fast and loose with their money.

To be effective, the teaching of ethics at business schools must be systemic, sweeping across the curriculum. In a new products course, equal weight must be given to the social responsibility of marketing $300 sneakers to ghetto youth and developing the market positioning for the sneakers. This is why business schools such as Columbia struggle with teaching ethics. It's treated as a course, not as a curriculum-wide philosophy. Systemic application is the key.

Incorporating ethical considerations into all courses can, in fact, lead to more profitable innovation procedures and, very importantly, improve innovation success rates. Since business schools stress maximizing shareholder value in almost every course, the most important shareholder contribution they can make is to produce ethically balanced students. The innovation game will welcome this new breed of manager.

The initiative for stronger emphasis on ethics must come from the dean of the program. He or she should encourage promising scholars to pursue ethics in marketing. The teaching of ethics must be a requirement, rather than a secondary elective. It is an opportunity for deans to differentiate their schools from the "sea of sameness" that typifies business schools.

Business schools screen potential candidates based on their GMAT scores (Graduate Management Admission Test). The test assesses "one's ability to give fast answers to little numerical and verbal problems."[16] There is also an analytical written test. Prospective students spend hours taking practice tests to pump up their GMAT scores. But there is a much-needed test business schools should also implement in screening applicants: why not have prospective students take an ethics test? The ethics score should carry equal weight with the GMAT score in screening candidates.

This demonstrates to students that ethics is important and represents a significant prerequisite for admission. It shows the commitment of business schools to not only raise admission standards but also their intent to integrate the teaching of ethics across the entire curriculum. And, most important, business schools start to produce students with a stronger moral compass—ones who don't lie, cheat, and steal when they cross the thresholds of corporate America or Wall Street.

Prescriptive #2: Humility, Not Mighty Big Attitudes

The innovation game requires managers with a superb set of soft skills. The most challenging part of product innovation is managing hundreds (or even thousands) of people in a vast network of resources. The innovation team must interact with both internal and external resources. The internal resources include engineering, manufacturing, research and development, purchasing, quality assurance, marketing research, legal, and sales. The external expands to resources outside the company environment—ad agencies, marketing research suppliers, sales promotion agencies, package designers, public relations specialists, outside legal counsel, technical specialists, and others.

Marketing tenderfoots, freshly minted from the MBA factories, are thrown into this cobweb of complexity. Their business school educations do not necessarily prepare them for the interpersonal challenges that will confront them in the innovation game. The *Wall Street Journal* annually surveys corporate recruiters who interview MBA students about prospective employment. Their annual refrain: MBA students need more humility.[17] This is sourced in the snobbish behavior and ego-driven attitudes displayed in job interviews.

This "MBA mentality" soon manifests itself in an inability to interact with other employees once on the job, especially those at lower levels. A marketing manager remarked that, "many MBAs can't interact effectively with lower-level manufacturing employees."[18] An MBA professor was surprised that students referred to lower-level employees as minions. One needs lower-level employees to be successful in the innovation game.

MBA graduates feel sure, and in fact are taught, that the hundreds of case studies and computer simulations in classrooms and study teams must stand for something. And it does—they have learned the basic jargon of business. What they don't understand—or choose to ignore—is that managing the complexities of the innovation process is not a computer simulation where buttons are pressed to get answers, nor a case study supplemented by a manual containing answers.

Successful managers understand that managing involves using soft competencies—a set of skills that receive relatively little attention in the majority of MBA programs.

As previously discussed, the innovation game is a discovery process that is very marketing research intensive. This requires a team effort between marketing and marketing research. When the MBA person brings to the process an attitude and a lack of soft skills, it makes true teamwork between marketing and marketing research difficult and, in many instances, impossible.

Remember the soft batch cookie fiasco at Procter & Gamble? The researcher recommended sales-wave testing to assess the long-term commitment of consumers to this new type of cookie. If the recommendation had been followed, the brand never would have been launched; Procter & Gamble and its investors would have saved lots of money.

Shareholders paid a hefty price because that recommendation was disregarded. An MBA recruiter commented, "MBAs should be more willing to show their flaws. When students are asked about difficult situations, things always turn out great, or how they wanted them to turn out. This cannot be the case and certainly isn't in real life."[19]

A CEO at a large consumer packaged-goods company accosted his vice president of marketing research in the hallway. He asked why a new product had failed, costing the company millions of dollars. The accosted employee went to his office and retrieved a report clearly indicating the product would fail. After briefly scanning it, the CEO looked the researcher in the eye and said, "You should have been more persuasive. That's what I'm paying you for." This hapless "poor persuader" was fired three months later. In this scenario, marketing sold a bad idea in the innovation game; research could not sell the truth.

There is a parallel between war and marketing research. In war, politicians often refuse to listen to generals in the months leading up to quagmires like Vietnam and Iraq. While marketing researchers are not generals, they often have incredibly good insights into consumers for the initiatives on the innovation menu. But their voices may not be heard, like our hapless persuader, leading to an innovation swamp fueled by the reasons discussed in this book. Innovation teams, like their political counterparts, often believe that they are the brightest guys in the elevator. No need to listen to what consumers have to say. The end result of this arrogance might be financially painful innovation debacles.

Some business schools offer masters programs in marketing research. While these programs produce technically competent graduates, the course they need most is not part of the curriculum—oral communications. Marketing researchers need to know how to present information persuasively and effectively to others. This does not imply that technical skills are not important. However, if management chooses to disregard important research findings, technical expertise is not going to make a sow's ear into a silk purse. The missing link is teaching students in these programs how to present value-added information persuasively, whether they get it in the form of a business course or one taught in a liberal arts department outside the program. They are going to need this capability to be truly effective.

The frayed edges in the MBA fabric that recruiters see is a product—warts and all—that many business schools produce with assembly line precision. Students are treated as if they were rock stars. One professor at an elite business school said, "We praise our students effusively." Another professor referred to the school's student stroking process as "a steady diet of the mush of greatness." To paraphrase an incident cited in the book *Managers Not MBAs*, a Harvard professor once remarked, "Our students make more decisions in a day than a general manager does in a month."[20]

While students may naively believe in statements like this one, decisions made in a sterile classroom are very different from decisions made in the messiness of the real world. One wonders if the professor would make the same statement to a room full of general managers.

A constant fare of the "mush of greatness" has unintended consequences. MBA students easily start to believe their "press clippings," fostering the problems that recruiters detect in the interview process.

Though not all MBA students become certified prima donnas, a sizable proportion do, and their MBA degrees morph into Mighty Big Attitudes.

Stewarding an innovation team is the last place to put the MBA person with months, rather than years, of experience. The soft skills are simply not there to motivate and inspire a vast network of resources—an art that requires dynamic and sometimes mothering leadership. The focus of the MBA person is too often on individual glory, not team results.

The guts of the innovation challenge—fatal mistakes, dubious forecasts, specious assumptions, ethical dilemmas, social responsibility, shareholder disregard, and the quest for personal glory—are rarely discussed in business schools.

Prescriptive #3: The Manager Myth

Is the glass half empty or half full? After spending over $100,000 and two years of their lives in an MBA program, are graduates ready to be managers? Are they ready to play the innovation game? Business schools would certainly vote in the affirmative.

In his book *Managers Not MBAs*, Henry Mintzberg, McGill's Cleghorn Professor of Management Studies, offers a contrasting view:

> If the business schools were really doing their job, were truly creating leaders, their graduates would be noted for their humility, not their arrogance. Certainly, they would graduate with an acute appreciation of what they do not know.[21]

Mintzberg's contentious, but simple, thesis is that MBA graduates are not Masters of the Business Acumen. Only time in the management trenches will tell whether they have mastered a delicate art form known as "the right to manage." What they lack is a graduate degree in experience.

Mintzberg noted that when Fredrick Taylor, the father of scientific management in America, was asked to teach his management concepts at Harvard, he refused the offer, noting his principles could only be learned on the shop floor, not in a Harvard classroom.[22] Taylor understood the value of a graduate degree in experience.

Mintzberg's book reveals a major disconnect between classroom discussions about business problems and the realities confronting practicing managers in dealing with messy real-world problems. Some colleagues view Mintzberg as a heretic. Others agree with him, but are less vocal, since they like their pay and tenure.

In discussing the MBA person, a vice chairman of a large consumer-goods company sits squarely in Mintzberg's corner: "They would throw their mothers off a moving train to get ahead. They can't make a decision without a marketing model. It becomes a substitute for using their brains." And, he might have added, it does nothing to develop critical-thinking skills.

In addressing a group of MBA students, Mintzberg noted that a CEO from a large pharmaceutical company once remarked, "My problem is that when I face a problem, I don't know what [business] class I'm in."[23] Business problems are like playing with Lego blocks (a Mintzberg analogy)—the pieces can be reconfigured in an infinite number of ways, but there are no pat answers like there are in the classrooms.

Business schools have quick-fix models for every business problem. While there is nothing wrong with a marketing toolbox of techniques, it takes experience to know when and how to use them. In the innovation game, this is why the marketer with the problem and the marketing researcher with the experience should be teammates rather than wary and sometimes friction-prone participants in the innovation process.

Mintzberg argues that managing is "basically a soft practice involving: experience, intuition, judgment, wisdom, and nuances."[24] Therefore, what has been taught in business schools is divorced from the important context of experience. In hiring an accountant or lawyer, or in visiting a cardiologist for chest pains, no reasonable person would randomly select names from the Yellow Pages. Experience would be an important consideration. Who wants to be rolled into the operating room for a surgeon's first angioplasty procedure?

Yet corporations are perfectly willing to throw "marketing yearlings" into the innovation game, all because they have the passport—an MBA degree. Many are not ready to play the game, but they will try, perhaps burdened by a lack of clarity from management about what is expected of them.

A *Harvard Business Review* article supports Mintzberg's early thesis about the deficiencies of MBA programs. One of its principle conclusions is that "graduating students are ill-equipped to wrangle with complex, unquantifiable issues—in other words, the stuff of management."[25] In the context of product innovation, the following episode crystallizes the naivety of business schools that emphasize science:

> One of America's most prestigious business schools hired a senior executive from a major consumer goods company to teach a new products course to MBA students. In his second week on campus, a faculty member, widely known for his work in mathematical modeling, grabbed the adjunct in the hallway asking, "Why are all these new products failing? We have wonderful models that could be so helpful in this area." The adjunct sat the famed professor down to explain the "birds and bees" of product innovation. Flawed product innovation surfaces from a range of human and organization issues—hubris, greed, the thirst for achievement, blind ambition, lack of accountability, misguided passion, attitudes, pressure, resume building, judgments, interactions—it's the soft stuff that Mintzberg harps about.

The professor cited above is uninformed about what drives product innovation failure. Marketing models are only as good as the motives of the people who use them.

In the earlier-mentioned *Harvard Business Review* article, a problem revealed with business school faculty members is their focus on scientific research that has little relevance to the business world. "A renowned CEO doubtless speaks for many when he labels academic publishing a vast wasteland from the point of view of business practitioners."[26] Most business executives start to yawn while reading mathematics-laden, ponderous articles written by business professors.

Business schools produce very little of practical value for corporate America because they are run like history or philosophy departments. MBA faculty members must publish or perish, generating a churn on quantity rather than relevance; the output tends to be a litany of boring, hard-to-read, sleep-inducing journal articles that nobody reads outside a small circle of business school academicians.

In addressing an audience of MBA program directors, Gary Hamel, management guru and former Harvard Business School faculty member, noted that "ideas that have altered the field of management (e.g., game theory and Six Sigma) have come from the industry or scholars outside of business schools."[27]

Test market simulation models, widely used and sometimes abused by consumer-goods companies, trace their development roots to Pillsbury and research vendors like Yankelovich and Elrick and Lavidge. W. Edwards Deming, an American scholar and statistician, set Japan on the road to better-quality products with advanced statistical techniques, and later Deming's quality movement was expropriated by American corporations in an effort to deliver quality satisfaction to customers. Wal-Mart perfected Just-in-Time delivery, a Japanese concept. Matrix organizations and cross-functional teams were developed in the aerospace industry.

Business schools preach these concepts in classrooms. However, with their emphasis on faculty research, there should be more. Business academicians have produced very little that has lasting significance for the business world, although their research efforts lead to an important personal goal—tenure. Medical schools set the pace for the practice of medicine. Shouldn't business schools be a catalytic agent for management innovation?

As it stands, if business schools have out-of-touch faculties and MBA curriculums that ignore the relevance of innovation, then many of their freshly minted MBA graduates may be ready to manage their checking accounts, but they are far from ready to manage new products.

NOTES

1. Ronald Alsop, "How to Get Hired," *The Wall Street Journal*, September 22, 2004, p. R8.

2. Jack Neff, "Don't Study Too Hard: MBA's Fail at Marketing," *Advertising Age* (March 20, 2006): 1, 40.

3. "Does P&G Still Matter?" *Advertising Age* (June 9, 2000).

4. Diane Brady, "The Immelt Revolution," *Business Week*, March 28, 2005, p. 64.

5. Kevin Maney, "Must-Win Attitude Gets Motorola Back on the Hip Track," *USA Today*, January 18, 2006, p. 3B.

6. Bruce Horowitz, "Crayola Draws on New Ideas," *USA Today*, December 6, 2006, p. 2B.

7. Ibid.

8. Brady, "The Immelt Revolution," p. 71.

9. Ibid. p. 64.

10. Horowitz, "Crayola Draws on New Ideas," p. 2B.

11. Bruce Nussbaum, "How to Build Innovative Companies," *Business Week*, August 7, 2005, p. 66

12. Altier, "From Experience: A Perspective on Creativity," p. 156.

13. Brady, "The Immelt Revolution," p. 64.

14. Jena McGregor, "The World's Most Innovative Companies," *Business Week*, April 24, 2006, p. 66.

15. Mica Scheider, "Poor Marks for Ethics Teaching," *Business Week*, June 14, 2004, p. 16.

16. Henry Mintzberg, *Managers Not MBAs* (San Francisco: Berret-Koehler, 2004), p. 13.

17. Alsop, "How to Get Hired," p. R7.

18. Ibid.

19. Ibid.

20. Mintzberg, *Managers Not MBAs*, p. 51.

21. Ibid., p. 75.

22. Ibid p. 39.

23. Ibid.

24. Ibid, p.13.

25. Warren C. Bennis and James O'Toole, "How Business Schools Lost Their Way," *Harvard Business Review* (May 2005): 96.

26. Ibid. p. 99.

27. "Hamel Challenges B-Schools to Stay Ahead of the Curve and Change the World," *Graduate Management News* (March–April 2004), http://www.9mac.com/2004/MarchApril.htm (accessed July 11, 2005).

(13)

[A FEW FINAL THOUGHTS]

We have reached our destination in the journey down the yellow brick road of innovation. The suggested guidelines discussed for investors, corporations, and business schools vary in terms of complexity. Some are easy to implement. Others are more demanding. All require commitment.

To quote the old farmer in Iowa, "Talk is cheap, but it takes money to buy whisky." Are the players in the innovation game—corporations, shareholders, and business schools—ready to act on what they claim to believe, or is it business as usual?

Shareholders are owners of the companies in their investment portfolios; they entrust professional management to make decisions in their best interests. Unfortunately for investors, innovation mistakes, sometimes involving billions of dollars, decimate shareholder value.

Our shareholder prescriptives enable investors to be more adroit observers of how their money is used and abused in the innovation game. The choice—and the truth—is in our hands as investors. Learn about and be smarter observers of the innovation game, or suffer the consequences.

America is in an innovation war. Emerging economies, especially China, are fundamentally reordering trade, manufacturing, and marketing. The rules of the innovation game are changing, but one thing is undeniable: muscle-flexing foreign competitors, such as Toyota and Samsung, aren't going away.

Over 90 percent of innovation attempts in corporate America fail to achieve targets for return on investment. This is not acceptable. Nor is it acceptable to lose important business sectors, like the automotive industry, to foreign competition because of innovation malaise. Innovation in America needs a major tune-up.

Corporations can't continue to make the same old innovation mistakes. Are General Motors, Ford, and Chrysler ready for the inevitable invasion of the North American market with cheap cars and trucks made in China? The innovation war demands authentic, creative products that emotionally persuade and reward customers. Just one well-conceived innovation, like Crest Whitestrips®, Prius®, or the iPod®, benefits companies and their shareholders more than a thousand lame ideas, like Coke® with lime or the Iridium™ cell phone, could.

With awareness of the most common viruses associated with flawed innovation, corporations can make better innovation decisions, avoid pitfalls, seize opportunities, and compete more effectively with global competitors. Modest improvements in the innovation process can easily double the bottom line of any company. Shareholders will be delighted with their newfound prosperity.

Business schools may find change more difficult. Top-of-the-line business schools have seduced corporate America as blue-chip companies fawn over their MBA graduates. The middle-tier business schools probably are more receptive to change, though this may not inspire recruiters to visit their campuses with the same fervor.

Corporations can force change by demanding more ethically

balanced students with less attitude and arrogance. Corporations can enhance compliance through the endowment of ethics chairs at business schools. Entry-level marketing positions can be filled with liberal arts graduates, not just MBAs. Recruiters can make ethical dilemma–type questions a major part of the interviewing process. Such efforts would shake things up in the corridors of business schools.

Business schools can respond in kind by making an ethics test part of their admission standards. At best, business schools receive—depending on the grader—a C+ to a C– in the ethics venue. In every barrel, there's an Andrew Fastow, Enron's chief financial officer, beyond the redemption of anything remotely associated with ethics. But business schools should feel uncomfortable about the moral compass of some of their graduates.

Business schools have let the scientific model drive out a sense of balance and common sense with respect to important issues like innovation, but there are a few promising ripples on the water. Gary Hamel from the Harvard Business School, lamenting the absorption of his colleagues who wallow in scientific papers destined for obscure research journals, is helping the London Business School launch the first "university-based management innovation lab" designed to bring companies and schools together to play the innovation game.[1] Hamel is attempting to walk the talk, since he has long been an advocate that business schools should be a driving force in management innovation.

Business Week noted that Stanford University has created a "D-school that will teach design thinking to business, engineering, and design students."[2] Such an innovative approach could give Stanford a competitive edge over conventional business schools in a corporate America starved for successful innovation.

Perhaps because this seems like the new strawberry shortcake, a few other schools have followed the Stanford model. "The power of this new approach, called design thinking, to promote innovation and open up business opportunities, is attracting the attention of corporations around the globe"—think of General Electric and Procter & Gamble as examples.[3]

The Lally School of Management & Technology at Rensselaer Polytechnic Institute decided its traditional business school model was broken—administrators threw it out the window and replaced it with a "new program teaming up professors to teach together in communities and guide students through real world business problems in a holistic way."[4] A headline from a *Business Week* article summarizes Lally's mantra: "This is not your father's MBA."[5]

It is encouraging to see some candor about the traditional MBA curriculum. These ripples should be watched; but remember, that's all they are—a few ripples in an ocean of academic contentment. Harvard is not going to abandon a curriculum heavily laden with case studies. There is no reason for elite business schools to change the rules when they comfortably reside at the apex of the pyramid. The best change agent is the final customer of business schools—corporations that eagerly recruit MBA graduates. They could fuel a positive chain reaction with some of the efforts previously mentioned.

Harvard economists John McArthur and Jeffery Sachs made the following observation: "Innovation is no mere vanity plate on the nation's economic engine. It trumps capital accumulation and allocation of resources as the most important contributor to growth."[6] So let the games begin for the players in the innovation game. Think about the prescriptives discussed here as well as those from other sources. Which players will really shake things up? Our bets are placed on the deadliest of games—innovation roulette. The outcome affects all of us—investors, corporations, employees, and, yes, America as a whole.

NOTES

1. Whitney Sparks, "A Lab Grows at London B School," *Business Week*, August 15, 2005, p. 12.

2. Jessi Hempel and Aili McConnon, "Special Report: Design Schools," *Business Week*, October 9, 2006, p. 64.

3. Ibid.

4. Geoff Gloeckler, "This Is Not Your Father's MBA," *Business Week*, May 16, 2005, p. 74.

5. Ibid.

6. Kevin J. Claney and Peter G. Kregg, "Surviving Innovation: Common Testing Mistakes Can Derail a Promising New Product Launch," *Marketing Management* (March/April 2003), http://www.copernicusmarketing.com/about/does/surviving_innovation.htm (accessed December 21, 2005).

[INDEX]